Writing Signs

Writing Signs

The Fatimid Public Text

Irene A. Bierman

UNIVERSITY OF CALIFORNIA PRESS

Berkeley / Los Angeles / London

This book is a print-on-demand volume. It is manufactured using toner in place of ink. Type and images may be less sharp than the same material seen in traditionally printed University of California Press editions.

University of California Press
Berkeley and Los Angeles, California

University of California Press, Ltd.
London, England

Library of Congress Cataloging-in-Publication Data

Bierman, Irene A.
Writing signs : the Fatimid public text / Irene A. Bierman.
p. cm.
Includes bibliographical references (p.) and index.
ISBN 978-0-520-20802-5 (pbk. : alk. paper)
1. Written communication—Egypt—History. 2. Arabic language—Social aspects. 3. Fatimites—Language. I. Title.
P211.3.E3B54 1998
302.2'244'096209021—dc21 97-50204
CIP

Printed in the United States of America

The paper used in this publication meets the minimum requirements of ANSI/NISO Z39.48-1992 (R 1997) (*Permanence of Paper*).

Contents

Illustrations

Figures

Maps

Preface

One visual sign found in contemporary multi-cultural cities is the public presence of different alphabets. Signs written in different alphabets appear on buildings large and small, on store fronts, on billboards flanking the road, on busses passing through the streets. In Los Angeles, along parts of Wilshire Boulevard, signs written in Persian, Korean, Greek, Hebrew, Spanish, and English differentiate places, marking zones. These written signs in public places indicate the presence of a community. They are embedded in a whole range of socially constructed institutions and practices. The full potency of what these writing signs convey depends on the social position from which you view them.

For some viewers, these signs with "strange" alphabets strengthen differences. They tell them what they are not, alienating them from information, and preventing them from participating in the social networks the writing signifies. For other, literate viewers, the signs support cohesion: a group identity that has as its index a written sign in the public space. Recognizing the alphabet is, however, only the beginning of understanding how writing signs convey their meaning.

Alphabet and language have a complex relationship which is socially defined in time and place. Today in Los Angeles, signs in Latin letters can be in English or in Spanish languages. The Arabic alphabet, in which Persian is written, so commonly seen on the Westside of the city, is testimony to the large Iranian community in the city, yet many of the signs are actually in English. "Corner market," "Hollywood café," "Video store" are the messages the Arabic letters convey. Addressed to an audience who can read that alphabet, the use of English words suggests the social integration of the community.

Beyond questions of alphabet and language, the display of writing signs in different alphabets in the public space signals for all members of the society social practices which enable the public space to be the site for such a display of difference. As natural as writing in the public space may seem, many societies of the eastern Mediterranean over many centuries in the Middle Ages did not use writing in the public space in significant ways, but, rather, used it inside communal spaces. Indeed, at many times, in different places, even in Los Angeles, when writing did appear in the public space, it was only the dominant alphabet and language.

The role of writing signs in the visual culture of societies is of primary interest to me. How do such signs mean?—is the question I mean to pursue. For my study, I have chosen the places in which they appeared, the times in which they were seen, and the people who wrote them and the people who saw them, the whole contextual framework. The signs whose meaning I pursue appeared on the outside, on the inside, on walls, and on floors of buildings. They were put there by people with power. They were intended to be seen, some by everyone who passed, some by limited groups who sought out the place, to meet there.

I am writing about the special achievement of the Fatimids 969–1171 C.E., because they expanded the use of writing addressed to group audiences, what I call writing signs, and left a lasting legacy of writing in the public spaces in Cairo. Other rulers in Cairo followed their practice, and today their medieval writing signs are displayed alongside contemporary, less permanent ones, in the public space. Part of my purpose is to clarify how writing in Arabic succeeded in that society by being caught up in the social relationships of power and equality.

Let me emphasize that in *Writing Signs*, writing is used as a neutral descriptor: it indicates the presence of script, or more technically, any written markings combined according to a particular set of linguistic conventions. "Writing" carries no judgment about grammatical or orthographical correctness, or the manner of production (incised, carved, drawn with a pen) or the medium (paper, stucco, mosaic, or ceramic), nor is any comment intended on the quality of the letters or the style of the writing. *Writing Signs* is not a study of Arabic "calligraphy." Calligraphy is a normative term. It involves a specific body of techniques for letter formation and script production. Writing that can be called calligraphy is hand-executed. Such "beautiful writing" requires for the writing of Arabic specially slanted pen points. Some writing addressed to group audiences in the eastern Mediterranean in the centuries studied here did have calligraphic qualities, but that fact is not the issue directly addressed in this study.

Nor is *Writing Signs* a paleographic or epigraphic study in the conventional sense. Both terms refer to the science of decipherment and stylistic evaluation of inscriptions. While, of course, the semantic meaning of writing as well as its style is relevant here, this study focuses on how writing made its meaning to its group audience, and for this purpose semantic meaning and style are only part of larger considerations.

In contrast to formal book-hand terms usual in the studies of calligraphy and epigraphy, the key terms in this study of writing are "officially sponsored writing," "group audience or beholders," and "sectarian" and "public spaces." These terms serve to highlight the specific contexts in which those in authority within groups addressed messages in writing to a group audience, and how those writings conveyed their meaning. These terms help to discover the probable meanings the Fatimid rulers intended when they made their written messages highly visible—perhaps even permanent—by embodying them in writing on the exterior of buildings, in public spaces, and thus made them into what I call Fatimid public texts.

Writing Signs addresses the following questions: What did a Fatimid public text mean? To whom? And how did it bring its meaning to those audiences? This focus shifts the emphasis from the seeming uniqueness of Muslim practice as a whole to an exploration of the social circumstances that particularized those uses of writing and the messages it conveyed. It begins with an analysis of the writing practices of various groups in the eastern Mediterranean, arguing for the equivalent uses of writing among sectarian and ruling groups from the sixth to the tenth centuries. These two categories, sectarian and ruling, were separate yet overlapping, since while some Muslim and Christian groups did rule during this period, others were among the ruled. In a chronological sense these practices are pre-Fatimid, but in a substantive sense the equivalencies in practice must be understood as a significant classification whose distinguishing marker is that they were communal practices.

This study then proceeds to a detailed, two-part analysis of the changes in the prevailing writing practices instituted by the Fatimid ruling group. Chapter 3, The Fatimid Public Text and the Sign of Ismaʿilism, covering the period 953–1073, details the changes in the uses of writing from the reign of the Imam-Caliph al-Muʿizz to the appointment of *wazīr* Badr al-Jamālī. Chapter 4, The Fatimid Public Text in a Changing Political Climate, 1073–1171, investigates the perpetuation of the older aspects of the public text, and the new changes in the public texts. The discussions in both these chapters attempt to show how Fatimid writing practices interacted in the social networks in the capital of Cairo, playing a visually significant role in the spatial hierarchies within the city. Indeed, as this study will argue, some aspects of the Fatimid public text were especially effective precisely because they addressed the whole Muslim population, sometimes creating distances, at times bridging differences, and at other times, helping to support new alliances within a population whose composition changed over the two hundred years of Fatimid rule, as did the nature of the ruling group. In the later Fatimid period, other newly introduced elements of the public text addressed the entire urban population—Jews, Christians, and Muslims.

For the purposes of this analysis, I have created a theoretical framework that enables us to understand writing addressed to a public audience as being full of meaning, conveyed in specific contextual ways—aesthetically, territorially, and referentially. This is a tool to analyze the range of meanings writing conveyed simultaneously to the people who interacted with their built environment and who participated in varying degrees in the socio-economic, political, and religious circumstances of the time.

Chapter 1, Initial Considerations, consists of a brief methodological and terminological discussion critical to explaining how the data were organized. The chapter explores the three primary functions of such written signs reflecting my conviction that form alone is not the only aspect through which written components of the visual environment related. Of course, it is true that form and content in art are not separate entities with their own histories and trajectories. But my analysis shows how the form of writing had various levels and dimensions of semantic denotation and connotation, just as the referential and territorial dimensions are shown to have complex yet specifiable and documentable manifestations. Finally, under this same rubric are found questions related to the corpus of materials and questions of defining criteria for the canon of the Fatimid public text.

Inquiries into the functions of officially sponsored writing in medieval societies in the eastern Mediterranean are still relatively few in number. The writings of Erica Dodd, Richard Ettinghausen, Oleg Grabar, Cristel Kessler, Stanley Morison, and Janine Sourdel-Thomine have helped light this not well-traveled road. I see myself walking in the same direction, in my own way.

The successful completion of this study reflects in part both the financial support from several institutions and the willingness of many colleagues in many places to discuss issues and share ideas. First I wish to thank that unique institution, The Center for Advanced Study in the Visual Arts, and Dean Henry Millon and former Associate Dean Marianna Shreve Simpson, for allowing me to participate in that stimulating and challenging atmosphere. There I explored some of the ways in which writing made its meaning. Several colleagues there, especially Peter Brunette, Donald Preziosi, and Barbara Stafford offered their insights into various theoretical issues relevant here. Oleg Grabar and Irving Lavin offered much-deserved and needed criticisms and invaluable pointers. They helped me find ways to build upon my understanding of Fatimid society laid down earlier in my studies with Wilfred Madelung.

A Fulbright Civilization grant, two summer grants from the American Research Center in Egypt, as well as support from the UCLA Art Council, the Academic Senate, and the Gustav E. von Grunebaum Center for Near Eastern Studies enabled me to travel the length and breadth of the eastern Mediterranean to see both the specific sites discussed here and, beyond them, those which formed the corpus from which the implications are drawn. This travel was particularly critical for this study because many sites have not been published, or published only minimally, and sometimes published in piecemeal fashion. Travel enabled me not only to see new sites but to reassemble old ones so that written signs were reinserted into their visual context.

The opportunity to investigate this subject also depended on access to materials in museums and in other collections. Among those who opened institutional doors as well as windows of understanding, I wish to thank and acknowledge the help provided by Esin Atil, Ursula Dreibholz, Marilyn Jenkins, Louise Mackie, Edward Meader, Abd al-Raouf Youssef, Naʿmat Ali Abu Bakr, and the late Larry Salmon.

My colleagues at UCLA and elsewhere have provided critical hearing over the last few years. I want to thank especially Donald Preziosi, Jere Bacharach, and Michael Morony; and also Ismail Poonawala, Donald McCallum, Cecelia Klein, Yoshiaki Shimizu, James Flanagan, Samy Shavit, Jaroslav Stetkevych, Paula Sanders, May Trad, Nasser Rabbat, and Rifaʿat Abou-El-Haj.

For suggestions for the final revisions of this manuscript, I owe thanks to Shreve Simpson, David Kunzle, Susan Downey, and to numerous students who have read sections as assigned readings for medieval Islamic art history, several of whom should be mentioned: Behzad Allahyar,

Shokrallah Ghoochani, Susan Sims, Patricia Kabra, Heghnar Zeitlian, and Abier Ziadeh.

Thanks are due also to the various reviewers of this manuscript, often nameless to me, who helped me sharpen my thoughts, and to Judah Bierman who reminded me to thread my thoughts and think my sentences. Lynne Withey of the University of California Press is due special thanks for her continuing support. Thanks also to Grace Wax and Sandy de Grijs who helped in various stages with typing this manuscript. And, finally, I wish to thank in particular Nasser Rabbat for the line drawings of the al-Hakim minarets and bastion, Nairy Hampikian for the other line drawings, and Carel Bertram for the many maps that help us walk through Cairo.

Help—even in the form of critical hearing—does not imply responsibility. All of those who in one way or another have helped me to walk my path and to avoid minefields are not responsible for those on which I stepped. This last version of the manuscript was written at UCLA, on the Pacific shore, where I often took heart from a wonderfully told tale that offered encouragement because it contained these poignant words: "We are accustomed to believe that our world was created by God speaking the Word; but I ask, may it not be that he *wrote* it, wrote a word so long we have yet to come to the end of it? May it not be that God continually writes the world, the world and all that is in it?" (J. M. Coetzee, *Foe*, emphasis added.)

CHAPTER I

Initial Considerations

"Public text" names the Fatimid practice of writing signs in Arabic.[1] It was, I shall argue, a socially and politically intensified use of writing in contrast to the practices of other societies in the eastern Mediterranean. In fact, the Fatimids made writing a significant public art. This study of the art of the public text explores how the Fatimid ruling group extended the use of writing in their capital of Cairo (969–1171 C.E. / A.H. 386–567) to support their political and hegemonic interests. It demonstrates how that extended range of writing signs became a visual legacy continually reiterated by ruling groups within a restricted area of Cairo.

For the Fatimids, every written sign in the public space was a public text: an officially sponsored writing addressed to a public audience which continuously reminded the viewers of the official Fatimid position. The phrase "Fatimid practice" also encompasses the new ways in which Fatimid patrons used writing as a visually significant sign on the interiors of the sectarian buildings they sponsored. For a period of almost two hundred years in Cairo, writing signs was a Fatimid gesture: Fatimid power, Fatimid community, Fatimid territory.

Because the time in which the public text flourished and the places where it was displayed were relatively limited, and because the buildings on which the writings were displayed and the cloths into which the messages were woven have not survived as well as one could wish, the idea of the public text may seem too well argued from too narrow a base. I think not. But the limitations make desirable some initial considerations of terms and ideas that create a conceptual framework enabling one to see and appreciate the power and uniqueness of the Fatimid public text.

First among these is the idea of space, public and sectarian spaces, and of what was included and what was rejected from the writings extant or known to have existed in each space. This study looks closely at the messages displayed in each to see if and how they changed over time. Next, after considering the corpus of these writings and understanding the nature of the spaces in which they were displayed, we need to consider the objects and materials on which the writing was presented. Third, we come to the central idea of this interpretation—how these writings made their meanings. These writings consisted primarily of Qur'ānic quotations, secular salutations, names and titles of sponsors, and similar simple and familiar short passages. What is important is the paradigm used to explore the possible meanings these group-addressed writings conveyed to the observers.

Finally, as part of the discussion of meaning, I explore briefly the idea of "contextual literacy," important to understanding how the Fatimids were able to address the diverse populations of Cairo with their systematic displays of writing in Arabic. These initial considerations make possible the close analysis of writing in Arabic and other languages in the eastern Mediterranean of which the Fatimid public text is the special focus.

In the eastern Mediterranean for millennia before the Fatimids came to Cairo in 969, writing was used for a variety of purposes.[2] Embedded in specific social institutions, writing was sponsored by various groups. Lists, tables, and business records helped commerce thrive. Notation systems stored mathematical and scientific knowledge. Essay-texts were developed to record philosophy, history, and myth. And Roman authorities put writing on the entablatures of the central buildings of the fora, and displayed letters on banners and standards in military processions.[3] That the Fatimids used writing in the extensive networks of their social organization was clearly not of itself a new practice in the eastern Mediterranean.

But to the eyes of Cairene beholders, the writing on the exterior of the minarets of the mosque of al-Ḥākim in the year 1002/393 (fig. 1) presented a significant departure in the conventional uses of writing because it was used to address a group audience in public space. Writing in Arabic was displayed on this structure in a highly visible format and on stone and marble, permanent and expensive materials, in contrast to the limited uses of writing in public space by previous and contemporary Muslim and Christian rulers in the eastern Mediterranean for some four hundred years and, in fact, even with the earlier Fatimid practice itself.[4]

1. Northern minaret, mosque of al-Ḥākim (drawn by Nasser Rabbat)

Generally speaking, before the change signaled by the writing signs on the mosque of al-Ḥākim, those in authority displayed writing in public spaces only in limited fashion, placing them at urban thresholds and on lintels over the entrances of some major buildings. Those who passed the exterior of the mosque of al-Ḥākim in 1002/393 witnessed some of the significant first steps taken by the Fatimid ruling group to use written signs actively to define urban spaces and to convey meaning to public audiences in the Fatimid capital area of Egypt.

In addition to this display of writing in the public space, Muslim beholders, especially those who were part of the Fatimid ruling group, witnessed another change in the use of writing—one that occurred inside the same mosque, an Ismāʿīlī Muslim sectarian structure. Those who entered the mosque of al-Ḥākim saw displayed on its interior writing larger in scale than that in other mosques in the capital area (fig. 2). But size was not the sole factor that signaled the change in the use of writing. The format, or the manner of display, set it apart from writing on the interior of earlier structures. In the interior of the mosque of al-Ḥākim, writing relatively large in scale for the practices of the time and place framed the architectural features almost unencumbered by other design elements, whereas in the interior of the earlier Fatimid mosque in Cairo, al-Azhar, writing small in scale framed depictions of plants and trees (fig. 3). In addition, the writing in the interior of the mosque of al-Ḥākim differed from the display of writing in the mosque of Aḥmad ibn Ṭūlūn, the large congregational mosque built in the ninth/third century in al-Qaṭāʾiʿ, south of the Fatimid royal city. There, writing had been used in a limited way in the mihrab area of the sanctuary, but not to fill the ornamental border running around the architectural features of the mosque (fig. 4).

The choice of the mosque of al-Ḥākim as the site for a manifestation of this shift in the uses of writing related in very direct ways to the structure itself and to the political and hegemonic features of Fatimid society of the time. These specific relationships are taken up in chapter 3. But what is relevant here is an understanding that writing outside and writing inside the mosque addressed different, and overlapping, audiences. The kind of group that could be addressed in a public space by the writing on the exterior of the mosque of al-Ḥākim, or in the public processions the Fatimids sponsored, was critically different from the group addressed inside the sectarian space, the Ismāʿīlī mosque. In this study, the two adjectives "public" and "sectarian" are used to denote spaces of contrasting accessibility.

Public space, as distinct from sectarian space, is where anyone—or everyone—could pass. That is, public space is accessible to the whole membership of the society, ruling and ruled, traders, servants, foreigners, Muslims, Jews, Christians, men, and women. Thus the act of putting writing in Arabic, in several places at pedestrian level, and in large scale letters on the minarets of the mosque of al-Ḥākim, itself located outside the royal city of Cairo, made that writing viewable by all who passed that public space. That writing was (and is) in that sense a public text.

2. Sanctuary, mosque of al-Ḥākim, after Creswell

3. Interior, sanctuary, al-Azhar mosque

Likewise, the writing in Arabic displayed on the clothing of the Fatimid ruling group, and on the trappings of their horses during official processions, was intended to impress those who watched the ceremonies from the public space, that is, mainly those from the urban complex of Cairo-Miṣr who watched along the route of the parade. One such spectator, Nāṣir-i Khusraw, visiting Cairo in 1047/439, during the reign of the Imam-Caliph al-Mustanṣir, has left us a clear account of one of those

4. Original mihrab, mosque of Aḥmad ibn Ṭūlūn

processions. He found the use of writing on textiles and clothing remarkable, describing with care the cortege of ten thousand horses whose saddlecloths had the name of the ruler woven into their borders.[5] Such systematic display of writing in public space seems not to have been paralleled in other Muslim or Christian practice.[6]

Sectarian space, by contrast, is group-specific space. It is a space where people of similar beliefs gathered in an official communal manner. In the societies covered by this study, sectarian space was mainly space for the gathering of members of religious groups: mosques, churches of various denominations, synagogues, and shrines.[7] These are the spaces where the main ritual ceremonies cementing communal life were enacted for the members of the group. Sectarian space was frequented only by members of that group, and, characteristically, one did not enter another's sectarian space, whether or not written rules governing such access existed. We know, for example, that the mosque of al-Azhar, within the royal city of Cairo, was a space intended for Ismāʿīlī prayer, sermons, and observances. Non-Ismāʿīlī Muslims would not usually have frequented this space for prayer because many practices, beginning with the specific manner of washing before prayer, varied from their own observances. Clearly, that mosque was not only a Muslim sectarian space, but in the time of the Fatimids, a specifically Ismāʿīlī Muslim sectarian space.

Before the changes initiated by the Fatimids most officially sponsored writing addressed to a group audience was placed inside sectarian spaces. Moreover, even within that space, writing was subordinate in visual importance to other signs of power displayed there. In Christian churches of all rites (e.g., Greek Orthodox, Armenian, etc.) and in mosques and shrines (e.g., the Great Mosque of Damascus, al-Azhar, and the Dome of the Rock), writing framed depictions of landscapes, biblical figures or foliage, and, in general, was subordinate in visual importance within the interior setting. Fatimid practice, beginning with the mosque of al-Ḥākim, shifted the role of writing on the interior of Muslim communal structures. By a dramatic use of writing, that is, by making writing on the interior walls of that mosque larger in scale than any previous writing similarly positioned, and by reducing the number of competing signs of power, the Fatimids began to make the Muslim sectarian spaces they patronized visually dissimilar from other sectarian spaces, Christian, Jewish, and Muslim. These changes in the role of writing were apparent primarily to the Muslim members of the society who frequented that sectarian space. In the sectarian spaces of the Christians and Jews in Fatimid society, writing practices seem to have remained traditional.

The Fatimid public text was a significant change from the traditional uses of officially sponsored writing, remarkable in its own time. I need, however, to clarify—even to circumscribe—the extent of the visual impact of those practices that constituted the public text within the built environment as a whole. The phenomenon of the Fatimid public text was geographically specific. It was a praxis observable only in the Fatimid Egyptian capital, a designation which in this study encompasses the area of the royal enclosure of Cairo (*al-Qāhira*) and the surrounding urban areas of Miṣr, a term used in the medieval texts to denote the urban areas south of Cairo (map 1). Yet even within this capital area, the public text did not function equally in all of the urban areas or at all times for all of the inhabitants. Rather, as the analysis of Fatimid practice will show, the public text was a dynamic phenomenon within the city.

Spatially, it involved changing relationships between various urban areas, distinguishing, for example, practices in Cairo from those in Miṣr. While all of the structures displaying this new use of writing were linked by the patronage of members of the Fatimid ruling group, their location and function varied, as did the presence of writing in specific areas on them. Similarly, the display or wearing of inscribed fabric in official ceremonial occasions was also limited to specific routes and structures, namely, those routes over which the Fatimid processions traveled. Thus only these areas were involved in displaying the public text on textiles.

Socio-politically, the public text was also a dynamic phenomenon in terms of group relationships and persons patronizing structures with writing on them and wearing inscribed garments. Wearing clothing with writing on it in public processions, displaying inscribed textiles, and patronizing Muslim communal structures with significant displays of writing defined, and was limited to, the members of the ruling group. The ruling group included the Caliph, his family, the *wazīr*, various dignitaries and heads of bureaus, poets and writers of the court, and the army.

Importantly, however, the composition of the ruling group changed substantially over time, as did the position of the individuals exercising power within it. Even the religious affiliations of members of the ruling group over the period of Fatimid rule changed, and toward the end of their rule in the twelfth century came to parallel more closely that of the population as a whole. Yet, the ruler-versus-ruled distinction remained stable and primary despite the fluid and variable inner dynamics of the ruling group.

Socially, the audiences for the various aspects of the public text also changed over time. While it was always true within the large urban setting of Cairo-Miṣr that the audience was mixed—different economic levels, different religious affiliations—the discussions in chapters 3 and 4 will make clear that in the initial periods of Fatimid rule some parts of the public text were aimed at Muslim audiences, excluding Christians. In contrast, in the later part of Fatimid rule, some equivalently placed texts in the public space addressed all members of the population, while others, namely, those in Fatimid sponsored sectarian spaces, addressed all Muslims.

How such writing related to the official sponsor obviously was equally dynamic. The astute beholder then, as today, could recognize that writing as a sign of power related to power in variously inflected ways. It explicated and dissimulated. The official sponsorship of writing at times indicated power where power existed. Equally clearly, the display of official writing could give the illusion of power to its sponsor where effective power no longer existed, or no longer existed in the same way. These aspects of writing will become clearer with the discussion of the later Fatimid practice which, although displaying the Caliph's name, indexed not his power, but that of his *wazīr*.

To turn then to its media, the Fatimid public text was displayed mainly on buildings and on cloth. We face strikingly different problems in trying to reconstruct and study the public text on each of these. The problems imposed by the textile fragments are somewhat less familiar, and so the situation in which we find them warrants a more extensive explanation, and will be treated second.

Only a limited number of buildings built before 969/358 in Miṣr are extant, and only a limited number of the buildings subsequently sponsored by the Fatimids themselves are extant. In addition, the medieval written sources are not detailed enough to add significantly to our knowledge of the corpus of extant structures. Problems exist, for instance, in trying to reconstruct them in detail, especially sufficient detail for this study.[8] These are not new problems and my reliance on later medieval, fifteenth century, sources, like al-Maqrīzī, to reconstruct aspects of the Fatimid-built environment follows familiar traditions. Al-Maqrīzī was one of the few medieval writers who talked a lot about buildings. But even he did not comment in sufficient detail to help us greatly. Given these limitations, my reference to the Fatimid-built environment is based on the extant buildings of the Fatimid period within the area of Cairo-Miṣr: those in Cairo, those outside it in the vicinity of the mosque of Aḥmad ibn Ṭūlūn, and those in the surroundings of the Muqaṭṭam hills, plus the textual references where appropriate.

These buildings are important to us not simply because they are extant

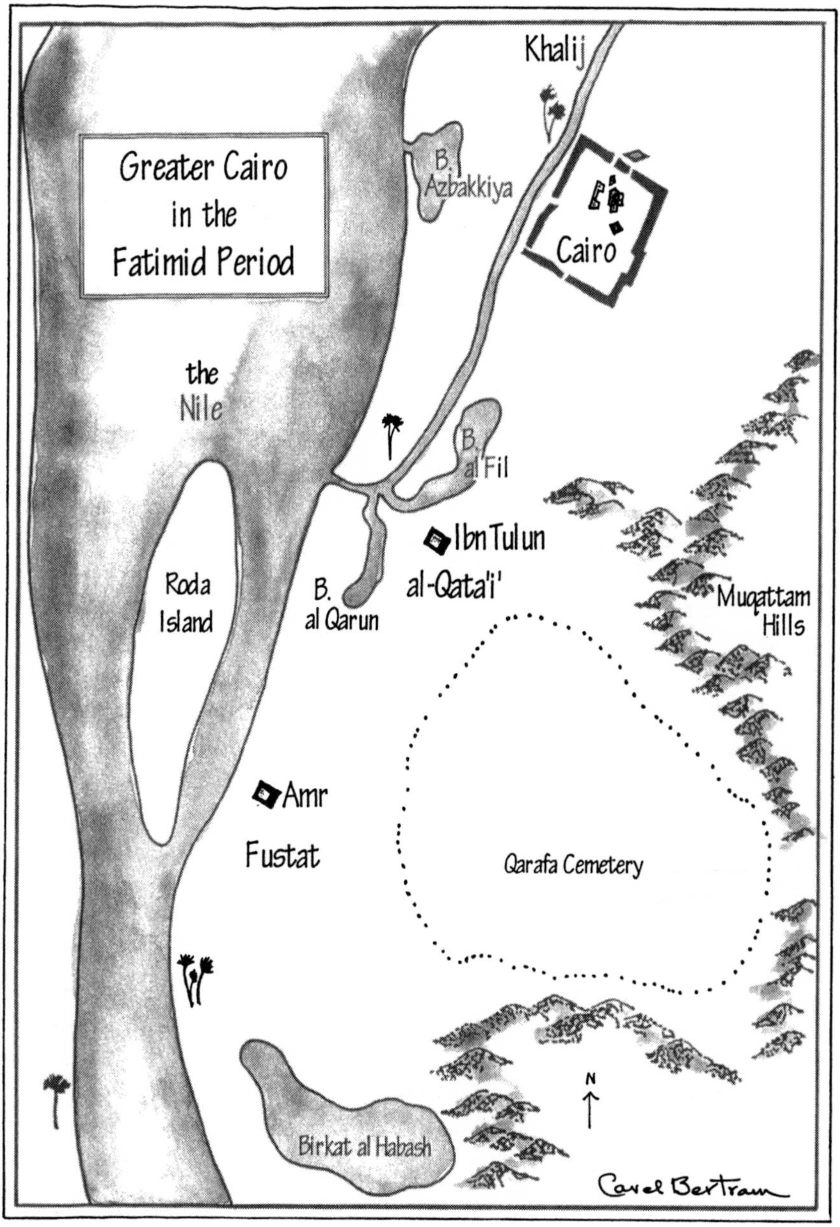

Map 1. Greater Cairo in the Fatimid period (drawn by Carel Bertram)

but because several of them figure in the official acts of the government which were aimed at a group audience. Others of the extant structures were passed (or nearly passed) in the procession. Many of the "missing" buildings were not focal points for official acts but, rather, were connecting links in the spatio-temporally extended rituals and ceremonies. What is a significant omission from the visible archaeological building record, and one not fully satisfied by mentions in the medieval chronicles, are the Fatimid Western and Eastern Palaces inside Cairo.[9] How or whether their facades differed visually from the neighboring mosques is something we simply do not know and cannot presently reconstruct.

On the other hand, cloth with writing on it remains from the Fatimid period in great quantities. The textile fragments with writing on them surviving from the Fatimid period number in the thousands. Most major museums throughout the world have some Fatimid cloth, usually labeled *tirāz*.[10] In spite of these extensive material remains, how what has survived functioned in Fatimid society is almost impossible to reconstruct.[11] We are hampered by a clear lack of correspondence between what we read in the medieval sources and what we see of the archaeological fragments. We are also hampered by the historical conditions of textile archaeology and the demands of the modern market place. These are factors seriously limiting the reconstruction of the many ways in which textiles with writing on them were made meaningful in Fatimid society, and the problem is serious enough to merit a more extended discussion here.

Except for one instance of a correspondence between an archaeological fragment and a textile use description in a medieval text,[12] inscribed cloth described as costumes for official processions, or hangings associated with them, cannot be identified among current archaeological textiles. For instance, among the hundreds of fragments I have examined in many collections, in many countries, not one displays a continuous quotation from the Qur'ān like that described by Ibn al-Ṭuwayr as flanking the mihrab in the mosque of al-Ḥākim during the Ramadan procession.[13] The luxurious silks mentioned in describing the attire of the Imam-Caliph have yet to appear—or if they have been dug up, they have not been identified. Not a fragment of the famous textile world map recorded by al-Maqrīzī in his account of the dispersal of Imam-Caliph al-Mustanṣir's treasuries (1061–69/453–62) has been revealed. According to him, this textile-map displayed all locations and was fabricated in gold, silver, and colored silks, displaying at the lower end the name of the Imam-Caliph al-Mu'izz and the date 354 (964 C.E.).[14]

Of course, some luxurious textiles have been found. They exist in the church treasuries and reliquaries in some museum holdings in Europe.[15] But except for certain individual textiles like the "veil of St. Anne,"[16] which is a complete loom length and which has been used in at least one manner we can identify, as a reliquary wrapping, the use of most of the other textiles represented now by their fragments is unclear. Even their final use is unclear, and that is in part the fault of the low esteem in which archaeology has held textiles until recently. Archaeological excavations have provided textiles primarily from burials and from refuse heaps. But the documentation of such textile findings in general has been poorly recorded.[17] Even in volumes like Kendrick's *Catalogue of the Textiles from the Burying-Grounds in Egypt*, where the title suggests a final use for the textiles, we are not told whether the textiles were found on skeletons (whose age at burial or sex also go unmentioned) or in the grave with, not on, the body. We are not told whether the graves were Christian, Muslim, or Jewish.[18] Perhaps the fragments came from a refuse heap in the graveyard: we are not told. And sadly, many fragments come to us without the benefit of an archaeological context no matter how vague. In short, the researcher of Fatimid cloth is dealing generally with evidence of unknown provenance, and for which the provenance is now forever unknowable.

The demands of the marketplace and of collectors have further complicated reconstructing textiles and their use. Most textiles which come on the market were cut to preserve only their embellished parts (the parts with the silk, gold, and writing), and with that cutting much technical evidence that usually provides data about textiles was destroyed. In proportion to the total number of extant fragments, few have selvages and finishes. Without them it is not possible to know the width of the finished fabric, or even where the embellished section that is preserved was displayed on the total fabric. At least one of the full length pieces that remain, the "veil of St. Anne," provides a base for understanding the design layout of relatively large fragments of similar design that are identified in the collections of the Metropolitan Museum of Art and The Textile Museum.[19]

All these caveats aside, much has been learned from the fragments of cloth with writing in Arabic on them. The range of messages and script styles has been described. Likewise, some studies have investigated the technology of gold thread, and others the range of colors and the source of fibres (linen, hemp, cotton, silk, and wool). But the factors described above do put serious limits on what can be learned from the textiles for this exploration.

The term "public text" also includes writing on coins because such writing was officially sponsored and it had a group audience by virtue of the sheer number of people who would have seen the writing. Obviously writing on coins is usually viewed in a more individualized manner than is either writing displayed on communal buildings, where many gather, or writing worn in official processions, where many watch. This difference accounts for the manner in which such writing is analyzed in this study. However, the fact that the writing on coins, officially sponsored writing, was a visual experience for a great number of people within and outside the territory of the issuing ruler brings that writing well within the focus of this study.[20] The Geniza records, for instance, provide ample evidence that writing on coins was meaningful for those engaged in money changing and transactions in the marketplace. Writing on coins was read for its semantic content, and the format of the writing (concentric circles or lines) was used for identification.[21]

"Official writing" and "public text" exclude from consideration non-officially sponsored writing with a group address, however much the writing practice might have been tolerated by officialdom. For example, these categories serve to exclude graffiti in Greek, Syriac, Latin, and Armenian left by pilgrims in the Sinai, which many reported seeing,[22] or in Arabic found on columns and other parts of structures at Jabal Says, Qaṣr al-Ḥayr al-Sharqī, and elsewhere.[23] In addition, they also exclude writing sponsored by the group leadership with a group address but not used officially in communal gathering spaces for the group, even though it played an elaborate role within the ruling class culture. Such writing on textiles and garments, as well as on a variety of luxury objects, was customary in the private practices among the ruling groups of most of the medieval societies of the eastern Mediterranean.

Greek-, then Latin-, and finally Arabic-speaking societies in the eastern Mediterranean, for example, all had finely blown glass vessels with writing on them. In each of these societies, and thus in each language and alphabet, some vessels displayed good wishes to the drinker, or beholder, or owner.[24] In addition, we know in detail that in Abbasid courtly society, handkerchiefs or headbands inscribed with verses of Arabic poetry were for a time the passion.[25] Even individuals not within the court seemed to participate in personalizing their clothing with writing.[26] All these uses of writing fueled fashionable taste and served individual interests, and it could be argued they served a limited group, but not in a manner to engender cohesion of the society as a whole by the reinforcement of beliefs and social relationships. In contrast to these uses, the writing on textiles and clothing that was part of the Fatimid public text was an officially orchestrated, systematic, group-addressed display of writing serving the interests of officialdom in the support of effective governance and, within its own terms, cohesion and stable social order.

In a more obvious way, several other kinds of writing also do not qualify as part of the public text. There is no public text in writing that constituted official government record keeping in which the audience addressed by the writing was not a group. Writing, of course, was an important part of official chancery practices of all ruling groups in the period. We know in detail that handwriting and the ability to compose in Arabic was an important factor in the choice of officials to staff Islamic government *dīwāns* (or bureaus). From al-Qalqashandī, we know in specific detail just how intensified these chancery practices became in the Fatimid period.[27] Nevertheless, official scribal practice, or its intensification, as in the Fatimid period, did not affect its audience. Chancery records were seen primarily by state functionaries or individual recipients of official missives, not a general audience.

This study of the functions of Fatimid public texts promotes a specific understanding of how officially sponsored writing (or any artifact or object or structure) makes its meaning. Meaning as understood here is not completely contained in the writing itself but, rather, grows in the web of contextual relationships woven between the official writing, the patrons, the range of beholders, and the established contexts in which that writing was placed. Take as a simple example what al-Ṭabarī tells us about one use of non-official writing in the early Muslim community. He says that ʿUmar ibn al-Khaṭṭāb had the phrase "reserved for [or devoted to] the way of God,"[28] branded on the thighs of his horses. What we are told about the writing is its semantic content and its placement. But how it communicated meaning to the beholder, who those beholders were, we are not told.

To answer the question, "What did this writing mean?" and to specify what meaning to whom, we need to know about a variety of relationships: for example, were all horses (those belonging to Muslims and those not; those belonging to leaders and those not) branded? Were all brands phrases, and if so, what was their content? Were some brands idiosyncratic marks, and this the only phrase? Were other objects or animals marked with this phrase? What did the brand look like in itself and in relation to others? And finally, what was the significance of the locus of this branding? Without elaborating this example any further, what becomes clear is that to understand the specific meaning of that writing as a brand, we must explore, at least, the network of relations between ʿUmar, his brand and branding practices, the beholders, and the operant social usages that encompassed them.

Of course, officially sponsored writings and the public text are quite different from al-Ṭabarī's story and ʿUmar's brand. But the story is a useful tool here for exploring the various networks of relationships that made that use of writing meaningful to the beholders of ʿUmar's horse. As such, it highlights for this study of officially sponsored writing, its content, its form, the reality of conditions of its being seen, and its beholders. This study suggests that these networks through which official writing communicated meaning to beholders had three primary dimensions: territorial, referential, and aesthetic. Each of these three dimensions, which could also be called functions, organizes many levels of relationships between official writing and the beholder, and social uses and practices.

Certainly, these three functions existed simultaneously. That is, the beholder of official writing derived meaning from each of these three sets of relationships at the same time, although each did not communicate meaning equally or in the same manner. At certain times, in certain historical circumstances, one of those functions of writing predominated. This text is not an attempt to say in words what the viewer saw. Rather, it builds from a fundamentally Gombrichian notion that writing relates to other writing and the reality of conditions in which these writings could be seen.[29] The major issues taken up in this text are understanding how the functions of the officially sponsored writing balanced one another, which one predominated to which group audience, and how those meanings changed within groups and between groups over time. Some preliminary discussion of these dimensions will clarify these networks of relationships.

The territorial function refers to the many ways in which officially sponsored writing reinforced and perpetuated to beholders both the solidarity of their group, binding it, and its exclusivity from other groups, bounding it from another or others.[30] By marking, and thus distinguishing for the beholder, one social territory from another, official writing signaled a boundary separating systems of different informational content. Officially sponsored writing as used by various societies or groups in the eastern Mediterranean communicated especially effectively through this dimension because the writing systems (of primary concern here, and to a lesser extent the languages) of many groups within this study were specific to that group. What is clear from the actions of various leaders of groups within the early medieval Mediterranean is that they recognized the effectiveness of writing as a sign of boundedness of a group, and consciously chose a writing system (what we might call simply an alphabet) because of its differences from, or similarities to, the alphabets of neighboring groups. This boundedness is not a startling revelation for us in the late twentieth century who have witnessed the break up of the Soviet Union, and the subsequent search for appropriate alphabets and languages to signal ethnic identities.

More to the point for this study, in the fifth century when the Armenian King Vramsapuh officially sanctioned the (current) Armenian alphabet created by Mestrop Mastoc', he consciously supported the adoption of a writing system that resembled no neighboring one. The previous writing systems used by Armenians had been based on Greek and Syriac forms; the new alphabet was fashioned of glyphs that looked significantly different.[31] Thus from the fifth century on, the Armenian alphabet was a sign by which Armenians as a group were distinguishable from all other Christians in the area, especially the dominant group, the Greek Orthodox Christians, whose language, like the Armenian language, is Indo-European.[32]

Contrast this choice on the part of the Armenian community to adopt an alphabet emblematic of complete difference from other Christians with the actions of the Coptic community in adopting a modified Greek alphabet. They chose to represent their Hamitic language, Coptic, in alphabetic characters that were visually close (although not totally identical) to those of the Greek alphabet, the alphabet of the dominant religion, practiced by the rulers of the territory and by the majority of the people within their empire. The Coptic alphabetic glyphs emphasized similarity or identification by blurring alphabetic boundaries between the Coptic Christians and the Greek Orthodox, although some boundaries were maintained through the discernible differences in the letter forms.

Of course, the issue here is not simply the adoption of alphabets, but their social use. Patrons, understood here also as beholders, marked Armenian sectarian spaces with the Armenian alphabet; Coptic was displayed in Coptic churches. Samaritan and Hebrew appeared only in synagogues. The fact that writing during the period of this study was used to mark space as exclusive to a group was a praxis we recognize today by the very fact that we use the presence of a specific alphabet (and language) in the identification of those sectarian buildings which otherwise are archaeologically indistinguishable.[33] Thus, it is the presence of Armenian on a mosaic floor in Jerusalem[34] that enabled contemporary scholars to identify its specific group audience as Armenian Christian, when the rest of the depictions in the mosaic floor were relatively common in the geographic area.

Some languages—mainly Greek and to a much lesser extent Arabic and Aramaic—did not function in this territorial or bounding manner, or not in this manner during all periods of this study. The mere presence of these scripts and languages did not immediately mark the space as sectarian specific to the beholder. Greek, for instance, was displayed in synagogues as well as in Greek Orthodox churches.[35] But the beholder could understand "territorial dimensions" from its placement or, more exactly, the pattern of its placement in social practice. For example, mosques directly sponsored by Umayyad rulers from al-Walīd on displayed only writing in Arabic on the *qibla* wall, whereas other languages were sometimes displayed elsewhere.

The second dimension or function of officially sponsored writing we call the referential. This term refers to those networks of meanings derived from the evocational field of the writing; its "content" or informational base. This base included the oral and written traditions of the society, as well as traditions of social relationships, like the names and titles of honored people (past and present) within the group, and dates and events of group significance. Writing on the interiors of sectarian spaces, whether they were Muslim, Christian, or Jewish, was taken from group-specific evocational fields. As will be argued in chapter 2, the semantic content of the most visually dominant writing in all sectarian spaces came from socially equivalent texts: the Qur'ān, New Testament, and Hebrew Bible. Officially sponsored writing within these spaces also gave donor and patron information that helped to organize and stratify the group within itself.

Similarly, the Fatimid public texts placed inside Muslim sectarian spaces were directed to Muslim audiences in ways that are detailed in chapters 3 and 4. In contrast, however, those public texts, displayed on the outsides of structures and in processions, addressed a public audience. These texts came from more than one evocational field and spoke to more than one audience. Importantly, the semantic content was accessible to beholders who were not familiar with the Qur'ān, who were not Muslim. Thus the public aspects of the public text conveyed information germane to subserving the Fatimid social order on a larger scale than a sectarian or group-specific one in a mixed society.

Among the groups considered in this study, written texts that supplied beliefs essential to group action, affirmation, and cohesion were script and language specific. For Muslim believers, God's revelation was and is in Arabic; for Jews, God revealed the Torah, oral and written, in Hebrew; to Christians, the New Testament came largely in translations. Thus for

Muslims and Jews, regardless of specific intra-group differences, Arabic and Hebrew, respectively, were the languages of the essential communal evocational field (or information base) that bound the group together.[36] Among Christian groups, in contrast, the language and, importantly here, the script chosen for the translation of the New Testament (Greek, Armenian, Syriac, Coptic, etc.) became the script and language of the group's belief-conveying evocational field. For Copts the New Testament of use was written in Coptic; for Armenians, in Armenian; for Latin rite Christians, in Latin.[37]

When the semantic content of the writing did not contain essential beliefs of the group, the writing did not (necessarily) function territorially to identify a sectarian group. Rather, the writing defined a group on a different scale, one bound by cultural traditions (written and oral) of a broader nature. Greek writing and language was for a time the primary example of this phenomenon because every time Greek was present in a sectarian space it did not necessarily convey content from the New Testament.

What enabled Greek script and language to be so widely appropriated by various sectarian groups were the social uses of the language in the eastern Mediterranean after Alexander. From the time of Alexander's conquest of this area in the late fourth century B.C., a varied constituency of Greek-speaking people developed. Even under Roman occupation, when the official language was Latin, so many people spoke Greek that official inscriptions in many places were written in Greek.[38] Thus, in the fourth century C.E., when Greek became the official language of the Byzantine empire, not only were the new written messages transmitted in it, but Greek also bound together the already existing classical cultural traditions with those of the Christianity that had diverged from it.[39] It should not surprise us, there is no evidence of comment at the time, to find writing in Greek in synagogues as well as in Greek Orthodox churches. In fact, as recent research confirms, Greek was the language used in public texts in the eastern Mediterranean well into the late eighth century.[40] Of course, the referential and territorial dimensions the writing conveyed to the beholder in each of these sectarian spaces was different.

In the Greek Orthodox churches, the evocational fields of the writing displayed to the beholder were from both the written traditions conveying essential beliefs and from those social relationships that supply the names and titles of historic and contemporary people important to the group. In the synagogues, however, Greek was never used to communicate the essential beliefs.[41] These were expressed in Hebrew. But the writing that did appear in Greek, such as the names and titles of donors, and similar information, evoked a variety of group-based social relationships. The different evocational fields of the two scripts (and languages) stemmed directly from the fact that the congregation was Greek speaking, and knowledge of Greek language played a cultural role in the society on a broad scale.[42]

The third dimension of meaning of officially sponsored writing, the aesthetic, organizes all those networks of relationships that beholders brought to bear when they saw the form, material, rhythm, color (what might be called style)[43] of the officially sponsored writing. I am concerned here, for example, not only with the gold and glass mosaic medium in which the writing in the Dome of the Rock appeared, but wherever else writing appeared in that medium, and where it did not. The linkages or relationships of where writing appeared in this style, or did not appear in this style, communicated meaning to the beholder as did the shape and form of the writing of the letters. In fact, as I will argue in chapter 2, the meanings derived from the aesthetic dimensions of officially sponsored writing in the Dome of the Rock were the predominant ones for the beholders. What will become clear over the next three chapters is just how important the aesthetic function was in communicating meaning to the beholder. When writing could not be read—and even when it could—its color, materiality, and form were prominent aspects of communication. One brief example from the Fatimid period illustrates this.

Ibn al-Ṭuwayr tells us that when the Imam went to the mosque of al-Ḥākim (known as al-Anwar) during Ramadan, textiles near the mihrab were embellished with writing from the Qurʾān. He even lists the *sūras*.[44] Thus, since he indicated the semantic content of the writing, presumably he saw, read, and understood it. But in telling this story, he gave equally many—if not more—details about the color, materiality, and form of the writing. These factors thus must have been important in conveying meaning to him, and presumably to those to whom he recounted the information in his own time, and to us today.

Ibn al-Ṭuwayr noted that the writing of the *sūras* had diacritical marks. This undoubtedly was a clue to his audience and to us, that the script was not Kufic. In all probability it was one of the cursive scripts—the scripts with diacritical marks. Why would he have made that comment? What does it tell a reader? It tells us that the writing on the curtains paralleled the scripts which we know were used in many of the Qurʾāns of the period. Conversely, it tells us equally clearly that the writing on the curtains contrasted sharply with the writing on the interior of the building in which it was displayed, (the Anwar mosque completed in the early eleventh century), and with the writing on and in the building sponsored by the Fatimids at about the same time that these curtains were displayed.[45] The writing in and on all of these structures was in Kufic, sometimes very elaborate Kufic.

But Ibn al-Ṭuwayr does not stop at that detail. He mentioned that the hangings were in silk. We know then that they were neither cotton, linen, nor wool. They were thus very costly, for the fabric was probably imported.[46] And, finally, he related their color—white. We know, and certainly his audience knew, that white was the official Fatimid color, as emblematic of their rule as the black (wool) was of their contemporaries, the Abbasids in Baghdad. Thus, from his comments (by placing what he described within the network of visual relationships and social practices for which we have evidence), we can begin to reconstruct the range of meanings that the official writing with diacritical marks displayed on white silk curtains had for Ibn al-Ṭuwayr and other contemporary beholders.

It seems appropriate at this point to inquire how this study of the Fatimid public text relates to scholarly inquiry in general and, in specific, to the study of writing in the disciplines that constitute Islamic Studies, for it is a part of both. The rubrics of analysis here are derived in part from elements of models of communication now almost three decades old.[47] Over the past years these categories have generated much scholarly debate, and scholars outside linguistic and literary studies in almost all social science and humanistic disciplines have attempted to digest, refine, rethink, and integrate this analytic paradigm.[48] This study of the Fatimid public text shares with such works an agreement that meaning involves the staging of specific relationships. But this study has a significant divergence from such a paradigm because it includes in its paradigm the sites or locations of meaning, a point of view that is absent from the narrower, linguistically oriented analysis.[49] *Writing Signs* includes the beholder, a group audience, as an essential element in its paradigm.

As such it takes inspiration directly from the pages of Ibn al-Haytham's (Alhazen's) theory of perception written while he was in Cairo at the court of Imam-Caliph al-Ḥākim (r. 996–1021/386–411) and beyond, teaching at al-Azhar mosque until his death in c. 1039. He claimed that *perception* of a form required discernment, inference, recognition, comparison with other signs (*amārāt*), and judgment by users to relate them properly.[50] His insistence that for all practical purposes forms were *perceived* and not seen, pointed the way to understanding the active role of the beholder in placing a given form in a network of memorized forms and associations.

Including the audience in the analysis in *Writing Signs* gives historical dimension to the meaning of official writing. Without an anchor in viewer (user) and place, the reconstruction of the meaning of the writing (or any artifact) takes on an ahistorical timelessness. When I said above that meaning was not completely contained in the writing itself but was also a function of the relationship of the beholder, the writing and social usage and practices, I asserted that the meaning of a particular example of writing was situated in a beholder in a specific historical moment: it therefore changes over time and with groups of beholders. Thus, the "same" writing on the minarets of the mosque of al-Ḥākim will carry different meanings to a Muslim than to a Christian audience in the same year, for example, in 1002/393 when the writing first appeared. So, too, the "same" writing on costumes and textiles in Fatimid processions would have conveyed different meanings to spectators along the route in 1060 than in 1123. These divergent meanings for the beholders were the result of shifting political, economic, geographical, and religious attitudes or circumstances, as well as changes in the composition of the audience and beholder.[51]

In addition to concern about the beholder's role in the construction of the meaning of written signs, this study understands writing practices in any society as subserving the hegemonic interests of officialdom, as defined by the given society. All societies with writing, then as well as now, have some mix of written and oral modes of communication. The uses of writing, whether extensive or limited, the modes and institutions through which writing is taught, and, in particular for the Fatimid emphasis here, the changes or shifts in the uses of writing within a society are all understood as socially constructed practices subserving the interests of those who institute the changes. That a society used writing to keep ledgers does not in itself supply sufficient reason for that same society eventually to put writing in or on buildings. Seeing writing practices as socially constructed, and fully understandable only in terms of the practices of a given society is supported increasingly by the research of psychologists, sociologists, anthropologists, and historians.[52]

These premises indicate that writing is approached in this study in ways unlike those used in most other works addressed to the understanding of writing in the Islamic world. Rather, *Writing Signs* is in the spirit of change called for by Michael Rogers,[53] and in the interests of contextual understanding of the role of writing advocated by Priscilla Soucek.[54] It has profited greatly from earlier studies, like those of Richard Ettinghausen, Oleg Grabar, and Janine Sourdel-Thomine that have approached some of the issues included here.[55] But it is fundamentally different from (and presents historical evidence to question) approaches based explicitly or implicitly on an organic, evolutionary model by which inevitably, at least quasi-mechanically, the public text would emerge by natural processes.

There are many kinds of compendiums and articles based on this evolutionary assumption. These include almost all scholarly works based on style analysis that postulates simple styles as "early" and elaborate styles as "late" or "developed." These compendiums have useful functions; such records form a base for this study. They do record difference, yet they understand difference as merely sequential and developmental, excluding the possibility that difference may simply mark contemporary variants caused by other production factors such as maker or use. In fact, beyond this explanation of change, most writers make no attempt to account for difference or change in any way. In other writings on writing, the organic metaphor is applied explicitly to the use of writing and the inevitability of its becoming more and more prominent not because of style but because it was launched on its trajectory by religion.[56] Yet, as a counter to this view it is useful to remember that the Qur'anic revelation is not the only one given directly by God to men. The Torah is understood to be uncreated and revealed by God in oral and in written form. Nonetheless, the trajectories of the uses of writing both within and between each group of sectarian believers varies over time and place. These evolutionary models usually conflate book hands with writing on all other artifacts and buildings, thus implying that when handwriting attained a high degree of elaboration in Muslim societies, it finally had to appear somewhere beyond manuscripts and chancery documents and was therefore placed on buildings.

As this inquiry will elaborate later, neither of these evolutionary models can be historically substantiated. The general argument made conventionally is that change occurred in the use of officially sponsored writing from the time of the Umayyad Caliph ʿAbd al-Malik (r. 685–705/65–86). In fact, in the Umayyad period, the uses of officially sponsored writing in Arabic in Muslim sectarian spaces appear more limited than those in Greek in Christian sectarian buildings during Byzantine rule. Moreover, the formats for the use of writing in Arabic had been established by early Muslim rulers; decade then followed decade with few changes. No exceptional or new use of officially sponsored writing addressed to a group appeared in the eastern Mediterranean. Fatimid Egyptian practice, the public text, then, was both distinct in its own time, and distinctly different from previous practice, even from Fatimid practice in North Africa and from that of their initial years in Egypt. The public text must not be seen as commonplace but, as my field observations suggest, as a unique, historically based occurrence not totally replicated elsewhere. We need only a cursory visual familiarity with the historical and geographical expanse of the practice of Muslim groups to know quite clearly that the official uses of writing were (and are) different, for example, in Safavid practice from those in Ottoman; in Ghana from those in the Philippines; in Detroit, Michigan from those in Pakistan.

One "evolution" or "development" that occurred in the eastern Mediterranean during the time of this study is supported by recent scholarly studies, namely, conversion to Islam. In the eastern Mediterranean, more people were Muslim at the end of the period of the study than at the beginning. More people were Muslim when the Fatimids ruled than when the Umayyads ruled. Egypt, Syria, and Iraq, by the time of the Fatimids, had a population that was dominantly Muslim, even if we adopt the late conversion date of 1010 C.E. argued for by Bulliet.[57] Even though significant Christian and Jewish minorities existed in Egypt, the population the Fatimids ruled was Muslim, and this study offers an understanding of how the public text was indeed related to the Muslim-ness of the society in the Fatimid capital. It seeks to highlight, in fact, that the specific composition of the Fatimid ruling group within the society, and that of the ruled population, and not simply its Muslim-ness, in part accounts for the presence and the meaning of the public text.

A language "development" is linked to conversion and Muslim rule: during the Fatimid period more people knew Arabic in Egypt than in the Umayyad period. "Knowing" Arabic involved several social considerations. On the one hand, knowing Arabic, in the sense of speaking the popular language, or *al-ʿāmmiya*, was important, but to participate in the hierarchy of the society, command of reading, writing, and speaking proper or pure Arabic, *faṣīḥa*, was mandatory. The hegemonic structures of the society, especially those representing the sciences of grammar and law, supported and fostered both what constituted *faṣīḥa* and, its corollary, rendered judgments as to those who had sufficient skills to rise to positions of importance. No charge was more damning against a reputation for those in or seeking prominent positions than not knowing Arabic (*faṣīḥa*). In the tenth/fourth century, and especially in the eleventh/fifth, the centuries of Fatimid rule, Cairo-Miṣr became a center for grammar and law, and Muslim students, especially from the western lands came there to study these sciences.[58] The size of the Fatimid government and record keeping in Arabic suggests the importance of knowing *faṣīḥa* and the number of people who qualified at least for bureaucratic positions.

Evidence for Christians and Jews speaking and writing at least *al-ʿāmmiya* is found in part in the nature of the anecdotes Abū Ṣāliḥ reports which indicate a significant level of spoken Arabic within the Christian communities.[59] The writing of the Geniza documents shows a familiarity with *al-ʿāmmiya* among some Jews in Fatimid society, even though many of the documents were written in Hebrew characters. This practice of writing Arabic language in Hebrew characters is yet another example of alphabet and not language bounding and binding a group. And finally we have the presence of Coptic texts and vestments that display writing in Arabic in addition to that in Coptic, which suggests the commonalty of Arabic as a spoken language in Fatimid society, as well as some reading knowledge of it.[60]

Clearly, issues relevant to the Fatimid public text are not simply the speaking of Arabic, but both the recognition of Arabic writing as writing in Arabic letters, and the ability to read Arabic. Doubtless, Jews, Armenians, Copts, and other non-Muslims in Fatimid society, all of whom had a different group-specific alphabet and language, recognized or could identify Arabic writing when they saw it. Thus all beholders could understand many aspects of the territorial and aesthetic functions of official writing in Arabic by recognizing the presence of writing in Arabic. But for beholders to derive meaning from the referential functions of official writing, they needed to know its semantic content. Clearly, for beholders to understand the referential aspects of officially sponsored writing, they needed to be literate.

This study assumes that the minimal literacy sufficient to enable at least the relevant urban people to fulfill their duties to act appropriately is one which enables many beholders to read names and titles, dates, and other similar data.[61] My argument is closely related to Brian Stock's hypothesis of a "textual community" where "texts emerged as a reference both for every day activities and for giving shape to the larger vehicles of explanation,"[62] for it includes both literate and illiterate beholders. But what I call "contextual" reading highlights the issues involved in beholders seeing the writing itself rather than simply knowing the text (either in oral or written fashion) and reacting to it.[63]

A contemporary ethnographic study by Sylvia Scribner and Michael Cole[64] testing literacy in Arabic offers substantial evidence supporting my assumption that a significant number of people in Fatimid society would have had "contextual" literacy, and therefore could have understood the referential meanings from viewing the Fatimid public text. This assumption follows from the evidence gathered by Scribner and Cole that Muslim males, in receiving even a minimal mosque school education, learned enough Arabic for "contextual" literacy. In the Fatimid capital in Egypt, the urban population was predominantly Muslim. Thus, among the males at least, we assume contextual literacy through minimal participation in mosque schools. In addition to this male group within Fatimid society, we are told that Muslim women, probably only upper class Ismāʿīlī, were educated. And, as mentioned above, some members of the various Christian communities and of the Jewish community read Arabic.

A few more words need to be said about contextual literacy and the findings of the Scribner and Cole study to clarify their relevance here. Scribner and Cole tested contemporary literacy in Arabic in a Liberian society where three languages and scripts (Vai, the main language and script; Arabic, known only to Muslim members of the society; and English, currently being taught in the government schools) were learned in different institutions, and used for different purposes within the society by differing although overlapping audiences. In Liberian society, Muslims, except those who excelled in Muslim studies, received only the usual minimal mosque school training. (Those who excelled were sent to the main cities and the universities.) What these psychologists discovered, and what is important for this study, is that Muslims with only minimal training in Arabic, that is minimal introduction into the writing system and evocational base of that writing system, could read the "official" writing in Arabic in their society. Because of the way they learned Arabic, they also had a greater memory-store of learned texts, mainly from the Qurʾān. Although these Muslims' knowledge of Arabic was not sufficient to read literature, or any range of "unexpected" material, nevertheless they could read all those materials in their society that were in Arabic, precisely because the material that appeared in Arabic writing in their society was expected. It came from a limited evocational base.

The critical element here is the range of expectation. In Vai society only very circumscribed material appears in Arabic. And Muslims within the society can read the range of Arabic that appears because the range of Arabic (the semantic content: the words) is expected. Literacy in Arabic does not extend beyond that ability. Chapters 3 and 4 of *Writing Signs* assume a "contextual" literacy and then detail the limited range, thus the "expectedness," of the evocational base of the Fatimid public text. It is not that the semantic content of the public text never changed over the period of Fatimid rule, but, rather, within elements of the public text (parts of the processions, inside and outside mosques and shrines) the evocational base was relatively constant. It could be read(ily) read(ily).

One final aspect related to the reading of writing in Arabic needs to be mentioned. Most, although not all, of the writing in Arabic that made up the Fatimid public text was displayed in Kufic. Kufic is a script which is instantly recognizable by its geometrical lines. But it is highly incomplete phonetically: in this script diacritical marks are usually not added to letters, and thus twenty-eight differing consonantal sounds are represented by only seventeen different graphic shapes. The possible ambiguities of reading that can result from an alphabetically incomplete script have led many contemporary scholars to regard Kufic as inherently difficult to decipher. But as Geoffrey Sampson demonstrates, incomplete scripts can convey fully clear meanings to readers knowledgeable of the contents.[65] Beholders accustomed to seeing incomplete scripts conveying specific semantic content in familiar contexts can read the writing. It follows, then, that the writing in Arabic in Kufic script on Fatimid buildings could have been read by the contextually literate of Fatimid society for precisely the reason those same beholders could read the semantic content. The context made the content expected. Thus, only some words and phrases—a limited vocabulary—appeared in the Kufic of the public text.[66]

What was special about the Fatimid practice of publishing its public text was the systematic display: how the Fatimids used the texts they chose in the public space, how they were guided in their choice by their sociopolitical needs, and their acute sensitivity to the diversity of their constituency. The public text, the Fatimid's special achievement, is best highlighted by observing the use of officially sponsored writing by others in the eastern Mediterranean.

CHAPTER 2

Signing the Community

For some five hundred years before the Fatimid public text first appeared, officially sponsored writing was used throughout the eastern Mediterranean to address group audiences. The archaeological remains from the time of the widespread building program initiated by the Byzantine Emperor Justinian (r. 527–565 C.E.) provide a sufficient base of communal practices—the specific uses of writing and the employment of specific alphabets—to discuss what we call "signing the community." Our first purpose, then, is to review how those in power used written signs addressed to group audiences, exploring and assessing both the official practice in the Byzantine, Umayyad, Abbasid, and early Cairene Fatimid reigns, and the relevant social practices in non-ruling groups of those imperiums where some assessment is possible. For some groups, such as the Jacobite, Malkite, and Syriac Christians, the lack of sufficient evidence makes assessment impossible.[1] Indeed, the evidence for the social practice of officially sponsored writing in the Greek Orthodox and Christian communities exists basically from the urban communities. Among the Jewish communities, destruction of synagogues during the fifth and sixth centuries leaves them represented largely by archaeological remains.

Although the evidence is large enough, much of it from these five hundred years is fragmentary and its contents unexplored. Detailed discussion of the producers of the texts or the expectations of the intended audiences remains difficult, sometimes impossible. Consequently, in this exploration of community writing my inferences are often drawn from practices widely spaced in time and place. The difficulties of interpretation are not simply the result of individual missing buildings like the Great

Mosques of Ramla and Aleppo,[2] or of buildings about which little is known beyond their location, such as Justinian's Nea cathedral in Jerusalem,[3] and whole categories of structures that represent official architectonic practices, such as *dār al-imāras*.[4] Nor is it simply a matter of buildings only partially extant, like most synagogues, or so badly damaged or changed by later restorations that they are not useful for this analysis, such as many of the churches.[5] Equally important, simply said, we often know little about what does remain. Critically, we do not know or understand many of the social practices.

We can only poorly identify or even describe the communities that used and supported some buildings we do know. We have known for some time that the small town of Umm al-Jimal, for example, contained fifteen churches. Yet only now are we beginning to understand the composition of the congregations that supported them, and how the various churches might have functioned in a larger social network.[6] Similarly, we know nothing of the communities that during the Umayyad rule built the small mosques which dotted the desert area of the *bilād al-shām*, like those found at Umm al-Walīd and Jabal Says.[7] Thus, in most instances, we not only do not know the rite used in the churches, or the specific beliefs of those using the mosques, we have little reliable knowledge of who sponsored the structures or of the socio-economic and political situation of their congregations.

One further example should serve. For some populations discussed in this chapter, both the producers and the audiences have to be inferred from the presence of an alphabet and language. The Syro-Palestinian Aramaic found in the church at Umm al-Ru'ūs near Jerusalem, in the monastery at Khirbad Mird in the Judaean desert, and in a mosaic inscription in a church at al-Quwaysma, south of Amman, indicate a Syro-Palestinian community distinguishable only by its writing.[8] Nothing else now currently known separates this community materially from others, and likewise nothing is known about the social structure of the community. In sum, then, although many hundreds of official buildings remain—churches, mosques, synagogues, baptisteries, hospitals, and the like—many are in such a fragmentary state that they are not useful for the purposes of this study. Often floors remain, but walls do not. All too often the original ornamentation is missing, or if plaques with writing on them are found at the site, little can be done to reconstruct the specific placement of the plaque. Writing in non-permanent materials by and large perished long ago.

Still, though not as fulsome as we would like, enough archaeological evidence remains to permit a beginning analysis. The time frame of this study, starting with the reign of the Emperor Justinian, also clearly brings some difficulties. But the practices of using writing addressed to group audiences both in the buildings sponsored by members of his imperium, and in the structures built by other groups within the broader social formation of Byzantine rule can here be examined as a base of Umayyad practice of writing signs. Byzantine did not become Umayyad practice. Rather, the systems of writing signs for group audiences embedded within the broader social formations of both Byzantine and Umayyad societies were equivalent but not identical. In both societies, and in those subsequent until the Fatimids, using writing was one factor among clusters of others that linked the social organization of small and large communities.

This time frame also helps us shift the consideration of the social practice of using writing away from explanations based solely on religion, Muslim versus Christian. Many scholars believe, incorrectly, a more expanded use of writing to be characteristic of Muslim visual practices from the late eighth century onward. To the contrary, using these particular five hundred years lets us examine the social uses of writing by societies that succeeded one another in a given geographic area. Imperium succeeded imperium, Byzantine, Umayyad, Abbasid, but the system of using the genre of written text discussed here changed little.

I am emphasizing that typical forms of writing linked similar kinds of producer, audience, topic, medium, content, and context regardless of alphabet and language, and regardless of the religion that dominated the society. In fact, a careful reading of the evidence demonstrates that officially sponsored writing with a group address served socially equivalent functions for all sectarian communities from the sixth through the tenth centuries. Rule appropriated the trappings of rule. Writ large is the truth that regardless of differences in religious beliefs, the pattern of the use of writing addressed to group audiences was equivalent throughout all communities.

What follows is a sifting of this uneven archaeological and artifactual evidence for observable regularities which can be understood as social rule or social practice whether or not prescriptive rules or regulations can be found in the records of the referent community. These observed regularities of practice are bracketed by the frames I call the territorial, aesthetic, and referential functions. Though considered here discretely, for a beholder all three aspects of meaning were present at once. However, in any particular historical context, one function was often the primary conveyor of the meaning.

Territorial Function

The universal social practice among groups in the eastern Mediterranean in this period was to use officially sponsored writing to mark sectarian spaces by placing writing inside those spaces, strategically. Christians of all denominations, Muslims, and Jews alike followed the same practice. In contrast, only to a very limited extent was officially sponsored writing addressed to a mixed audience used as a territorial marker in the public spaces.

Indeed, writing placed on the outside of structures, or invading public spaces in any way, was rare. In fact, one significant earlier use of writing, the inscribing of milestones along major highways connecting commercial centers, was virtually discontinued by the opening years of this study and was not programmatically revived by any ruling group.[9] Thousands of milestones are extant from Roman–early Byzantine practice, whereas only a few are extant from as late as the Umayyad and early Abbasid periods.[10] The practices of the Byzantines, Umayyads, Abbasids, and early Fatimids, as ruling groups, were similar in their minimal use of written signs in the public space. Those minimal uses will be reviewed here first, before the more significant territorial functions of writing within sectarian spaces will be analyzed.

The most consistent way in which writing was addressed to a mixed audience in the public space, one that was renewed and continued throughout the entire period, involved the marking of thresholds of walled urban areas. Byzantine, Umayyad, and Fatimid rulers and governors placed writing on the outsides of the gateways through which access into cities was controlled.[11] Examples of this practice are found in the seats of imperiums like Constantinople and Cairo, as well as in more rural, although commercially strategic, areas like Aqaba.[12] Rulers continually updated inscriptions, such as those on the city gates into Constantinople, and writing was placed on the gates of walled cities newly constructed late in this period, such as Cairo.

The presence of Greek or Arabic alphabets on the exterior of city thresholds was a sign of power marking boundaries; it indicated not that the group within was bound by a common language or common beliefs, but that the group was bound by a common rule. Moreover, that alphabet on the gate was a visual index of both the official language of rule, and, by extension, of the language of the belief system of the ruling group. Cities visually linked by similar writings became units in a chain which indexed the extent of rule, and often—in the sequence of inscriptions—the succession of rule.[13]

Less frequently and less consistently, rulers also used writing in the public space to mark the perimeter of their territory. Highly uneven archaeological data suggests that only Byzantine rulers among all those studied here consistently marked the forts on the frontier of their territory in the eastern Mediterranean with writing.[14] Recent analysis of these forts and their inscriptions by Thomas Parker suggests that this specific practice was especially important to Byzantine rulers primarily because they often reused Roman forts which already displayed other officially sponsored writing. Thus the re-making or re-writing by Byzantine rulers was one way of updating the written signs of power and rule. Highway markers functioned in a similar way. Umayyad rulers do not seem to have used writing as a consistent sign on structures serving similar perimeter or border functions, possibly because they seem to have built new buildings for new types of border services. Likewise, the Abbasids and Fatimids apparently did not mark their borders in the eastern Mediterranean in the same fashion.

Officially sponsored writing on coins is the only other significant use of writing in public space during these centuries before the emergence of the Fatimid public text. The coins minted by all rulers and governors from the sixth to the eleventh century displayed writing. Since coins circulated mainly within the territory of the issuer, many urban residents in all cities throughout the area, and over the centuries, would have been exposed to writing on coins as a sign of power that governed them, even taking into account Philip Curtin's hypothesis that coins were circulated far less widely than we thought.[15]

Two incidents from this period involving the writing on coins illustrate, first, the use of alphabets as a group identity sign and, second, the dangers of easy generalizations about significantly augmented uses of writing by early Muslim rulers. Umayyad copper coins of the Damascus mint (phase two coins) displayed a Byzantine royal portrait on the obverse, typical of the seventh century Constantinopolitan folles (copper coins), and on the reverse the capital M, which on the Byzantine prototype represented the numeral 40, their nominal denomination. These coins were minted with three different writing formats giving the mint name: one with Greek as the sole denomination (DAM), one with Greek (DAMAKOC) and Arabic (*dimashq*), and one solely with Arabic (*dimashq*), which according to Michael Bates represents their probable date of issue (figs. 5, 6, 7).

5. Copper coin, Umayyad period, phase II, Greek language (1954.112.4 Collection of the American Numismatic Society)

These Umayyad copper coins follow the Byzantine prototype closely in image and in weight. Only the presence of writing distinguished the Umayyad issues from the Byzantine because no Byzantine folles displayed the Damascus mint name, even in Greek, as part of their image. We can understand the shift in alphabets and languages on the coins as the issuers' attempt to relate the image on the coin (and thus the coin) to the group of Arabic speakers, especially the Muslims within their territory, rather than to the Greek speakers, especially the Orthodox Greek Muslims.

An equally interesting analogue, and perhaps one more familiar, is the Umayyad silver coin issued from the Damascus mint with Sassanid imagery. The obverse of these coins displays the image of the Sassanian emperor Khosraw II. On the right of the image is his name written in Pahlavi script (middle Persian language), and behind his head is a laudatory inscription also in Pahlavi script. This entire image, then, complete with its original writing, is Zoroastrian Sassanian, relating rule to a specific religious culture. Coins issued in A.H. 72 (fig. 8) bear in addition the inscription in Arabic, "In the name of God, Muḥammad is the Messenger of God," (those issued in 73 and 74 display a slightly longer inscription). Here, again, writing in Arabic served as a territorial marker.

The second incident in coinage history, one from which much has been extrapolated in assessing the uses of writing in Arabic by Muslim rulers, occurred in 696–97 C.E. / A.H. 77–79 when the Umayyad Caliph ʿAbd al-Malik began to mint coins which displayed only writing in Arabic (fig. 9).[16] Instituting this new epigraphic format provided a readily distinguishable marker that enabled users to differentiate his new dinars (gold coins) and dirhams (silver coins) which were lighter in weight from the others in common currency.[17] The "other" heavier coins in circulation were those minted previously by himself and earlier Umayyad rulers, and

6. Copper coin, Umayyad period, phase II, Greek and Arabic languages (1917.215.3314 Collection of the American Numismatic Society)

those of other rival Muslim leaders, as well as those of Byzantine leaders. ʿAbd al-Malik's decision to put more writing on coins needs to be seen as an isolated act in developing a set of signs indicative of his own and of Umayyad power. He did not use writing in any other visual medium either more frequently or in more visually significant ways than other rulers of his time.[18]

We do not fully understand what made ʿAbd al-Malik choose a solely epigraphic format for his coins and not also for the buildings he sponsored, but obviously one of his intentions was to create a visual difference from other coins, thus helping his own new issue. That other Muslim leaders minted coins in the epigraphic pattern he established at the Damascus mint, beginning with his governor of Iraq, al-Ḥajjāj, is best understood in the light of political alliances. Those adopting the new epigraphic format aligned themselves with the Umayyad Caliphate and with Caliph ʿAbd al-Malik. A totally epigraphic format in Arabic was an innovation that denoted a specific group in the social matrix and was an effective tool to set the Umayyads and those who supported them apart from others. The continued adoption of this format by the Abbasids and their governors is likewise a political decision that understood the format as a legitimating sign of Muslim power associated with a specific sociopolitical tradition. The break with this format by the Fatimids in the tenth century needs to be seen as a conscious manipulation of a widely adopted sign of Muslim political power.

One looks in vain in the archaeological and supporting textual records for other *systematic* uses of written signs in the public space beyond the limited ones described here. Extant buildings from Salonika to Cairo reveal an equivalent absence in the practice of all ruling groups in the use of writing in the public space. Written signs were not used systematically

7. Copper coin, Umayyad period, phase II, Arabic language (1970.107.26 Collection of the American Numismatic Society)

to differentiate Christian sectarian buildings according to their rite;[19] nor to mark buildings of different religions; nor to indicate different functions for structures—even in large, prosperous cities with populations representing several sectarian groups and economic levels.[20] Even the placement of writing on the lintels of entrance doorways is done irregularly. In the late fourth century, in the reign of Theodosius, the Roman temenos in Damascus was purified for Christian use. At that time inscriptions were carved into already existing lintels of the triple-arched doorway in the facade of the south wall of the temenos. These inscriptions are still visible today on the outer face of the walled-up door of the mosque. But it was even more frequent for lintel inscriptions to be on the inner face, or inner of the two doors if the doors are double, as at the Dome of the Rock.[21] One can point to exceptions: the Armenian church on Achtamar, unusual in its island setting and in its ornamentation within Armenian conventions, and the so-called Three Door Mosque in Qairowan for which full archaeological data is lacking, both somewhat removed from the geographical area considered here, but both displaying writing on their exteriors.[22] Yet these rare instances only underscore what was the normal practice of not using writing as a visually significant marker in the public space.

Investigation into public ceremonies—Byzantine, Umayyad, Abbasid, and early Fatimid—reveals a similar absence of *systematic* uses of writing as visual signs of power.[23] Descriptions of public ceremonies are infrequent and not systematic and thus only preliminary judgments can be put forth. What can safely be said is that textiles with writing on them, or standards with words or letters, did not play a significant enough role in any ceremonies of this period to elicit substantial comment. By contrast, from these same written sources we do understand the importance of cer-

8. Umayyad silver coin, Khosraw II (1971.316.35 Collection of the American Numismatic Society)

tain colors: for example, the importance of wearing black, usually black wool, for officials in Abbasid public ceremony. Color also played a role in Byzantine ceremonial, especially in Constantinople, as did statuary, which was often carried in processions. What little is known about Umayyad public display suggests the lack of a consistent system of displaying this power to a public audience.

Strikingly different in frequency and consistency was the use of writing placed *inside* sectarian space, marking that space as group specific. Here extensive archaeological evidence exists for most groups, even though again it is uneven. Within sectarian spaces, beholders, already community members, came prepared with a common contextual frame of reference. Within their space, the presence of the group-specific alphabet served to the sectarian beholders as one of several signs of their group's identification. In fact, the importance of the alphabet as a communal sign is reinforced by what we know of the writing practices of Jewish and Coptic communities as early as the tenth century in Egypt. Within these communities, Arabic, the language of rule, was written in the alphabet of the group, known today as Judeo-Arabic and Copto-Arabic.

We can expand that statement to say that writing in the group-specific alphabet was an emblem of the group because the presence of that same alphabet marked all the group's sectarian spaces. Directly stated, the Coptic alphabet and language was placed in all Coptic churches, and Copts as a community were reinforced by accepting those spaces and the writing therein as appropriate to their group, and their group alone.[24] The territorial function of the use of Coptic was reinforced by the social practice of Egyptian society as a whole, for Coptic was used in no other sectarian space except those frequented by Copts.

Yet although writing was a ubiquitous territorial sign used by all groups during these centuries, it was a secondary sign or site for conveying ter-

9. Reform coin, ʿAbd al-Malik (1002.1.406 Collection of the University of Pennsylvania Museum in the Cabinet of the American Numismatic Society)

ritorial meanings. Depictions occupied far larger areas inside all sectarian spaces. For example, more space on the walls of the Dome of the Rock (fig. 10) and the Great Mosque of Damascus was devoted to the depictions of trees and plants and, in the Great Mosque of Damascus specifically, to the depictions of buildings, than was allocated for writing. The same could be said for Christian sectarian spaces. Writing was secondary to the depiction of biblical and New Testament figures. To the beholder within whichever sectarian space, Muslim, Christian, or Jewish, depictions, much more than officially sponsored writing, served as group-specific emblems, marking that space and others like it as belonging to the group.

Though visually less important, officially sponsored writing did mark the space as group specific, and the presence of a particular alphabet often signaled to the beholder a transformed or community-specific message for depictions that were common in the society as a whole. Take, for example, the closely similar depictions in several mosaic pavements on the floors of diverse sectarian structures—both synagogues and churches—from the sixth century, as noted above.[25] These floors, in various states of preservation, are located at the church of Shellal, at the synagogue at Gaza, at the Maʿon (or Nirim) synagogue, on an Armenian mosaic floor in Jerusalem, and in abbreviated versions in a few other places (figs. 11, 12, 13, 14). How writing functioned to specify the depiction becomes clear when we compare three of these pavements within three different types of communal space: the pavements in the synagogue at Maʿon, in the church at Shellal, and in the Armenian church in Jerusalem.

These three floors all depict a grape vine (flowing from a vase) which has little foliage, abundant grapes and, in its loops, a range of beasts, birds, and objects. All have peacocks framing the vase: those at the Maʿon syna-

10. Interior, Dome of the Rock (drawn by Hampikian after photo by Creswell)

gogue and the church of Shellal break through the confines of a single loop; those in the Jerusalem pavement have tails that break out of a single loop but do not enter a second. The central vertical registers of all three display similar motifs: a bird in a cage, various containers of fruit, and perhaps also an eagle.[26] Basically, in formal terms, the depictions are strikingly similar. What visually distinguishes them, and makes them group specific, is the presence of writing as part of the whole depictive framework.

The script is Armenian on the pavement in Jerusalem, Greek on that at Shellal, and Aramaic at the synagogue at Maʿon. To the beholder standing

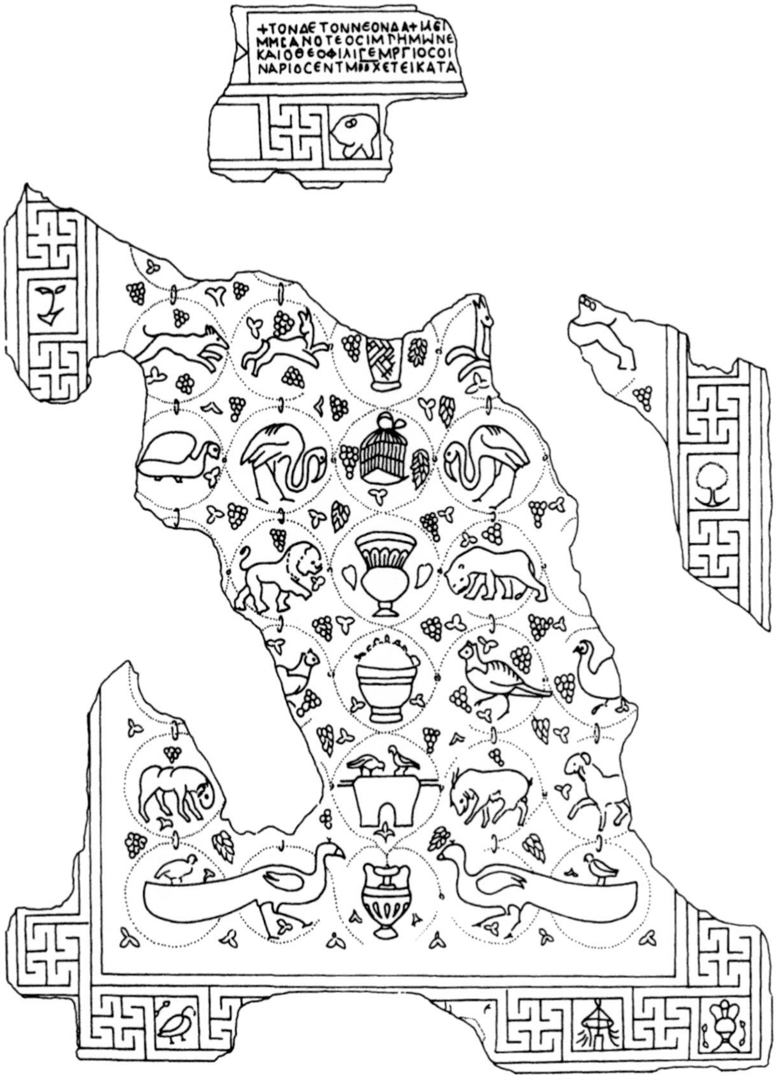

11. Floor mosaic, church of Shellal (drawn by Hampikian after photo by Avi-Yonah)

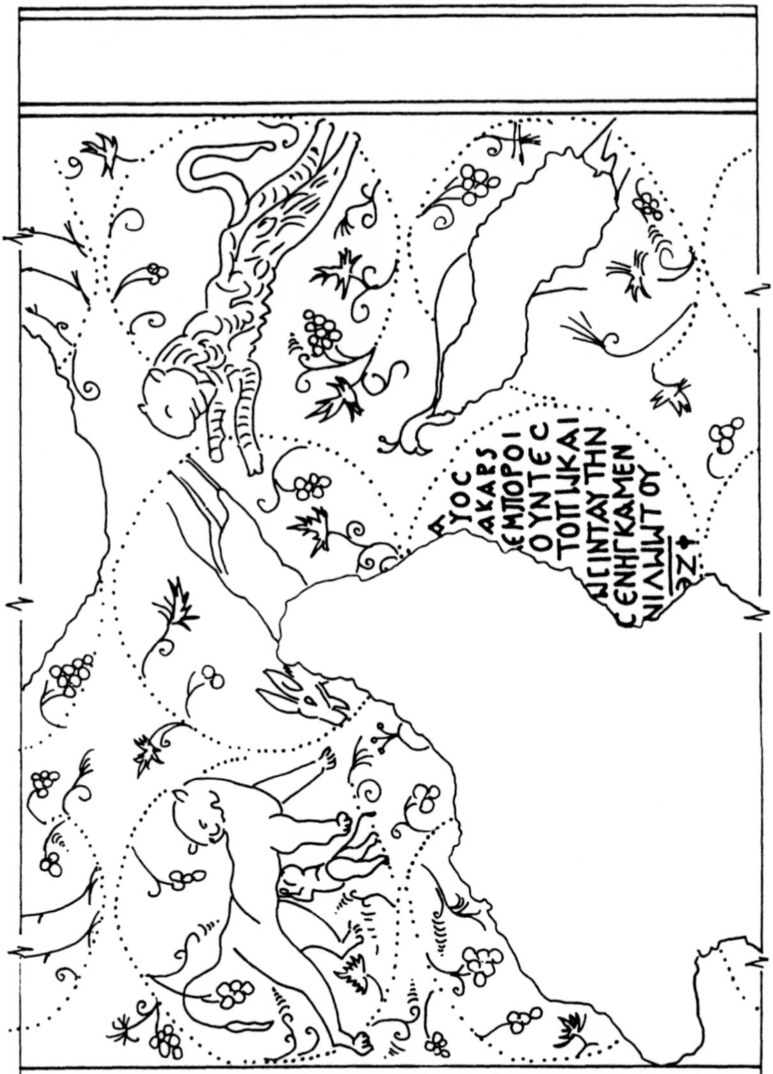

12. Floor mosaic, synagogue at Gaza (drawn by Hampikian after photo by Avi-Yonah)

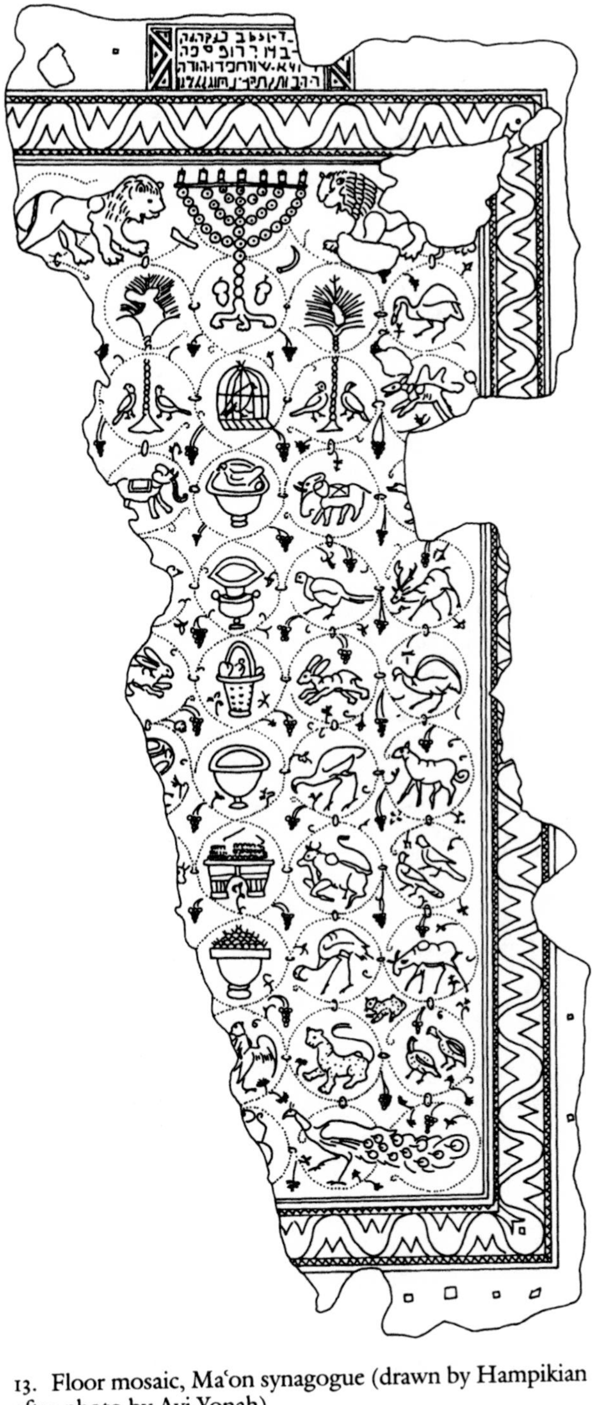

13. Floor mosaic, Ma'on synagogue (drawn by Hampikian after photo by Avi-Yonah)

14. Floor mosaic, Armenian church, Jerusalem (drawn by Hampikian after photo by Narkis)

within the group space, the script was part of the territorial content of the depiction. Among the common images of the whole depiction, the specific alphabet was a visual clue for the beholder. It placed the images in the mosaics in a territorial or group-specific context, evoking by its presence the meaning of the images appropriate to the individual sectarian group. Thus, the images were read as "Armenian" or "Jewish" or "Greek Orthodox."

The depiction of the bird in a cage which appeared in all of the mosaics, for instance, represented a common neo-platonic allegorical theme of a soul as a prisoner of the body. Each of these sectarian groups, having adopted the theme, transformed it in group-specific ways.[27] The presence of the alphabet of the group informed the beholder and indexed the group-specific referents. In fact, we, the contemporary beholders, understand the meaning conveyed by the presence of the alphabet in a similar way. We see (and publish) one as Armenian Art, one as Jewish Art, and one as early Christian Art based on the presence of the group-specific written sign. I should mention here as an aside that writing functioned in similar ways on the early Umayyad coinage, as mentioned above. On those coins, writing in Arabic, and in one instance Greek and Greek-Arabic, cued the beholder that the familiar image had a new group referent.[28]

Evaluating the archaeological evidence from several vantage points strongly reinforces our contention that it was the mere presence of the group-based alphabet, and not its content or its placement, that was the definitive territorial marker for the group-audience. Take, for instance, Abbasid Caliph al-Maʾmūn's tampering with part of the inscription of Umayyad Caliph ʿAbd al-Malik in the Dome of the Rock.[29] Caliph al-Maʾmūn added his name over that of ʿAbd al-Malik in the inscription on the east end of the intermediate octagon, south face. The semantic content now reads: "hath built this dome the Servant of God, ʿAbd Allah the Imam al-Maʾmūn, Commander of the Faithful in the year two and seventy." That al-Maʾmūn substituted his name for that of ʿAbd al-Malik has long been recognized by scholars, but in substituting his name, he did not change the date. It still reads A.H. 72 (691–92 C.E.), some 140 years before the time of the substitution of names in 831/216. In ways recalling Ettinghausen's argument more than a decade ago,[30] the semantic content inconsistencies only highlight the importance of the presence of officially sponsored writing for a group-audience, however important the presence of his name was to the Caliph.

The social practices that orchestrated the placement of writing within sectarian spaces were similarly operative for all groups.[31] In sectarian gathering places sponsored by the ruling groups, such as churches and mosques and shrines like the Dome of the Rock, writing was most frequently placed within the roofed enclosure, on walls, primarily within a position bordering mural representations which were significantly larger in scale. This format of writing framing depictions was usually placed in certain focal architectural features like niches, apses, mihrabs, or central areas, especially those defined by a dome. This arrangement appears, for example, in the following extant structures built during our era and in which mural ornamentation survives:[32] (Byzantine) St. Polyeuktos, the Hagia Irene (fig. 15),[33] and Sts. Sergius and Bacchus, all in Constantinople (fig. 16);[34] the Hagia Sophia in Salonika (fig. 17);[35] (Umayyad) the Dome of the Rock in Jerusalem (fig. 10);[36] the Great Mosque in Damascus;[37] (Fatimid) al-Azhar mosque in Cairo (fig. 3).[38] Abbasid additions and restorations to the structures in the eastern Mediterranean maintained the same format as in the initial construction.[39]

A simple comparison of the mural arrangements of three structures demonstrates the point: in the Hagia Sophia in Salonika (fig. 17), the depiction of the virgin and child enthroned occupied the semi-dome of the apse, and the writing borders the depiction along the bottom; in the Dome of the Rock, Jerusalem (fig. 10), the depictions of trees, plants, and royal jewelry occupy the main part of the wall areas, and the writing borders the depiction along the top. Similarly, in the al-Azhar mosque, (fig. 3), the first mosque built by the Fatimids in Cairo, depictions of trees and vines are large in scale and occupied the main wall sections, and the writing, significantly smaller in scale, borders these depictions.

In addition to framing depictions, all groups used writing by itself to frame focal areas. Consider, for example, the writing in Greek carved into the marble niche in the church of St. Polyeuktos (fig. 15)[40] or the writing in Arabic that framed the mihrab in the mosque of Aḥmad ibn Ṭūlūn in al-Qaṭāʾiʿ (fig. 4). A particularly visually impressive example of this practice is the band of writing in Greek carved into the entablature under the dome of Sts. Sergius and Bacchus in Constantinople (fig. 16).

One use of writing on walls of sectarian spaces, however, appears to have been specific to Christian practice. Only in the extant mural articulations of Christian spaces from this period was writing placed within the depiction, either to identify or label, a kind of *tableau parlant*. But describing this practice as peculiar to Christian groups is an assessment based on absent evidence. The mural articulations of Muslim and Jewish spaces are very unevenly preserved from this period. In the Great Mosque, Da-

15. Niche, St. Polyeuktos, Hagia Irene, Istanbul (photo by Terry Allen)

mascus, for example, less than 15 percent of the original interior articulation of this period remains, and the walls of most synagogues are not extant, and thus any generalizations for these groups are risky.

In contrast to the ubiquitous practice of placing writing on walls, displaying writing on floors was a practice more limited in time, medium, and in group conventions. Writing was displayed in the mosaic floors of synagogues and of most churches until the eighth century. Writing does not appear to have been put on mosque floors. But even within the practice of the Christians and Jews, writing does not appear on the floors of all sectarian structures and cost may be the most relevant explanation for the absence or presence of writing on the floors. For example, in imperial churches, or those endowed with substantial funding, the floors were constructed with *opus sectile*, quartered and matched slabs of marble or occasionally limestone.[41] Sometimes floors were constructed out of stone selected because of its close resemblance to the costlier *opus sectile*.[42] In displaying such beautiful flooring, the patron demonstrated an ability to afford a costly medium and to command the technologically expensive process of quartering marble. The practice was not to "break up" this expensive surface by smaller designs such as writing, although patterning

16. Interior, Sts. Sergius and Bacchus, Istanbul

on a large scale was often achieved by different colored and grained marble. By extension, the absence of writing on the floors in the Great Mosque of Damascus and the Dome of the Rock could possibly be attributed in part to the presence of marble floors.

On floors writing appeared in mosaic, a less expensive flooring. Thus in synagogues, monasteries, and local churches with mosaic floors writing was part of the floor design. The archaeological evidence for practices within spaces built as mosques (and not converted churches) is quite fragmentary, yet little evidence suggests that as a general practice writing was placed on mosque floors that were mosaic.[43]

While it is clear that the presence or absence of writing on floors in the practice of these communities followed the use of material, materiality and cost alone cannot totally explain the practice. Writing could have been displayed in *opus sectile*, and mosaic floors could have been monochrome or color patterned without writing or depictions. Various social factors, such as the displacement of Greco-Roman culture by an Islam-based one, are issues which must be considered.

Beyond the embellishment of floors and walls within sectarian spaces, little evidence exists to suggest that artifacts used within sectarian spaces during these centuries systematically or significantly displayed writing. We

17. Interior, Hagia Sophia, Salonika (drawn by Hampikian after photo by Cormak)

make this judgment based mainly on the written record because very few portable artifacts used in the sectarian spaces of any group remain from this period. One of the exceptions is the fifth or sixth century polycandelon displaying writing in Aramaic dedicating it to the synagogue of Kefar Hananyah.[44] Most often, however, we are dealing with mentions of the presence of writing such as that on an altar cloth in the Hagia Sophia in Constantinople,[45] and, although it is outside our eastern Mediterranean geographic area, the displaying of the Caliphal name on the *kiswa*, the textile covering the Kaʿba in Mecca.[46] Apparently various basins, containers, and lamps from churches, synagogues, and mosques displayed writing, but the use of writing on such objects does not seem to be a consistent pattern.

In sum, the pattern of extant officially sponsored writings from this period indicates both the importance of its presence and of its presence in the group-specific alphabet. Primarily, all communities used such writing as a territorial marker within their own sectarian spaces. All groups, ruling and ruled, marked walls, and most floors, with officially sponsored writing. By contrast, using writing to invade the public space appears to have been the domain of ruling groups, both imperial and local. And finally, the pattern of use clearly indicates that officially sponsored writing served as a territorial marker of lesser visual prominence than depictions, but one that evoked important relationships.

Aesthetic Function

Confronted by the officially sponsored writing in sectarian or public spaces, beholders found the reinforcement of group identification in the alphabet, but also saw the form and materiality of the writing itself. "Style" conveys meaning to beholders by the system of writing forms they see, as well as through their awareness of the whole process that supported the finished product: the technology, cost of materials, and the status and training of the artists.[47] In addition, the presence of a specific style conveyed meaning by the pattern of its social use within the society.

An analysis of the aesthetic dimension of this writing reinforces the patterns that emerged from examining the territorial function of officially sponsored writing, namely, an equivalency of practice among the various sectarian groups in the eastern Mediterranean. During this period no sectarian group developed a style of script specifically to be seen by its group audience. Officially sponsored writing followed conventions for handwritten forms and manner of orthography,[48] but, of course, was larger than the writing in books and was executed in and by entirely different materials.[49]

Careful observation reveals a remarkably specific consistency between officially sponsored writing and one specific book hand in the social practices of all groups: between the officially sponsored writing of any sectarian group and the book hand in which their group-based text was formally written (that is, the Qur'ān, the Hebrew Bible, or the New Testament).[50] We are speaking here, for example, of what is called Kufic script for writing Arabic, squared serifed in Greek, and old or squared or formal Jewish for Hebrew (fig. 18).[51] All these script styles can be characterized as geometric or squared. They were distinguished from coeval script styles in these same alphabets that were cursive, and were used for government record keeping, business records, and the like, as well as from various versions of geometric writing that were less precisely rendered.

Unfortunately, the relation between the script of officially sponsored writing and the Book hand remains very problematic. Neither in Byzantine practice, where we might expect the clearest evidence, nor in Umayyad, where we know evidence to be elusive, can we speak with certainty about the extent or specific ways the script practice of officially sponsored writing and that of the book were related.[52] Given the state of our evidence, we need to avoid adding any more limitations to our understanding of this period. We must be prepared, if necessary, to abandon inherited assumptions that officially sponsored writing imitated, or followed the lead of, the handwriting of the sectarian Book. In fact, I suspect that as with other complex relationships interdependence is a more useful concept than causal development.

A few scholars have already remarked on the resemblance between the script of officially sponsored writing and the Book hand, although most of them confined their remarks to specific cases. Cristel Kessler, for instance, has described in detail what she terms the dependency of the inscription of the Dome of the Rock on the Qur'ān book hands of the period.[53] She demonstrated that the writing of the inscription, in addition to letter shapes, displays the diacritical marks that parallel the writing practices in the early Qur'āns, even to the extent that the letters were shaped to mimic the markings formed by the cut of the early *qalam* (reed pen).[54] Even the ornamental devices separating Qur'anic phrases in the Dome of the Rock parallel those found in Qur'anic texts, although she does not note this latter aspect. And, of course, the format for this inscription, as indeed with all other inscriptions from this period in any language, was linear as on a manuscript page.[55] In general, letters were displayed against a plain background.

Stanley Morison, taking his observations in a direction different from Kessler's, has examined the relationship of certain official book hand styles and monumental inscriptions as indexes of relations between the Western-

18. Writing samples, formal style (drawn by Hampikian)

Latin and Eastern-Byzantine Churches.[56] And, finally, Joseph Naveh has pointed out that the same formal script was used for writing the Hebrew language on monuments and in texts.[57] The minimal evidence available for the comparison of the practice of writing in manuscripts and in sectarian spaces suggests a similar practice within the Armenian and Coptic communities as well.

What is remarkable about this practice is its consistency. Geometric letter style, association between officially sponsored writing and the book hand, as well as the preservation of a linear format were all maintained for almost five hundred years. Yet while members of the communities could see these consistencies—or at least see them within the practice of their own group—differences existed that created contrasting patterns, setting up new relationships that evoked more nuanced meanings. Diachronic and quality differences are apparent.

A diachronic examination of the officially sponsored writing in the sectarian spaces sponsored by members of the ruling groups indicates that small script changes were consciously made to distinguish and identify a specific group or ruler. For instance, the letter terminations in the officially sponsored writing in the mosque of al-Azhar are slanted, and medial and ending letters often elaborated (fig. 3), while these features are not present in the writing in the Dome of the Rock some three hundred years earlier (fig. 10). Most of the differences in the officially sponsored writing practices in Greek and Arabic, like those in the example above, consisted mainly in variations on terminations of letters, in proportions of width to height, and of relative thickness and thinness of the vertical and horizontal lines of letters. Of course, despite these changes, the geometric nature of the letter formation was preserved.[58]

In addition, the evidence indicates differences in the fineness—in the trained quality—of the letter formation of officially sponsored writing. Officially sponsored writing, beautifully formed and skillfully executed, like that of the Greek displayed in the central areas of Sts. Sergius and Bacchus (fig. 16) in Constantinople, existed at the same time that more modest letters in Greek were displayed in the church of Mt. Nebo. The officially sponsored writing in the mosque of Aḥmad ibn Ṭūlūn (fig. 4) from the ninth century is not as fine as that in the mosque of al-Azhar in the tenth (fig. 3). Of course these readily observable differences represent different social hierarchies. Sts. Sergius and Bacchus was sponsored by Empress Theodora (and Emperor Justinian) and is in the imperial capital; the church on Mt. Nebo was a monastery church in the provinces. The mosques of Aḥmad ibn Ṭūlūn and al-Azhar are both within the urban expanse of Cairo-Miṣr, but the former was sponsored by a provincial governor and the latter by a Caliph. And, of course, the two churches and the two mosques were constructed to serve different types of congregations within their sectarian groups.

But however extensive the variation in script styles related to changing times, different places, and different social practices, the overriding pattern of these similar visual signs evoked a relationship between ideology (or belief) based in the communal text and the social structure that maintained those beliefs. Beholders thus understood ideology and social structure in terms of their own group Book-based practice. These understandings naturalized authority—that is, they reinforced as normal and appropriate both the beliefs and organization of the group to the sectarian beholders. In so doing, these understandings situated those specific sectarian beliefs and social organization within the larger social network.

The very large diachronic stability of these visual signs of power—officially sponsored writings within sectarian spaces—presented to the various sectarian beholders the stable nature of their communal authority. By the preservation of form, authority was presented as conservative and unchanging. Formal consistencies thus masked very real shifts both within the beliefs and the social structure that developed in the eastern Mediterranean from the sixth through the tenth centuries.

If the diachronically observed stability of some formal patterns of officially sponsored writing supported and reinforced Book-based communal authority, there were real and repeated exceptions that probed these rules. I will attempt to explicate the relation of writing to authority and audience when Fatimid practice is the focused subject, but there remain some unanswered questions worth not forgetting. For example, writing and depictions are displayed in the floors of a large number of Greek Orthodox churches, despite the promulgation by the Byzantine emperor of laws forbidding the placing of writing and images on floors.[59] What is the nature of authority (of communal practice) that could disregard such laws? Concerning Muslim practice of the seventh and eighth centuries, the *aḥādīth* (Traditions) tell us that a number of people—Mālik ibn Anas was one—spoke out about the appearance of writing on the walls of mosques. Specifically, the writing of Qur'anic verses is mentioned as a distraction for those at prayer.[60] Yet despite the opposition of some people and of some *aḥādīth*, writing of Qur'anic verses was displayed in mosques. What does this tell us about the nature of authority in early Muslim practice?

Also, we must recognize that no matter how significant the formal elements of officially sponsored writing appear to have been, the materiality of the writing weighed more heavily in the aesthetic dimension of their meaning. I will offer two examples, one from Muslim and one from Jewish practice, which explicate different linkages of relationships both within and between groups that were based on the materiality of the writing.

The example from Muslim sectarian practice, which concerns five of the buildings sponsored by the Umayyad Caliphs ʿAbd al-Malik and (his son) al-Walīd, demonstrates the importance of the materiality of the writing in Muslim sectarian practice itself and its links with the practice of some groups of Christians. The sequencing of the buildings is relatively well documented.[61] Caliph ʿAbd al-Malik built the Dome of the Rock in 690[62] articulating the inner walls with officially sponsored writing in Kufic letters, in a linear band which surmounts depictions (fig. 10). Both the writing and the depictions were executed in gold and glass mosaic (with some cabochon jewels within the depictions) all of which surmounted marble wall paneling.

The Dome of the Rock remained the only Muslim structure so articulated until Caliph al-Walīd began his program of building and reconstruction of 705–15, during which he undertook, almost simultaneously, the construction and reconstruction of four major mosques: two in the eastern Mediterranean (the Great Mosque in Damascus and the al-Aqsa mosque in Jerusalem) and two in Arabia (the Prophet's mosque in Medina and the *ḥarām* in Mecca.)[63] In these, in gold and glass mosaic, writing in Arabic and depictions were displayed.

What was conveyed by the aesthetic dimension of officially sponsored writing to its Muslim beholders? On one level, of course, by using gold and glass mosaic and the format of depiction and writing in the four mosques, al-Walīd created visual linkages "backward" in time to the Dome of the Rock his father sponsored, and linked the latter to the "present," that is, with his own structures and his own power. On yet another level, by adopting the pattern of so marking some specific structures, al-Walīd also perpetuated and augmented the visual inequalities between Muslim sectarian spaces he and his father had sponsored directly and all others (those sponsored by previous Caliphs and former and contemporary provincial governors) where the gold and glass medium was not used. In short, they created a hierarchy within Muslim sectarian spaces based in significant measure on the medium of ornamentation. In visiting the capital city of Damascus and then the religious pilgrimage centers of Mecca, Medina, and Jerusalem, Muslim beholders could not escape seeing the visual link made among the main Umayyad-sponsored Muslim sectarian spaces in these cities.

Yet still another level of meaning was conveyed to Muslim beholders by the materiality—the gold and glass mosaic—of the articulation of these Muslim sectarian spaces. We could, in fact, deduce this meaning from the pattern of the use of gold and glass mosaic within the society as a whole, but in this instance we have reported conversations that also suggest these understandings. The conversations took place during the inspection tour that Caliph al-Walīd made after the completion of the restorations he ordered to the Prophet's mosque (*masjid al-nabī*) in Medina. He spoke then to ʾUbān ibn ʿUthmān ibn ʿAffān, whose father had been the third Caliph. Al-Walīd asked him what he thought about his restoration to the Prophet's mosque relative to the changes ʾUbān's father (ʿUthmān) had made to the same mosque.[64] ʾUbān's reply, "We built it in the manner of mosques, you built it in the manner of churches," suggests a reference to the meaning conveyed by the materiality—the gold and glass mosaic medium—used in the interior.

Obviously, ʾUbān, in speaking of "the manner," did not allude to the spatial arrangement of that mosque. No one entering that Muslim sectarian space could have mistaken it for a Christian church. Nor did he allude to the depictions of the architecture and trees and the writing *per se*, because they resembled the mosaic format in the Great Mosque of Damascus more than that in any Christian church. We are thus left to conclude that ʾUbān was referring to the gold and glass mosaic medium itself.

In commenting on the medium, 'Ubān's words implied more than a direct reading—that al-Walīd had made the mosque of Medina resemble churches—would have us understand. 'Ubān, speaking these words in the early eighth century, was undoubtedly noting—and the Caliph was undoubtedly hearing—what the archaeological evidence tells us. Al-Walīd's restoration made the mosque resemble churches sponsored by the Byzantine ruling group. Only that level of authority could have afforded such a medium. In a McLuhan sense, here the medium was indeed the message. And the message was power—power to command expensive glass technology with all that suggests of furnaces and other equipment, color expertise, and gold, and the power to cause the movement and support of highly trained artists.[65] Thus a specific, extravagant aesthetic display linked ruling authority with ruling authority across sectarian boundaries, and it also distinguished socio-political levels of authority within the Muslim sectarian group.

Materiality of officially sponsored writing also conveyed information about the hierarchy within a group's social structure on less spectacular levels. This is especially apparent in Jewish sectarian spaces where officially sponsored writing in more than one alphabet (and language) were likely to occur. Here the patterns of materiality, alphabet, and script fineness combine to give us today some insights which are all the more valuable because we know these communities mainly through their archaeological remains.

Looking at the archaeological remains of the synagogues that were in use in the coastal cities of the eastern Mediterranean into and during the early part of the sixth century, we find it not unusual to see officially sponsored writing displayed in three languages: Hebrew, Aramaic, and Greek.[66] The orthography and letter shape of the writing in Aramaic inscriptions, like the fragmentary one preserved in the synagogue of the village of 'Isfiya, was most likely to be the most poorly executed of the three alphabets.[67] The Greek alphabet, on the other hand, was most likely to be the most finely executed, as we find in the synagogue of Caesarea.[68] Inscriptions in Hebrew were relatively even in fineness. All were modestly well rendered—correct spelling and letter shape, a pattern obviously linked to the social stratification of various members of the congregations.

In one synagogue or another, all of these alphabets appeared in stone mosaic. Sometimes the stone was augmented by local green glass as it was in 'Isfiya.[69] When writing appeared in a yet more expensive medium, Greek was the only alphabet and language displayed.[70] In the practice (and socio-economic level) of these sectarian communities, more expensive medium meant marble. What do these patterns of fineness of script and its materiality signify to a beholder who can distinguish the alphabets and languages present as Greek, Aramaic, and Hebrew?

At that time, and until well into the eighth century, Greek was the socially predominant language and culture. Although a large proportion of the Jewish population was Aramaic speaking, Greek almost always was used as the official language for inscriptions and documents.[71] Greek was everywhere tied to those elements of authority within the community who had the financial ability and the willingness to express that power within the communal space. This seems an obvious and direct conclusion. But if we state the relationship between authority and medium in another way, we reveal more nuanced webs of signification. Among Jewish congregations of the coastal area in the sixth century eastern Mediterranean, Greek was the language in which power within the community was demonstrated. Power was represented on a minimal level as economic ability—to afford marble over stone. Power was also linked with a specific education and knowledge of literature written in Greek, rather than Aramaic.[72] This educated authority had the ability to command the language and script and oversee its fine execution. Clearly such an education represented a knowledge broader than familiarity with texts directly related to Jewish communal life.[73]

How then do we assess the patterns presented by officially sponsored writing in Aramaic and in Jewish script (Hebrew language)? Obviously the authority signified by the writing in Aramaic was less powerful (less financially able, or less well educated) in the activities of the society as a whole and within the Jewish community than that represented by the other two officially sponsored writings. Clearly it did not/could not even sustain the vigilance necessary to guarantee a finely executed and properly spelled Aramaic script. We could argue that mosaicists and stone and marble carvers were more used to producing writing in Greek than Aramaic, and that alone might account for poorly executed script. While that may indeed be an accurate assessment of the skills of the artists, I still would argue for understanding the poor quality of the inscriptions as representing the lack of power (financial or educational differences) to sustain the necessary vigilance, because the writing of Hebrew in Jewish script was uniformly fine. Since many mosaicists were Christian, no need existed within their own sectarian communities for them to know either language. And, perhaps more significantly, the alphabets and letters of these two languages are similar. What is known as Jewish script—what most people today would call Hebrew letters—developed in the Roman period from the Aramaic alphabet.[74] Thus any artist able to render the letters of one alphabet (language) could easily render those of the other.

The inscriptions in Hebrew evoked an authority in the middle ground between the two. The constancies in the quality of the inscriptions in all the Jewish sectarian spaces throughout these ten cities represented an authority with sufficient power (education or social) to maintain such uniformity. The constancy in the quality of the script also communicates a social practice where the maintenance of a uniform alphabetic sign was important. We cannot forget that officially sponsored writing in Hebrew was a sign of the Book of all of the Jewish communities, whereas the other two alphabets (languages) were not. Hebrew was the language of the Book-based belief. Greek, on the other hand, had a wide and common currency.

Referential Function

I have argued that the group-specific alphabet, as a familiar emblem, functioned primarily to mark the space as specific to the beholder's sectarian group. At the same time, of course, the style of the writing, situated in the social patterns of aesthetic values within the broader social system and within that of the specific sectarian group, communicated authority and evoked for viewers nuanced understandings of social, political, and economic hierarchies. Officially sponsored writing functioned in these ways whether beholders "read" the writing for its semantic content or not. Of course, when beholders "read" the writing for its semantic content, it signified meanings that both reinforced and augmented those conveyed by the other functions of officially sponsored writing. But we suggest that the referential dimensions of writing remained secondary to the other two dimensions in conveying meaning to group audiences.

Given our evidence that the social practice of the sectarian communities in the eastern Mediterranean was equivalent, we are prepared for the pattern that emerged from analyzing the semantic content of the officially sponsored writing in sectarian spaces and public spaces. The referential bases of the officially sponsored writing of all of the groups were also equivalent. The semantic content of the writing was drawn basically from only two evocational categories: one based in the written Book of the group, and the other, based partially in written sources other than the Book, and partially in a restricted code of names, dates, places, and phrases important only to the group.

In this latter configuration we classify the following: the names of people who because of their social rank or their activities had an importance within the referent system of the group (rulers both past and present, wealthy or holy personages, prophets, martyrs, artists, saints, even enemies); the names of places or structures important to the group; dates important in the history of the group or the specific community's life, calculated by the calendar system of the group, or by references to an earlier event common to the group; and common aphorisms or phrases.

Materials from these two evocational categories were not presented in an unvarying order in the official writings. For example, officially sponsored writing did not always begin with words from the group's Book and end with the patron's name and date. But writings taken from certain evocational categories were more likely to be placed in some areas of sectarian spaces rather than others. In the social practices of all of the groups, writings based on the written Book were more likely to appear both on the wall and in the focal area of the structure than elsewhere. No sectarian community placed writings from the communal Book on the floor.

So placed, writings from the Book in mosques and churches (no evidence exists for synagogues) framed depictions. In no extant instance do the writings from the Book directly explain the image they frame. Rather, they have to be understood as appropriate juxtapositions, similar to those Grabar noted in Seljuk pottery and in contemporary Christmas cards where the greeting does not always explain or directly relate to the image on the front of the card.[75] For example, in the Hagia Sophia in Salonika, the writings from the Psalms do not explain the image of the Virgin and Child enthroned which they frame, nor do the lengthy passages from the Qur'ān in the Dome of the Rock explain the depictions of hybrid plant forms or of royal jewelry which they surmount.

Writing based in the second evocational category was more likely to appear on objects, on the floors of the structures, on lintels or door frames. These are the locations where we usually find donor or patron information, or information commemorating events of the group. A few examples will suggest the ubiquitous nature of this practice. First consider that on the mosaic floor of the synagogue in Gaza the following inscription appears, "Menahem and Yeshua the sons of the late Isses, wood merchants, as a sign of respect for a most Holy Place have donated this mosaic in the month of Loos 569."[76] An inscription of similar content is found on the choir door in the Coptic church of al-Adra in Deir al-Baramus where "the blessed Patriarchs Mar Cosmas and Mar Basil" are mentioned.[77] On the lintels of two of the inner entrance doors of the Dome of the Rock first the Umayyad Caliph ʿAbd al-Malik and later the Abbasid Caliph al-Maʾmūn placed their names as patrons.[78] Objects, such as basins found in synagogues and in mosques, also displayed donor information: for instance, the basin inscribed in Greek found in the synagogue at Gaza,[79] and the one inscribed in Arabic with the name of Umm Jaʿfar, daughter of ʿAbd al-Faḍl Jaʿfar, son of the Caliph al-Manṣūr who donated it for Muslim pilgrims.[80]

This pattern was not a rigid one, of course. Often patron or donor information and dating was placed at the end of the inscription from the communal Book in the focal area of the communal space. Such was the practice in the Dome of the Rock where ʿAbd al-Malik added his name and date. In fact, in one notable exception, the patron, "our sceptered Justinian," publicized himself and his rule in the inscription of the focal area in Sts. Sergius and Bacchus as much as he did the honoree (fig. 16):

> Other sovereigns, indeed, have honored dead men whose labor was useless. But our sceptered Justinian, fostering piety, honors with a splendid abode the servant of Christ, Creator of all things, Sergius; whom nor the burning breath of fire, nor the sword, nor the constraints of trials disturbed; but who endured for the sake of God Christ to be slain, gaining by his blood heaven as his home. May he in all things guard the rule of the ever-vigilant sovereign, and increase the power of the God-crowned Theodora whose mind is bright with piety, whose toil is unsparing efforts to nourish the destitute.[81]

What were the meanings these referential dimensions conveyed to beholders? Mostly they supported and specified the meanings conveyed by the territorial and aesthetic dimensions of the officially sponsored writing. Yet we believe there was a critical difference in the accessibility of meanings between those conveyed by the territorial and the aesthetic dimensions on the one hand, and the referential on the other. Not only did the beholder have to be contextually literate, and within some groups the mechanisms for ensuring this were minimal, but had to understand the group-specific context of the text to derive its meaning from its referential function.

In light of these observations, I cannot agree in this instance with such scholars as Grabar, who suggest that the semantic content of the Qurʾān-based inscriptions in the Dome of the Rock was meant to missionize, to invite people to submit.[82] Instead, I suggest that the language of the Qurʾān, a highly specialized written language, was addressed to sectarian believers. Who else would understand its semantic framework? Who else would believe that it was the word of God and thus understand its importance? Impressing to missionize and to entice was the task of the aesthetic function, and to a lesser extent the territorial one. The aesthetic function offered readily accessible socio-economic messages which situated a given officially sponsored inscription within a broad social practice.

This demur extends also to semantic content not based in the communal Book. Who else but a sectarian beholder could understand the implications of the semantic content of the Coptic inscription that gives the date of the death of Papa Stephanos as "tenth month after the passing away of . . . "?[83] Who is this person? Why was he important? What does the title mean? When is this? That Menahem or Umm Jaʿfar donated something is publicity that is meaningful for the social context of the sectarian group. To non-group beholders these names, dates, places, and titles lack a meaningful poignancy and immediacy.

The core of what we have tried to effect in this chapter is an understanding of the practices of writing signs during the centuries before the Fatimid conquest of Egypt in 969. Paradoxically, the functions of writing were simultaneously cohesive and differentiating. All the communities within the society used writing signs in similar ways, the traditions of centuries, to mark territory, to reference the Book, and to commemorate people and places. Styles of script were analogous, and the communities shared a hierarchy of materials and technology. The communities also shared a range of uses for such writing: most prominently, marking the interior of sectarian spaces. Such continuity of functions and range of uses of writing signs only strengthened the ability of these signs to be comprehended by those within and without a given community. The appearance of a group-specific alphabet—or a combination of alphabets—reaffirmed for the group in that space who they were, and by the absence of other alphabets, who they were not.

That alphabets were used by communities as visual signs of differentiation in a shared system of writing signs is critical to know because they were among the most effective visual signs signalling difference between communities in a visual culture that was largely shared. While imagery, and not writing, dominated the visual culture of urban life in the eastern Mediterranean, a point underscored by Peter Brown in demonstrating the constancy and reiteration of classical themes,[84] it was writing in the alphabet of the community that strongly differentiated that imagery, orienting it to its audience—for example, the mosaic floors mentioned above.

This chapter also serves as a *mise en scène* for the augmented range of uses of writing signs the Fatimid ruling group effected. Their change in the traditional uses sketched above alerts us to new kinds of choices made in that society and to the political and ideological interests which imposed them.

CHAPTER 3

The Fatimid Public Text and the Sign of Ismaʿilism

From the Reign of Caliph al-Muʿizz to the Appointment of Wazīr *Badr al-Jamālī (953–1073/341–466)*

The key to understanding the Fatimid use of writing signs as a public text is the recognition that the Fatimid rulers were Ismāʿīlī Muslims, a sect of Shīʿī Islam. From the time they declared their Caliphate in North Africa in 910/297[1] until the end of the dynasty in 1171/567, they ruled over a population predominantly Sunni Muslim.[2] Their position as leaders of empire was fundamentally different from that of the other major contemporary Muslim rulers, the Abbasid Caliph in Baghdad and the Umayyad Caliph in Cordoba. This difference was not simply a matter of numbers of adherents to different sectarian positions within Islam. It was, rather, that the Fatimid Ismāʿīlī ruler functioned in a dual role: both as Caliph to all those within his empire (all Muslims, Jews, and Christians), and as Living Imam to Believers (Ismāʿīlīs).

As Caliph, the Fatimid ruler exercised the same prerogatives of office as other Muslim rulers: his name was read in the *khutba* (the sermon at the Friday midday prayer) in the mosques of his realm; coins were minted in his name *(sikka);* and textiles woven at government establishments *(tirāz)* displayed his titles. However, only to Believers was the Fatimid ruler a divinely guided and infallible Imam, vested with ultimate authority to interpret the Qurʾān in his lifetime.[3] His ability to interpret rested on his knowledge of the true reality found in the esoteric dimension (*bāṭin*) behind the literal or obvious (*ẓāhir*) words of the Qurʾān. His ability to function as interpreter was traced to his direct descent from the Prophet Muḥammad through his daughter Fāṭima and son-in-law ʿAlī.

For Fatimid Ismāʿīlīs, interpretation (*taʾwīl*) was a *system* of allegorical or symbolic understanding. It was the vehicle for reaching the dimension of the esoteric from that of the exoteric. This system was both written down and passed on orally. Ultimate interpretation was the prerogative of the Imam. He was the final authority, after the Prophet Muḥammad, for interpreting God's laws, and the promulgator of rules of social conduct.

Believers came to know the *ta'wīl*, and thus the dimension of the esoteric, through formal and gradual training or initiation. The Fatimid ruler, the Imam, established institutions in Cairo such as the *dār al-ʿilm* or *dār al-ḥikma* (House of Learning or Wisdom) in a part of their palace where such instruction took place. The Fatimid Imam was the head of the organization, or *daʿwa*, of religious dignitaries established to help initiate Believers. The core of inner beliefs was revealed only to those properly initiated. In fact, Ismāʿīlī missionaries (*dāʿī*, sing., *duʿāt*, pl.) traveled from the edges of the empire, even into northern India, to properly initiate Believers.[4]

As the foregoing suggests, the position of the Fatimid Imam-Caliph involved an especially complex interweaving of roles. As Caliph, like rulers everywhere, he was the center of socio-economic power. Those who were members of the ruling group participated in the benefits that such a status conferred. The Fatimid ruling group included Sunni Muslims, Shīʿī Muslims (Ismāʿīlī and Imāmī), Coptic and Armenian Christians, and Jews. But the Fatimid ruler was the infallible Imam only to Believers. Originally, Believers constituted a significant proportion of the Fatimid ruling group, especially as members of the army. However, over the course of the two hundred years the Fatimids ruled from Cairo, the numbers of Ismāʿīlīs, within both the ruling group and the population, greatly diminished.

From the point of view of the audience, or population, and especially the Muslim population in the Fatimid empire, this Caliph-Imam role of the ruler, and all the networks of associations related to each role, created groups with different bases for perceiving the laws, building programs, communal actions, and so forth of the ruler.[5] The important issue here is that Fatimid public texts—that is, writing signs placed prominently in the public space—were viewed by a broad general audience. But the meanings those signs conveyed depended on the differing perceptual judgments of the varying groups within this audience.

Of course, during the two centuries the Fatimids ruled from Cairo, these dual roles of Imam-Caliph were not static, nor was the composition of the ruling group stable, nor were the socio-economic conditions continually prosperous. Obviously, many factors contributed to making the social situation in Cairo particularly receptive to the use of writing signs as public texts. But all that the dual nature of Fatimid Ismāʿīlī rule entailed was certainly primary among them. Accordingly, the Fatimid creation of the public text is described in terms of the actions of the Imam-Caliphs in the first century of Fatimid rule, and primarily in terms of the activities of the *wazīrs*, in the second one hundred years.

The Sign of Ismaʿilism: Concentric Circles and Coins

The first example of the Fatimid public text was the display of writing in the format of concentric circles (fig. 19) on new coins minted in Ifriqiya.[6] The choice to display writing in this format was a brilliant strategy, one that came to be used not only on coins, but on precious objects and on buildings throughout Fatimid rule, especially in their Cairene capital. What made the choice of the concentric circle format a vehicle useful in supporting Fatimid rule was the referential function of that format. To those who saw the concentric circle format, it was a sign of Fatimid rule and law. To Ismāʿīlīs among them, it was that and more. It was a sign of Ismāʿīlī ideology.

That ideology may be said to have been written large in the circular city that Imam-Caliph al-Mansur (r. 946–53/334–41) ordered to be built outside Qairowan in 948. Though today it survives only as an archaeological site, evidence reveals that the city was circular in design, and even more important for my argument here, the Imam's palace was in the center.[7] Moreover, al-Mansuriya was a wholly Ismāʿīlī city. Residence was limited to the Ismāʿīlī members of the government, the army, and the chief Ismāʿīlī qāḍī. For Ismāʿīlīs there, the structure of the city provided a template for Fatimid rule and law; they all knew that the Imam-Caliph lived at the center of their lives.

It remained for Imam-Caliph al-Muʿizz (r. 953–75/341–65), the son of al-Mansur, to impose the concentric circle format on his coins in order to emblematize Ismāʿīlī rule and law as well as ideology.[8] By adopting the format of writing in concentric circles on his coins, al-Muʿizz made it possible for all to distinguish coins of the Fatimid Ismāʿīlī realm from those of the Abbasid lands. Al-Muʿizz issued these coins throughout the remainder of his reign. In the first year, there was writing which displayed a forthright, aggressively Ismāʿīlī message in the inner concentric circles on the coins.[9] In all subsequent coins for the next twenty-three years

19. Dinar, al-Muʿizz (1002.1.1178 Collection of the University of Pennsylvania Museum in the Cabinet of the American Numismatic Society)

(953–75/342–65) that central space contained only a raised dot (fig. 19). Al-Muʿizz reinforced these references on coins by changes in the aesthetic dimensions, specifically the purity of gold in the dinar. The use of the format not only on coins, but also on objects and buildings related to Fatimid patronage, strengthened the linkage between format and Fatimid Ismāʿīlī rule.

The years of Imam-Caliph al-Muʿizz's rule (953–975), spanning the conquest of Egypt and the foundation of the royal city of Cairo (*al-Qāhira*), also witnessed the works of two major scholars, the philosopher and *dāʿī*, Abū Yaʿkūb al-Sijistānī (d.c. 971),[10] and the jurist Qāḍī al-Nuʿmān (d. 974).[11] These two scholars made major contributions to the discourses within Ismaʿilism of that time. Al-Sijistānī's writing were part of the discourse of metaphor,[12] the esoteric dimension. Qāḍī al-Nuʿmān's writings were substantial in both discourses, but his position within the Fatimid government as *qāḍī*, provided him with a venue for making lasting contributions in law (*fiqh*).[13] It is his contributions to the discourse of law, the exoteric (*ẓāhir*) dimension, that are relevant here.[14]

Both scholars used concentric circle diagrams within their texts as what can be called memory devices.[15] They appear to be the first Ismāʿīlī scholars to use such memory devices, one copied by later Ismāʿīlī writers such as al-Kirmānī[16] and Nāṣir-i Khusraw[17] in the eleventh century. The memory devices used in each of these two discourses, while sharing the basic typology of concentric circles, were nevertheless geometrically different. Likewise, the audiences these texts and memory devices reached, while overlapping, were different. When this essential form—that of concentric circles—was used not as a memory device in an intellectual discourse but as an element of an appropriately placed public text, it was intended to be apprehended by viewers who were Ismāʿīlī as referring to a whole system of associations specific to Ismāʿīlī belief. To Muslims who were not Ismāʿīlī, and to non-Muslims, this same form was perceived in a variety of other, different contexts.[18] Exploring the relevant writings of al-Sijistānī and Qāḍī al-Nuʿmān allows us to explore the differing networks of references in which the concentric circle memory device functioned for its varying audiences.

As used by al-Sijistānī within the discourse of the *bāṭin*, the discourse of metaphor or truths (*ḥaqāʾiq*), the concentric diagram related to the mode of explication by analogy. In his *Kitāb al-yanābīʿ* (The Wellsprings of Wisdom), al-Sijistānī uses four different concentric circle diagrams.[19] The concentric circle diagrams are used intentionally to help the reader perceive at a glance the correspondences among the dimensions of the universe. They function to stabilize, fix, and order sequences, oppositions, and relationships, and in so doing aid the memory in the mind's intellectual journey toward the central truths.

The esoteric realm itself formed a system based on a cyclical interpretation of hierohistory and a cosmology. In that system, time is a limitless progression of cycles within seven major cycles. Each of the seven cycles (of varying duration) is begun by a Speaker-Prophet (*nāṭiq*) who announces a revealed message constituting the exoteric religious law of that period. Adam, Noah, Abraham, Moses, Jesus, and Muḥammad, in turn, were the Speaker-Prophets who began the first six cycles. In each era, the prophet was succeeded by a Spiritual Legatee (*waṣī*), also known as a Foundation (*asās*) or Silent One (*ṣāmit*), who interpreted the esoteric meaning of the revelation. For example, Aron was the *waṣī* (*ṣāmit* or *asās*) of Moses, Simon Peter that of Jesus, and ʿAlī of Muḥammad. Each *waṣī* in turn was followed by seven Imams, or a series of heptads of Imams, who maintained the revelations and the laws in both their *ẓāhir* and *bāṭin* dimensions. We live in the penultimate cycle for which Muḥammad is the Prophet, as the Fatimid Ismāʿīlīs did then.

The cosmology in this discourse involves a heptad of letters (KUNI-QADR) relating to created things as well as the cycles of hierohistory.[20] Each letter of this heptad stands for a Speaker-Prophet (*nāṭiq*): K for Adam through R for the *nāṭiq* beginning the seventh era. Similarly, the physical realm is analogized by important letters such as those making up the word "Allah"—a-l-l-h (*alif, lām, lām, hā*).[21] In *The Wellsprings of Wisdom*, for example, *hā*, the final letter in the word "Allah," described as shaped in the form of a circle, relates symbolically to the *Asās* (or the Imam), to *taʾwīl*, and to the earth. The second *lām* corresponds to the *nāṭiq* and to water, and so forth in a complex inter-relationship.[22]

In addition, every word and letter of the *shahāda* (the profession of faith)—*la ilāh illa allah* ("no God but The God")—as well as the negation and affirmation of its grammatical structure—were highly symbolic. Its letters and syllables, like those in KUNI and QADR and in Allah, corresponded to numbers which in turn related to hierohistory, nature, and the creation of the cosmos.

Looking at one of al-Sijistānī's diagrams helps explicate how the diagram functioned as a memory device for the complex realms of the esoteric dimension (fig. 20). This device diagrams the thirty-fourth "wellspring" which discusses the perfect number six.[23] The text explains in detail what is compressed here into very abbreviated form. Six is understood as a perfect number because the sum of its divisors equals itself, that is, 3+2+1=6. Six indicates that there are six Speaker-Prophets. God created the world in six days. Nature has six powers—motion, rest, prime matter, form, place, and time. The effects of these powers abide in six directions—above, below, right, left, front, and back. The human form has six members—two hands, two legs, a back, and a belly. Six also represents the hierarchy of Speaker-Prophets (*nātiq*), Imams, and Adjuncts, a total of twenty-one. This number is reached by adding together the numbers 1+2+3+4+5+6.

The diagram fixes the correspondences of these realms. Each of the six is represented in its own sphere. The elements of the spheres move counterclockwise around the circle, a direction dictated by the decision to have the center be the viewing point for reading the writing.[24] The center circle indicated by words written in lines is the fixed center of the universe: God and the seventh, final Imam or Mahdi. Each of the elements in each realm also corresponds to a specific element in the other realms, and each is also fixed in the diagram in its appropriate wedge. This structural patterning serves as an aid to memory.

Concentric circle diagrams with typological equivalencies to the one discussed above are presented by al-Sijistānī in two other sections of *The Wellsprings of Wisdom*—one in the section discussing the qualities of the Intellect,[25] and two in the section discussing the manner in which mankind worships the Originator.[26] In the second of the two latter diagrams, the profession of faith, the phrase *la-ilāh, illa allah*, is meticulously related by letter and syllable to the intellect and cosmos. Each of these diagrams help the Believer make an intellectual journey, though they are not maps in the modern sense of that word. They do not *represent*, that is, stand for, either the words or concepts in the text or a model of the real universe. Rather, they are devices to remember with, which Ismāʿīlīs as a group were

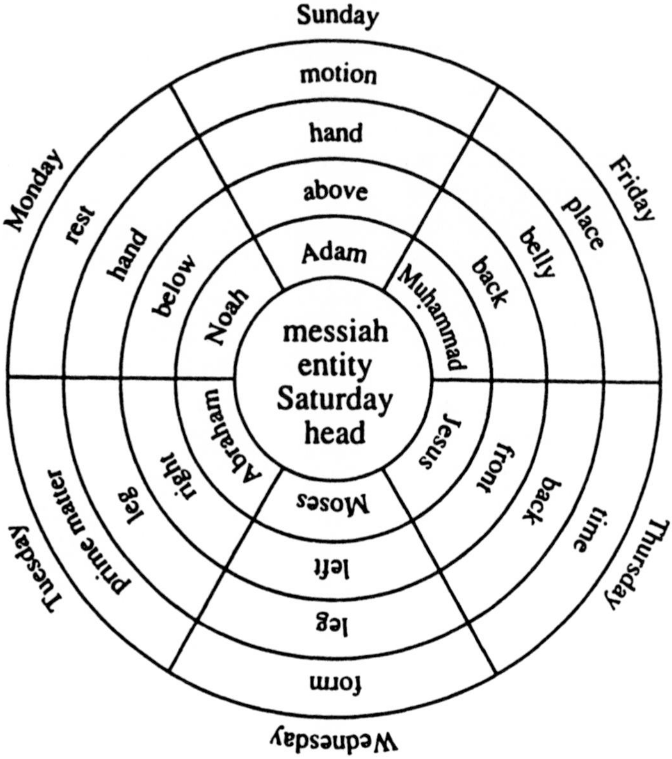

20. Diagram, thirty-fourth wellspring (Paul Walker, *The Wellsprings of Wisdom*. Courtesy of the University of Utah Press)

trained to use when they thought about the realities (*ḥaqā'iq*) of the world. As such, they were a community memory device, the sign of Isma'ilism.

The concentric circle diagram was used at the same time in the discourse of the exoteric. Qāḍī al-Nu'mān used this same basic form to illustrate an important point about the relationship of Belief (*Imān*) to Islam in his widely disseminated text The Pillars of Islam (*Da'ā'im al-Islam*).[27] In this text, Qāḍī al-Nu'mān expounds the basic tenets of Belief (Isma'ilism): Expression, Attestation, and Work. Expression is minimally fulfilled by utterance of the *shahāda*. Attestation is recognition of God's messengers and Knowledge, and the recognition of the Imam of the Time (*Imām al-Zamān*), at this time, Imam al-Mu'izz. Work is doing all that God commands (*zakāt, ṣawm, jihād*, etc.) as well as obeying and accepting the words and actions of the Imam of the Time.

Islam is also characterized in this text, although less space is devoted to its explication than to Belief (*Imān*). Qāḍī al-Nuʿmān presents Islam, as the title of the book suggests, in terms of the pillars, *ṣalāt, zakāt, ṣawm, ḥajj, jihād*, and in the metaphors of the marriage contract, rules for inheritance, and settlement of feuds. Qāḍī al-Nuʿmān reports that Abū Jaʿfar (an earlier Imam) first drew on the palm of his hand a circle representing Belief (Imān), and then he drew around that another circle showing the relation of Islam to Belief (fig. 21). This second, outer circle is exoteric, and its range is more constricted. It includes many elements but not Belief.

Qāḍī al-Nuʿmān characterizes the inner circle as *bāṭin* because it involves recognition of the Imam of the Time and Knowledge of historical revelation. Such a recognition was an acknowledgment that the Fatimid ruler, at that moment al-Muʿizz, was more than simply a Caliph with the power to collect taxes: he was the Imam, the final interpreter of the Qurʾān. Acknowledging the ruler as the Imam of the Time was an act of Ismāʿīlī Believers only, and both in Ifriqiya where this text was written, and later in Egypt where the Muslim population was overwhelmingly non-Ismāʿīlī, the interface between Ismaʿilism and the rest of the Muslim population was an important issue both for the government and for those who lived within the society.

In addition to the description of Abū Jaʿfar drawing these circles on the palm of his hand to demonstrate to his audience how these relationships are visually manifest, Qāḍī al-Nuʿmān drew concentric circles in the text of his manuscript, represented in all known copies by a central dot-circle and another, outer circle. No writing is included in this memory device. But no writing was necessary, not simply because the diagram ostensibly indicated the correspondence of only two elements, Belief and Islam, but primarily because of the use Imam-Caliph al-Muʿizz (and succeeding Fatimid rulers) made of the text in which it was embedded. They made the text and its diagram accessible to a broad audience by the sponsorship of its reading. Long after Qāḍī al-Nuʿmān's death it was read to those who came to learn about Ismaʿilism in the al-Azhar and al-Ḥākim mosques in Cairo, and the mosque of ʿAmr in Fusṭāt. It was also read in Cairo at the sessions of the *majlis al-ḥikma* where Ismāʿīlī doctrine was taught. Held on Thursdays and Fridays, these sessions and those in the mosques were important for conveying Ismāʿīlī knowledge.[28]

These sessions were performative. Readers at the sessions read the texts out loud and explicated them. One phrase in *The Pillars* particularly associated with the drawing of the concentric circles reinforced the diagram of the circles drawn on the hand, and helped to fix the key element in the memory of the hearer. Just before drawing the two circles on his hand,

21. Diagram, from the *Daʿāʾim al-Islām* of Qāḍī al-Nuʿmān

Abū Jaʿfar is reported as saying: *al-imān yashrik al-islām waʾl islām la yashrik al-imān* (Belief embodies Islam while Islam does not embody Belief). This phrase is repeated in *The Pillars* (and in other writings of Qāḍī al-Nuʿmān) almost as a refrain whenever the relationship between Islam and Belief is discussed. In fact, this phrase is repeated so often in *The Pillars* that it is impossible not to wonder whether it was spoken in a special voice. Perhaps it was chanted.

In addition to its repetition, the powerful association of its verb *yashrik*, translated here as "embodies," immediately relates this phrase to Qurʾanic usage, where it refers to those who *associate* others with God, a negative reference.[29] Using the verb first in the positive and then in the negative, a kind of grammatical construction that echoes the *shahāda* itself, strongly emphasizes the sense of association and then of disassociation of the two parts, Belief and Islam. Belief embodies Islam, that is, a Believer (Ismāʿīlī) is a Muslim, but Islam does not embody Belief, that is, a Muslim is not (necessarily) a Believer.

Imam-Caliph al-Muʿizz used this concentric circle format on coins—a public text—not by replicating the diagrams in either of the two discourses of Ismāʿīlī writings (either *bāṭin or ẓāhir*), but by strategically creating a three-dimensional sign consisting of the salient visual features of each: concentric circles and central dot-circle. At the same time, he maintained the commonly used Kufic style for the writing within this new sign. In this way, Imam-Caliph al-Muʿizz changed the format on his coins from one that imitated Umayyad-Abbasid traditions to one that emblematized Ismāʿīlī ideology.

Imam-Caliph al-Muʿizz further melded the aesthetic and referential dimensions of the new coin in support of the rule and ideology behind it, by making the gold in his dinars more pure than that in the coins of neighboring, competitive authorities.[30] Fatimid dinars came to be valued in the market for their purity and that purity guaranteed that the coins would pass readily into neighboring as well as distant lands. Then as well as now, sound coinage strongly suggested a sound economy and a strong government.

The content of the writing on the new coins presents the relationship of Belief to Islam, and as such relates to Qāḍī al-Nuʿmān's text, *The Pillars of Islam*, and its intent. That text was aimed at expressing the interface of Ismaʿilism and Islam both to Ismāʿīlī audiences and to others beyond the Ismāʿīlī community. It was used as the text in the introductory level class because it dealt with the religious law according to the system of the Ismāʿīlīs. Intended as a primer, its message reached a broad audience.

From the outer to the inner circle, on both the obverse and reverse of this new coin, the sequence of the reference bases relates the general or obvious to the more specific, recalling the differences between Islam and Belief and *ẓāhir* and *bāṭin*.[31] All the referents of the writing are found within Ismāʿīlī *taʾwīl*, except for the date and mint site. The outer rings contain the mint name and date (obverse) and a Qurʾanic verse (reverse). This Qurʾanic verse, 9:33, has a bi-valent referent. The verse, "Muḥammad is the Prophet of God. He sent him with guidance and the true religion to prevail over all other religions," is meaningful to all Muslims because it is a quotation from the Qurʾān, and as such belongs in the realm of the *ẓāhir*. To Ismāʿīlīs, in addition, the verse is one specifically referred to in *taʾwīl*. In Qāḍī al-Nuʿmān's interpretation it relates to the Qāʾim (Righteous Imam who ended a cycle) and the triumph of Ismaʿilism over other religions.[32] The inner rings contain the name of the Imam (obverse) and the *shahāda* (reverse).[33] Thus, on both sides of this coin, the inner circle relates to the Imam and the Originator (or God), just as the central core of the diagram. In looking at the format as a whole, with all of the writing presented in a circular format so that it has to be turned to be read, one is tempted to suggest that this format resonates also with the Ismāʿīlī cyclical view of history.[34]

That all the specific aspects of the Fatimid ideology expressed by the change in the format and in the content of the writing on these coins was understood by everyone is clearly doubtful. Ismāʿīlīs viewing these coins undoubtedly recognized the referent of the concentric circles. A portion of the general public in greater Cairo who attended the readings and discussions of Qāḍī al-Nuʿmān's writings—a sizable number documented into the early decades of the eleventh century—would have been made aware of the emblematic aspects of the concentric circles.[35] Texts, such as the writings of al-Sijistānī and Qāḍī al-Nuʿmān, as well as those of al-Kirmānī and Nāṣir-i Khusraw many decades later, carried the knowledge to scholars and to advanced students beyond the empire. In addition, ample evidence confirms that the circular format on coins itself was recognized as a part of the public text in the service of Fatimid rule, and some suggests that the format was viewed specifically as an emblem of Shīʿism.

When the Mirdasid ruler of northern Syria, Ṣāliḥ ibn Mirdās (r. 1023–29/414–20), recognized the power of the Fatimids, he struck dinars in Aleppo imitating the design.[36] Likewise, when Abū al-Ḥārith Arslān al-Muẓaffar al-Basāsīrī (r. 1058–60/450–51) revolted against the Seljuks in Iraq in support of the Fatimids, he struck coins in Baghdad[37] with concentric circles and writing. These represent a break with minting coins in the Umayyad-Abbasid format. Two Buyid rulers, themselves Shīʿī but not Ismāʿīlī, struck a "bulls-eye" type coin as a silver dirham.[38]

Imam-Caliph al-Muʿizz and the City of Cairo

Imam-Caliph al-Muʿizz's armies led by the general Jawhar conquered Egypt in 969/358. That conquest ended Ikhshidid rule in Egypt that had lasted only three decades (935–69/323–58). Jawhar began at once to make overtures to the conquered populations in the existing urban areas, and at the same time he undertook construction of a walled, royal urban center, ultimately known as *al-Qāhira* (Cairo), "the Victorious" (map 2).

The existing populations lived in a series of urban centers built on the east side of the Nile.[39] Fusṭāṭ, the southernmost section, had originally been built as a garrison town for the conquering Muslim armies in the mid-seventh century, and expanded from that time forward. The population, initially comprising soldiers, their retainers and families, soon began to include Christians (mainly Copts) and Jews who had lived in the areas in the pre-Muslim times. By the tenth century, this area housed a large Jewish and Christian population, as well as Muslims, mainly Sunni.[40] The central focus for the Muslims of this area was the mosque of ʿAmr ibn al-ʿAṣ, named after the conquering general. The mosque was located close to the channel (*khalīj*) of the Nile which served as the western boundary of this city (map 1).

North of Fusṭāṭ another urban center, known as al-Qaṭāʾiʿ, was built during the rule of the Tulunid governors (868–905/254–92). It was the site of the largest mosque in the area named after its patron, the governor Aḥmad ibn Ṭūlūn (r. 868–84/254–70). The administrative seat (*dār al-imāra*, literally "house of the princes") was attached to the mosque, forming the locale for much of the administrative business during the ninth century. The public treasury for the Muslims (*bayt al-māl*), nevertheless, remained to the south, in Fusṭāṭ, in the mosque of ʿAmr ibn al-ʿAṣ.

No walls separated these parts of the urban area from each other,

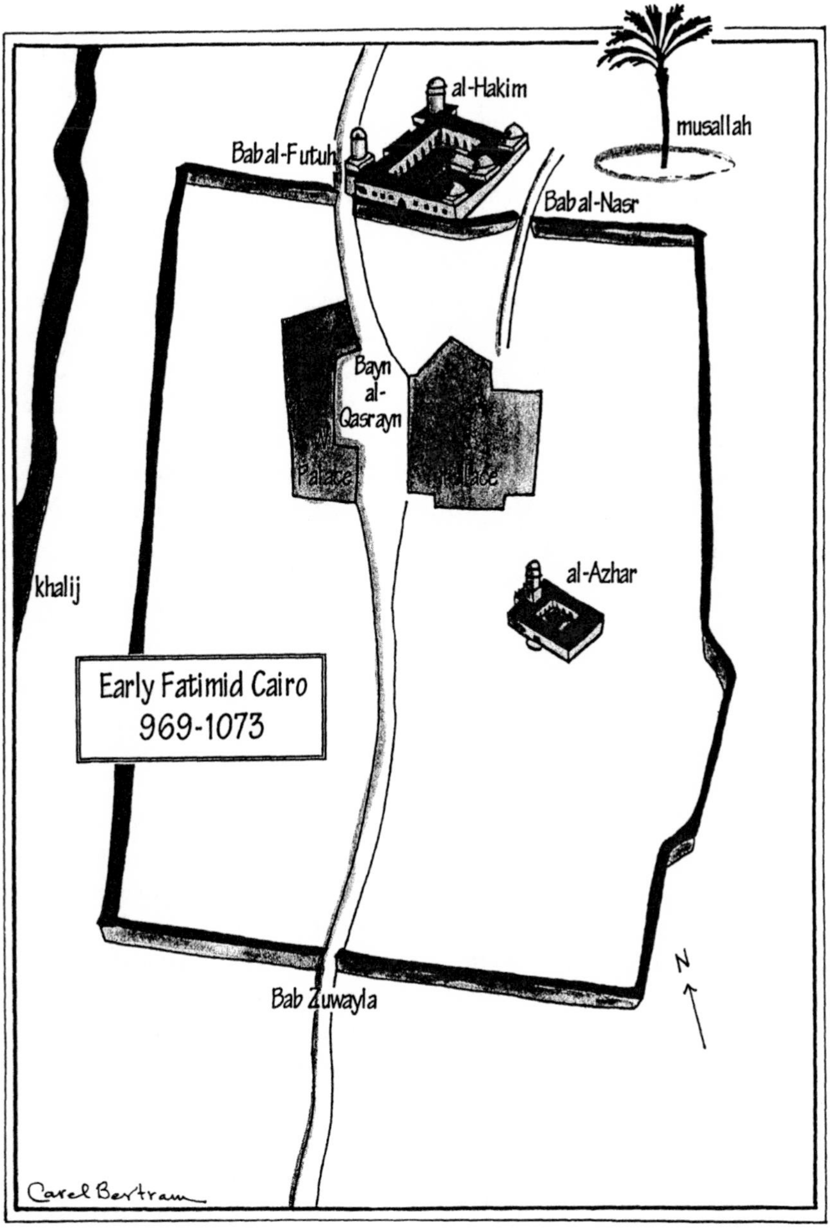

Map 2. Cairo, early Fatimid period 969–1073 (drawn by Carel Bertram)

although in the inundation season some depressions throughout the area gathered water, while still others held water almost year round. Rather than creating boundaries, these areas, known as *birak*, became recreational magnets bringing populations from all areas for boating, bathing, and parties on the water's edge.

Mixed populations, members of the provincial ruling groups, as well as merchants and traders, glassmakers, tanners, potters, and the like lived in both these areas. It also appears that neighborhoods were mixed; Muslims, Jews, and Christians lived in the same areas and even in the same apartment complexes.[41] Social considerations did shape this pattern, however. Jews lived close to their synagogues. But the main mosque complexes, serving the major portion of the population, dominated the areas spatially and socially, reflecting the administrative activity. The practices of Islam shaped the pace of the days and the year. The *ādhān* or call to prayer, formulated according to Sunni practice, was heard five times a day throughout both areas.

These two areas—Fusṭāṭ and al-Qaṭā'i'—were known collectively as Miṣr, although some later writers called it Miṣr-Fusṭāṭ. The inhabitants expressed preferences for prime locations within these linked areas.[42] North of these areas stretched plains dotted with monasteries and retreats where the more leisured groups often hunted. North was also the area of agriculture and gardens, and fresh air, as the prevailing winds come from that direction.

When Jawhar conquered Egypt he dealt with the existing populations reasonably and with great care. He allowed them to continue the call to prayer in their own fashion, and allowed them privileges that eased the transition to the new rulers of the area.[43] That this predominantly reasonable relationship on several social levels was sustained throughout the rule of Imam-Caliph al-Mu'izz is attested to by the pages of the *History of the* [Coptic] *Patriarchs*.[44] At the same time, Jawhar was preparing a walled royal enclosure north of these population centers for the Imam-Caliph, his family, retainers, and army. It was an urban area for Believers (Ismā'īlīs).

Although a segregated city,[45] this new area of Cairo had walls that were permeable like those of the central core in Abū Ja'far's diagram as shown in Qāḍī al-Nu'mān's text. Cairo's walls were symbolic, indicating a boundary; they were not defensive. It is almost possible to suggest that at this moment the urban geography of the area resembled a wedge taken from that concentric circle diagram and laid alongside the Nile, narrow end or core pointing to the north. In the north was the core, the royal city where the Imam-Caliph and the Believers lived. To the south, and larger in size, was the rest of the population, primarily Muslim. Echoing the phrase, "Belief embodies Islam while Islam does not embody Belief," those in the north were Ismāʿīlī Muslim; in the south, Muslims were not Ismāʿīlīs.

The royal city of Cairo was a rectangle oriented to the northeast, and divided almost in the center lengthwise by a street known as the Great Street (*shāriʿa al-aʿẓam*).[46] In the south the street met the double-arched gateway, the Bāb Zuwayla; in the north the street branched (map 2). The main path continued to the gate popularly known as the Bāb al-Futūḥ, and a branch went northeast to a second gate, the Bāb al-Naṣr. Within this large enclosure, somewhat north of center, on the east side of the Great Street, a palace was built for the Imam. Some years later, across this street, on the west side, a second palace was built. Together these two palaces framed the Great Street, making an area between them known as "between the two palaces" (*bayn al-qaṣrayn*). South of the Eastern Palace, across an open area (*raḥba*), and off to the east of the Great Street, the mosque known as al-Azhar (the shining) was built.

This mosque, also called the mosque of Cairo, was relatively small in size and primarily served the Ismāʿīlī population of the royal city, although as mentioned above, lectures and readings of Ismāʿīlī writings drew interested members of the population from outside the royal city.[47] The call to prayer from this mosque included the formula "come to the best of works" (*ḥayy ʿala khayr al-ʿamal*), a Shīʿī formula. North, outside Cairo at the Bāb al-Naṣr was a *muṣalla* (a defined open space) used for prayer during Islamic holidays. The major part of the Fatimid troops were also stationed outside, and north of Cairo. Imam-Caliph al-Muʿizz came to this city in 971/362 from his capital in Ifriqiya, Sabr al-Manṣūriyya, in procession and bearing the bodies of his ancestors, the first three Fatimid Imams. They were interred in the southern section of the Eastern Palace which became the mausoleum for subsequent Fatimid Imams.

Beyond his coinage and its newly devised sign of Ismaʿilism, Imam-Caliph al-Muʿizz appears to have used writing both territorially and referentially in more conventional ways. An anecdote discussed below reveals contemporary recognition of the range of his practice in regard to the public text.

In conformity with the practice continuing over many centuries in the eastern Mediterranean, he put inscriptions over the main thresholds or gates into Cairo. He used writing to frame depictions inside the mosque of al-Azhar.[48] As in earlier practice, that writing was smaller in scale and less visually prominent than the depictions it framed. Its referential base was the Qurʾān. The medium of both the writing and the depictions was stucco, continuing the aesthetic practice of the capital area. Judging from some aspects of the archaeological remains, it is possible that he put the sign of Ismaʿilism in this mosque.[49] What is reported clearly, however, is that the year after he came to Cairo, 973/362, Imam-Caliph al-Muʿizz displayed a gift for the Kaʿba prominently in his palace.[50] This gift did display the sign of Ismaʿilism.

Al-Maqrīzī describes this gift, a *shamsa* (sun, ornament, or collar), which Imam-Caliph al-Muʿizz raised on high so that it could be seen both from inside the palace and from the street. Close attention to the description indicates that the design of this ornament and the sequences of references on it—from the inner to the outer rings—both have equivalences with those on the coinage, and the diagram of Abū Jaʿfar.

Further, in describing the *shamsa*, al-Maqrīzī recounts that on a background of red brocade, twelve spans in each direction, an open-work golden ball was displayed inside a circle of writing in Arabic. Inside the central golden circular ball were pearls the size of dove's eggs and red, yellow, and blue precious stones. The writing around this center displayed the *sūrat al-ḥajj* written in emeralds. Stuffed with musk granules, the whole gave off a costly perfume. Ismāʿīlīs who saw this precious object undoubtedly would relate its concentric circle format to that of the coins and the diagram. Others saw it simply as a precious gift, a fact that al-Maqrīzī records.[51]

On this *shamsa*, the golden orb stuffed with pearls and gems can be understood to function as an aesthetic metaphor for the Imam, resonating with the center raised dot-circle on Imam-Caliph al-Muʿizz's coins. This reading of the metaphoric center is plausible in the context of Imam-Caliph al-Muʿizz's experience with his early issue of coinage in Ifriqiya and with the intended destination of this gift. The coinage on which Imam-Caliph al-Muʿizz first placed names and titles directly and exclusively relating to Ismaʿilism might have drawn great protests from the Sunni population in Qairowan, the population center near his capital in Ifriqiya, or, for other reasons, negative reaction from the Ismāʿīlī population in al-Mansuriya. For whatever reason, he chose to alter the references of the inscriptions to ones which would be acceptable to all Muslims, although he chose ones which would carry meanings in the dimension of the *bātin* for Ismāʿīlīs.[52] It was clearly appropriate for al-Muʿizz as Caliph to give a costly gift to the Kaʿba. But, on a gift intended for the Kaʿba at Mecca for the pilgrimage month when all Muslims would gather, reference to his role as Imam would most effectively be metaphoric.

Some sense of Imam-Caliph al-Muʿizz's attitude toward public texts can be gathered from an anecdote in Ibn al-Muqaffaʿ's *History of the Pa-*

triarchs. The anecdote suggests how the contemporary population understood the ruler's power to play with the public text. Written from the point of view of the Christian inhabitants of Miṣr, it also gives us insights into the role of public texts on impermanent materials, here a *sijill*, or decree, written on paper.

The story is as follows.[53] Caliph al-Mu'izz is reported as having occasion to give the population of Miṣr a test. He commanded that a large roll of paper (like that upon which a *sijill* was written) be rolled up without being written on and sealed. He then sent the bearer of this roll, along with the town crier and a trumpeter, to Miṣr to present the "decree," and sent trustworthy spies to report back. The trumpeter played and the crier called the local inhabitants to gather around because the *sijill* of the Caliph was to be read. Some inhabitants wanted to hear the *sijill*, but others said not to bother because the decree was blank. The news that the inhabitants knew the *sijill* had no writing on it was brought back to the Caliph who marveled exceedingly.

The story presents the Caliph as playing a trick with the text-ness of the *sijill*. The aesthetic dimensions of a *sijill* were present: the roll of paper, the trumpeter, the crier. But the local residents were not persuaded by the aesthetics of this public text without its writing. The story suggests public texts such as *sijill*s convey their meaning primarily through their writing, the close link of writing and authority, the referential dimension.

This story provides a contrast to the argument made in chapter 2. There, the referential bases of the writing on the interior of the imperial sectarian spaces in the eastern Mediterranean of all groups was equivalent. I argued then that the aesthetic dimensions of the writing—gold and glass mosaics the most costly—were the primary conveyors of meaning by such "expected" sectarian texts.

This story recorded by a member of the local population portrays that society as smart—because it is a text-based and literate society. In such a society even if many cannot read, the actions of the educated elite by their writing, by their knowledge of what is written and what that writing can effect in society, serve as a guarantee or proof that authority is vested in writing. The local population demonstrated that they knew that where there was no writing there was no power and authority.

Imam-Caliph al-Ḥākim and the Public Text

Imam-Caliph al-Ḥākim was the ruler who significantly augmented the way officially sponsored writing was used in the urban social network. He used writing in the urban areas of Cairo and Miṣr as a visual sign that defined and re-defined his relationship—as an Imam and as a Caliph—to the population he ruled. He used it to define his authority as Imam to certain audiences; he used it to express his power to all beholders. In highly visual ways, Imam-Caliph al-Ḥākim's uses of writing signs were part of Fatimid shaping and using the new capital area, both the royal city, Cairo, as well as the adjacent urban area.

In the early part of his reign, Imam-Caliph al-Ḥākim used writing in the public space in dramatically new ways in each of the two zones of the capital city. North of Cairo, in the royal enclosure, he placed writing on the outside of the minarets and on the monumental portal of the mosque he completed which had been begun by his father Imam-Caliph al-ʿAzīz in 990/380 (fig. 1).[54] This mosque was known by its location just outside the Bāb al-Futūḥ, and also as the al-Anwar (the lights) mosque, although it later was named after Imam-Caliph al-Ḥākim who completed it. The minarets and portal of this mosque remain tangible archaeological evidence for this display of writing.

In contrast, in the south, in Miṣr, Imam-Caliph al-Ḥākim placed at about the same time writing in gold letters and colors on the outside and inside of all the mosques and Muslim tombstones, and on the doors of the houses and of the bazaars.[55] Al-Maqrīzī records this official act whereby writing which cursed the companions of the Prophet Muḥammad and the first three Caliphs was placed on all these structures in 1004.[56] We are told specifically that this writing was executed in gold pigment and color, but not the style of the script. We are told about its semantic content—not its specific words. For this display of writing, however, no archaeological evidence exists.

These two uses of officially sponsored writing, on the mosque of al-Ḥākim and on the mosques, houses, and bazaars in Miṣr, can be seen as successive messages conveying various aspects of Fatimid ruling power, while at the same time supporting certain permanent values of maintaining social order in a mixed population.[57] These two uses of writing are different parts of the same ideology, both related to each other and to the nature of Fatimid authority and rule in Egypt. The two different populations and zones within the urban social networks to which they were addressed together made up the whole of the urban environment. It becomes clear from observing how writing in public space—public texts—was used, that those who orchestrated it were conscious of actively shaping the urban social networks of the capital to establish varying relationships of the parts under the regulation of the Fatimid ruling group.[58]

Both these initial sets of Imam-Caliph al-Ḥākim's officially sponsored writings (on the al-Ḥākim mosque in the north, and on the mosques, houses, and stores in the south) were officially sponsored writing occupying the public space, visually accessible to the whole range of the population. The referential bases of these writings, extracted from Islamic evocational fields, were addressed only to Muslims and not to Christians and Jews. Clearly, in Miṣr, the widespread display of the golden curses must have saturated the visual environment for all inhabitants, but they were not put on churches and synagogues.

The semantic content of the writings on the minarets and doorway of the mosque of al-Ḥākim was based primarily in the Qur'ān. But on the mosques, houses, and stores in the population centers of Miṣr south of the royal city, the referential base of the writing was Ismā'īlī Muslim practice.[59] This practice of cursing the Companions of the Prophet and the first three Caliphs, although sometimes written, was very much an oral practice coeval with al-Ḥākim's publishing or making the curses visual.[60] In attacking the leadership within the early Muslim community who took political authority away from the 'Alī immediately after the death of the Prophet Muḥammad in 632, it must be recognized that these curses attacked those Muslims in Miṣr who believed legitimate authority in the Muslim community followed from the succession of the Rashidun Caliphs to the Umayyads and Abbasids, thus bypassing the lineage of 'Alī. Primarily then, these curses were aimed at the Sunni Muslims, and the ruling authorities who derived their legitimacy from such a lineage—for example, the Umayyads in Spain and the Abbasids in Baghdad, the primary Muslim rivals of the Fatimids.

Clearly Imam-Caliph al-Ḥākim made these officially sponsored curses function territorially by marking only certain places within a specific zone of the greater urban complex. By marking them uniformly with officially sponsored curses written in gold letters, he bound them together visually. While other color pigments were also used to inscribe the curses, gold, because of its costliness, drew attention both to the importance of the message and to the economic position of the Imam sponsoring the writing. The golden medium and the curse-filled message also drew attention to the nature of the power and authority of the ruler who in that society was able to write such signs on buildings and make that writing last, in this case for some twenty-six months.

It should be noted in support of the interpretation here, that al-Maqrīzī transmitted these curses because he understood them as creating a boundary that was spatial and a territorial zone that was socio-political. He understood the act as an action aimed against Sunni Muslims.[61] Himself a Sunni Muslim, al-Maqrīzī saw the Fatimid period (some three hundred years before his time) as an interlude of rule by outsiders.

It seems that in the early years of the eleventh century, Imam-Caliph al-Ḥākim was very conscious of maintaining this socio-spatial boundary distinguishing north from south, Ismāʿīlī from non-Ismāʿīlī, in the urban area. Another account of his actions relates other ways in which he visually reinforced that boundary, even as it demonstrates just how dynamic were his uses of public texts, by creating successive messages that support the primary permanent value of maintaining the ruling group in power. After the defeat of the almost successful rebel, Abū Rakwa, Imam-Caliph al-Ḥākim had Abū Rakwa's head displayed on a *manẓara* (belvedere) outside the royal city, on the south side, facing the population centers.[62] The placement of this rebel's head between the royal city and the population centers visually reinforced the separation of group spaces within the urban complex that the previous writing had already demarcated. By this action, Caliph al-Ḥākim and the ruling group in the north, displayed to the others—the ruled in the south—the consequences of revolt.

This rebel and his severed head—in the sense that the latter indicated his defeat—are important for the reconstruction of the dynamic aspects of how the public text functioned during this period of Imam-Caliph al-Ḥākim's reign. It is ironic that this very rebel caused the socio-spatial boundary marked by his head to begin breaking down. Simply put, the defeat of Abū Rakwa, who claimed the title of Caliph through Umayyad lineage, was extraordinarily costly to Imam-Caliph al-Ḥākim both in monetary outlay and troops killed.

Imam-Caliph al-Ḥākim needed all the goodwill and support he could generate from the population of the entire capital area. As al-Maqrīzī recounts, in making rapprochement to the Sunni Muslims, he was compelled, in 1007, to erase the very golden curses he had put up on the mosques in the south.[63] Further, he appointed Shāfiʿī and Mālikī scholars to the *dār al-ʿilm* within the royal city. By this act, more Muslims from the southern areas had official reason to be in the northern royal enclosure, and access to the northern zone became somewhat easier.

Obviously this example of a public text disappeared in the wake of Abū Rakwa's revolt. But the writing on the mosque outside Cairo's Bāb al-Futūḥ remained. Punctuating this northern space, it addressed all Muslims, not dividing audiences along sectarian grounds, in the commonly accepted reference of the words of the Qurʾān. Like the golden writing, it excluded Jews and Christians by marking territory that was Muslim.

The mosque of al-Ḥākim, as far as we can reconstruct, was the only mosque in the entire capital area, as well as in the northern zone, that displayed visually prominent writing on its exterior (fig. 1).[64] This was not the only distinctive feature of the mosque. To any pedestrian, this structure was strikingly different from any other sectarian structure in Cairo or Miṣr, especially any other mosque. It had two differently shaped minarets, one on each corner of its facade; other mosques had only one (fig. 22). It had a monumental doorway; other mosques had none. Its facade was constructed of stone; others were of brick and stucco. This display of officially sponsored writing may have seemed at first to be only another difference in construction practice. But his subsequent use of writing on the bastions of this mosque is further indication of how central writing was to his political praxis and role of Caliph as well as to his role as Imam.

In the early years of the eleventh century, the mosque and the route in front of it were not the common ground for the general population. This mosque and the way in front of it were the central area for only some members of the social order, mainly those having official business with the ruler in the royal city who entered through that door. Located in the northern part of the northern zone, it was almost as far away as possible from the old centers of population in the south. Yet although the major part of the population of the capital area did not have reason to pass this spot daily, the mosque occupied a public location. It was outside the Bāb al-Futūḥ, a gate of the royal city, and thus access to it was not physically limited by walls.[65]

As to the congregation of this mosque, written accounts indicate that the Imam-Caliph al-Ḥākim and his entourage from the royal city attended this mosque exiting the city through the Bāb al-Futūḥ. They did this on ceremonial occasions, and often at the start of processions. Dignitaries visiting the palace in the royal city of Cairo passed by this mosque because they customarily entered the city through the Bāb al-Futūḥ, near the palaces, which served as a formal, official threshold.[66] And we assume that the regular congregation of this mosque was the Fatimid army which was mostly settled in the north, the direction from which the military threat was greatest (e.g., Abū Rakwa's major foray was in the Delta). The size of this mosque alone suggests the army as a congregation because it was the only mosque of considerable size in the northern zone.[67] The mosque of Cairo, al-Azhar, was small in comparison and large numbers of troops would overflow it. Indeed, for an army whose various contingents were uneasy cohorts, a mosque outside the walls of the royal city offered distinct safety advantages to the ruler.

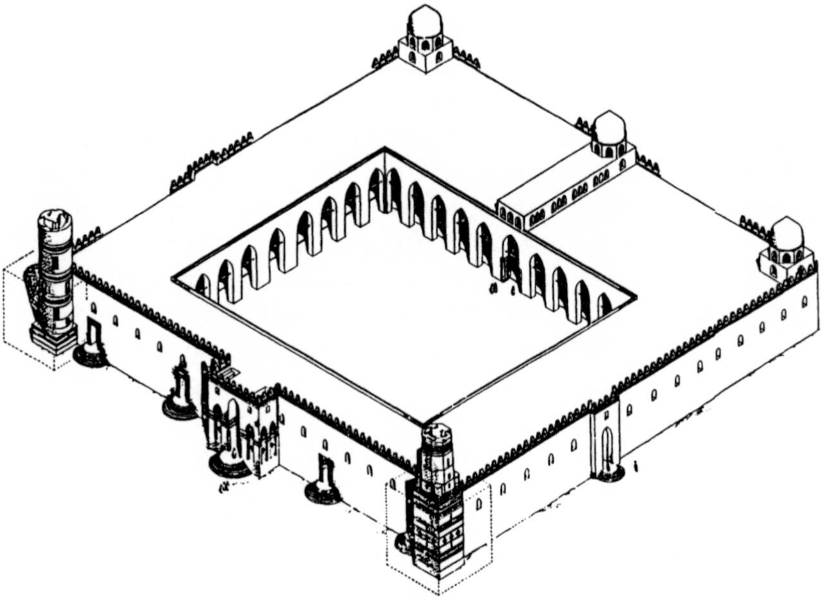

22. Al-Ḥākim mosque, after Creswell, *Muslim Architecture of Egypt*, vol. 1

The genius of the public text on the mosque of al-Ḥākim rested in the choice of its semantic content and in its aesthetic strangeness. Writing with a semantic content from the Qurʾān was the one sign of power around which all Muslims could rally because of its profundity. To all Muslims the Qurʾān is the word of God, and it makes possible varying levels of signification defined by the exegesis and interpretation of each group. Unlike the golden curses, which came from specific sectarian practice, the semantic content of this officially sponsored writing expressed permanent values for *all* Muslims. As Paula Sanders points out, the writing from the Qurʾān in this mosque must be analyzed for its meaning in both its *ẓāhir* (exoteric) and *bāṭin* (esoteric) dimensions.[68] The analysis she has done points to the rationale behind the choice of the *āyas* (verses) on the part of the Ismāʿīlī patron, and for the impact of the semantic content on Ismāʿīlī beholders. It is important not to let the knowledge of a specific Ismāʿīlī meaning mask the fact that the semantic content of this writing was directed to a Muslim group audience in a public space. This message, then, was permanently accessible to all Muslims, whether Ismāʿīlī or non-Ismāʿīlī, who would have understood it through *tafsīr*, or *taʾwīl* or somewhat later, through *asbāb al-nuzūl*.[69]

In fact, the very choice of writing based in the Qurʾān was probably the only fundamental reference that would rally all Muslims of the ruling group together, as well as Muslims within the population at large. Introducing and using such an emblem was in itself an important decision especially in the reign of Imam-Caliph al-Ḥākim. He had to maintain the Fatimid power base which demanded balancing the various Muslim elements, including various Sunni *amīrs* whose strength was land based and whose power pre-dated the Fatimid conquest of Egypt, as well as the new elements of the army which Imam-Caliph al-Ḥākim, himself, was supporting and introducing.

Imam-Caliph al-Ḥākim reinforced the changes in the composition of the army begun by his father, Imam-Caliph al-ʿAzīz, which sought to balance, really to undermine, the power of the *maghariba*, or Berber North African forces (literally, "westerners") who had been part of the conquering force of Egypt. They were Muslims, and more specifically, Ismāʿīlīs.[70] They believed in the Imam as the authority who preserved the permanent truths (*ḥaqāʾiq*) of the Qurʾān and the relationships in the universe, in addition to their support of his rule. The newly recruited troops, mainly Turks, Daylami, and *mashriqiya*, or Easterners, were mostly non-Ismāʿīlī Muslims. They supported and enforced the political rule of the Imam-Caliph, but did not recognize Caliph al-Ḥākim as Imam. All of the army, of course, and the members of the bureaucracy (many of whom were non-Muslims), were members of the Fatimid ruling group. All these groups sought their own interests in a system headed by a Fatimid Ismāʿīlī Imam and the Imam, in turn, preserved his power by balancing these various factions, as well as the factions within the palace structure itself.

When this audience passed by the mosque of al-Ḥākim, they saw officially sponsored writing based in the Qurʾān not only placed prominently, but displayed in an innovative assemblage.[71] In addition, this innovative assemblage included the sign of Ismaʿilism. From the evidence presented in chapter 2, we know that many of these formats were new to the public space.

From the viewing stance of the pedestrian, the writing most readily visible on the northern minaret was displayed in two signs of Ismaʿilism, two concentric circle medallions (fig. 1). Rather than adopting Imam-Caliph al-Muʿizz's format for these medallions, one that combined the visually salient features from the diagrams in the discourses of both the *bāṭin* and *ẓāhir*, Imam-Caliph al-Ḥākim used a format with the salient feature of the diagram from only one discourse—that of the *bāṭin*, found in al-Sijistānī's writings, and reinforced in his own time by ones used in the *dāʿī* al-Kirmānī's writing in the same discourse.[72] Those diagrams, as the medallions on this mosque, displayed a center filled with a line (or lines) of writing, fixing an orientation for the concentric circles. This is the format for the sign of Ismaʿilism that Imam-Caliph al-Ḥākim also adopted for his coinage, and one that subsequent rulers maintained for a number of decades (fig. 23).

In the center of the small medallion closest to the street, the word "Allah" is displayed in very clear, unadorned Kufic (fig. 24).[73] This appears to be the first time that the word "Allah" framed in this manner, highly visible and easily readable, only 6 feet (2 m.) from the ground, is displayed in a public space.[74] In a society where Christians and Jews were also using Arabic, the word "Allah" (The God) was also used by them to refer to the Supreme Being. It is, for example, found in churches and on Christian objects from this period. Framing it as a single word for display is traceable in Muslim use to Fatimid practice.

The word "Allah," and the letters and the syllables of the word, have elaborate significance in Ismāʿīlī *taʾwīl*, even as they are important to every Muslim. Al-Sijistānī records the importance of this word in five sections of *The Wellsprings of Wisdom*, one of which is perhaps most relevant here.[75] In the first chapter the letters of the word are related to what they resemble in the physical world, to the exaltation of God, the elements and the Speaker-Prophets, as well as to the numbers four, ten, seven, and eight. These serve to underscore the importance of placing this word in the concentric circle format closest to the pedestrian, a concentric circle format where points along the circle relate to significant numbers.

The next writing on this same minaret also appears within a sign of Ismaʿilism. Here the reference to the diagram and to the format on Imam-Caliph al-Ḥākim's coins is rendered large in scale, almost 1 meter (3.28 ft.) in diameter (fig. 25).[76] Qurʾān 5:55 is displayed in the outer circle, and in the center the Qurʾanic phrase "from the shadows into the light" is written in two lines.[77] The choice of this Qurʾanic phrase about light relates directly to Ismāʿīlī understanding of creation, when God made the single command, "Be" (*kun*) and God made darkness light. This formulation from al-Sijistānī was reinforced by the *dāʿī* Abū ʿIsa al-Murshid, who wrote at that same time, elaborating that God produced out of light a creature.[78] Indeed the centrality of this conception is underscored by the writings of *dāʿī* al-Kirmānī, a contemporary of Imam-Caliph al-Ḥākim. In his text, *Rāhat al- ʿaql*, one of the diagrams displaying only two concentric circles relates to this concept (fig. 26). This attention in Ismāʿīlī discourse relates

23. Dinar, al-Ḥākim (1002.1.890 Collection of the University of Pennsylvania Museum in the Cabinet of the American Numismatic Society)

to the several mentions in the Qur'ān of the specific phrase "from the shadows into the light," and of light in general.

The sequences of references of the writing in the concentric circle medallion parallel those on the coins. In the outer ring, *āya* (5:55), "only God is your Friend and His messenger and those who believe, those who keep up prayer and pay the poor-rate and they bow down" can be understood as relating to Islamic practice.[79] The inner circle, with its direct relation to Ismā'īlī *ta'wīl*, fixes the position of Isma'ilism in the center as the more encompassing element.

Above the medallion on the minaret, writing displaying *āyas* from the Qur'ān frames four windows (figs. 1, 27). In aesthetic terms, how the writing was placed around these windows serves to highlight how closely the writing in the medallion they surmount replicated the sign of Isma'ilism. In the medallion, the writing in the outer circle, like that on the coins and in the diagrams, runs counterclockwise continually around in a circle. The writing at the bottom of the circle, therefore, is upside down to the viewer. On the windows, however, the inscription begins on the lower right-hand side of each window, and runs counterclockwise until the bottom frame of the left-hand side of the window, where the direction is reversed and the phrases are produced upright to a beholder in the street. The *āyas* (24:36–37) chosen to surround these windows also refer to light, and to prayer. They are taken from the *sūrat al-nūr*, or the chapter on light in the Qur'ān. Placed around the windows they relate both to the physical light that comes in the windows lighting the stairwell of the minaret as well as to Ismā'īlī hierohistory as related by Qāḍī al-Nu'mān.[80]

Further above, a band of writing in large letters (68 cm./24.8 in.) displays the name and titles of the Imam.[81] This band was particularly highly visible for reasons which we can know, but which would not have been

24. Roundel displaying the word "Allah," after Flury

obvious to the beholder in the street, namely, that the band cants slightly outward.[82] Thus the writing was intentionally made more visible to a pedestrian than it would have been had the band of writing been kept parallel to the minaret as was that on the medallions.

The western minaret, different in shape from the northern one, also displayed writing in a different pattern, although the references of the inscriptions were equivalent (fig. 28). No sign of Ismaʿilism appears on this minaret. The name and titles of Imam-Caliph al-Ḥākim, and the year and the month are displayed at greater distance from the ground, but larger in scale (almost 1 m./3.28 ft.) While this band was not canted, the moulding above it projects more than any other moulding, and could have served as a kind of awning in the direct sunlight, giving some shadow to the writing which is carved deeply into the limestone.[83] Below this band is another one displaying Qurʾān 9:18, and although partially effaced, the name of al-Ḥākim. This, too, is a prooftext from Qāḍī al-Nuʿmān.

The writing in the bands of the two minarets can be understood as reinforcing each other and offering visual and semantic support for al-Ḥākim's claims to place "this mosque in the hierarchy of mosques, and reiterate the link between this mosque and the Ismāʿīlī mission (*daʿwa*)."[84] He further reinforced these claims made to an Ismāʿīlī audience by the writing in bands by placing the sign of Ismaʿilism on this mosque. To other Muslims, and to all others who beheld the large concentric circle medallion on the northern minaret, its resemblance to al-Ḥākim's coinage must have been obvious.

The monumental doorway of the mosque also displayed writing in

25. Roundel, mosque of al-Ḥākim (drawn by Hampikian after photo by Creswell)

Kufic (fig. 29).[85] Just how much writing was displayed, and its layout in Imam-Caliph al-Ḥākim's time, we cannot now reconstruct. Presumably, however, there was much more than survived into the early twentieth century when all that remained was a part of a Kufic inscription (3:199) on the north side of the monumental gateway.

What has been stressed in the above is primarily the referential function of the writing on the outside of the mosque of al-Ḥākim, and to some degree its aesthetic functions. Other ways can be reconstructed to indicate how this writing functioned to convey meaning to its primary audience, the ruling group. The formal distinctiveness of the assemblage of writing on the exterior of this structure called attention to the structure itself and its location. Yet, despite the distinctiveness of the whole, some additional elements—beyond those discussed above—did relate to other social patterns for displaying officially sponsored writing within Fa-

26. Al-Kirmānī, memory device *rahat al-ʿaql*

timid society at that time. First of all, the writing itself was in a basic geometric style; all of it was Kufic. As the evidence in chapter 2 indicates, the traditional script for such writing was a geometric one. Except for the signs of Ismaʿilism, the remainder of the writing on both minarets and the door was displayed in band format familiar to all because, as noted above, it was the common format within sectarian spaces. The semantic content of this writing was the most accessible to the beholder, in addition to the single word "Allah" on the north minaret. The accessibility of the semantic content was due, in part, to the linear format, which lends itself more readily to being read than writing around a window frame, or upside down in a concentric circle.

What could be read in these bands was more than *āyas* from the Qurʾān. More space in these bands was allocated to the name of the Imam al-Ḥākim, his titles and date, than to words from the Book.[86] This difference in semantic content is tied to a difference in aesthetic content of the writing. While the basic style of the script in these bands was also

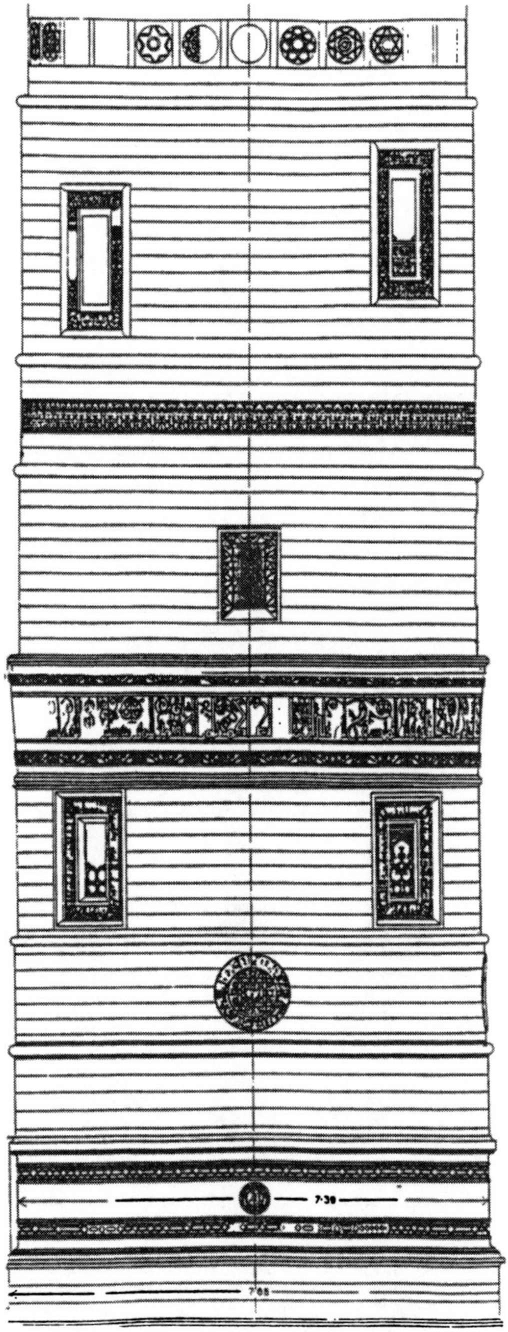

27. Northern minaret, after Creswell, *Muslim Architecture of Egypt*, vol. 1

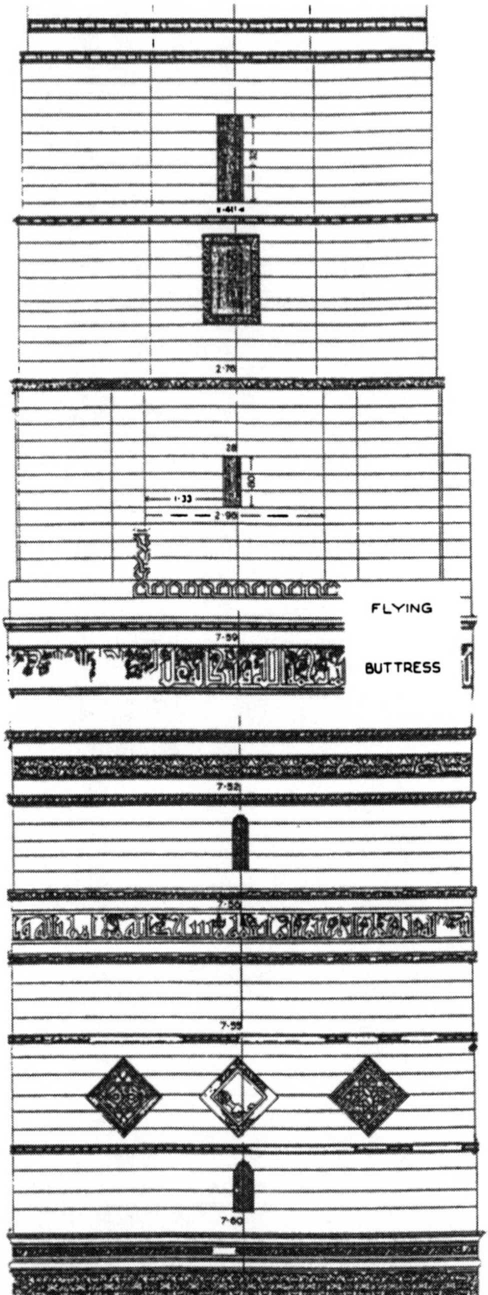

28. Western minaret, after Creswell, *Muslim Architecture of Egypt*, vol. 1

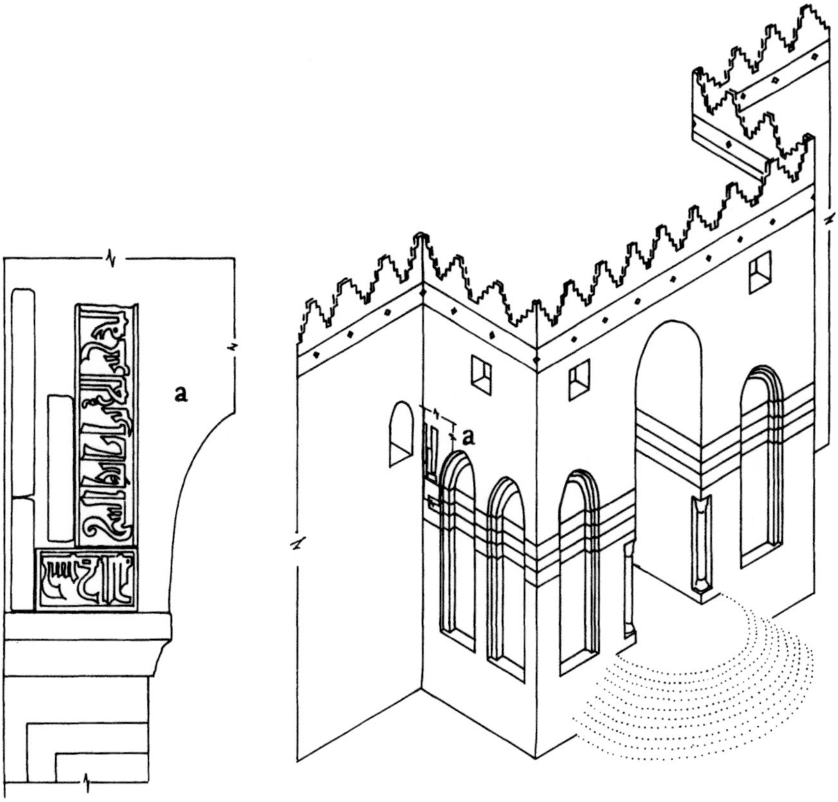

29. Monumental doorway, mosque of al-Ḥākim (drawn by Hampikian)

geometric, vines and floral terminations extrude from various letters and fill the background. This is especially apparent in the topmost band on each minaret (figs. 30, 31). This augmented aesthetic display was an innovation that separated the writing in these bands from the traditional script of officially sponsored writing; moreover, it broke the traditional linkage between officially sponsored writing and the Book hand.

Judging calligraphic practice from Qurʾāns of the period, letters forming the words of *sūras* (chapters) were unelaborated (fig. 32).[87] Elaboration was reserved for *sūra* headings, and for the functional devices that aided recitation which were usually presented in the margin, although some were placed intertextually. Until this time, officially sponsored writing was scripted in the same unadorned manner as the writing in the Book. Undoubtedly the elaboration of the innovative-looking writing in the

30. Inscription, top band, northern minaret, mosque of al-Ḥākim (after photo by Creswell)

bands served to call the beholder's attention to the writing, attracting people to read and thus to know that: "Imam al-Ḥākim bi Amr Allah, Commander of the Believers, may the blessings of God be on him and on his pure ancestors, ordered to be done in the month of Rajab of the year 393." Thus in these bands the aesthetic dimensions of writing served to emphasize the semantic content.

Yet the link between this stylistic elaboration of the writing and its semantic content displaying the name and titles of the Imam may have evoked another level of associations to Ismāʿīlī beholders that further indexed the authority of the Imam. What suggests this association is the even more elaborated writing on the interior of this mosque that permanently framed Imam al-Ḥākim (and those that succeeded him) when he visited this mosque on ceremonial occasions (fig. 2).[88] The members of the ruling group who entered this large prayer space on such occasions entered a mosque where the Imam prayed, delivered the *khutba*, and sat on the *minbar* at the *qibla* wall, in which position he was revealed to the congregation. The mosque of al-Ḥākim, in particular, was a showcase for the Imam-Caliph in an Ismāʿīlī Muslim context. As the large mosque outside the walls of the city closest to the Imam's palace, it was a space where

31. Inscription, top band, western minaret, mosque of al-Ḥākim (drawn by Hampikian after photo by Creswell)

prayers, sermons, and lectures were conducted according to Ismāʿīlī formula. Moreover, as Sanders has pointed out, to Ismāʿīlīs, the mosque and especially this mosque, as understood through its *bāṭin* dimensions, was the initiation house (*bayt*) into the Ismāʿīlī mission.[89]

Here Imam al-Ḥākim was surrounded by writing that was especially visually prominent, accessible, and elaborate. In this mosque, writing did not frame depictions, as in conventional practice or even earlier Fatimid practice. Rather, it was a solitary feature, larger in scale than previous writing in sectarian spaces, almost two feet (60 cm.) high. In addition, efforts were made to facilitate the visual accessibility of this writing, especially in the central aisle under the dome where the Imam-Caliph sat on the *minbar*. There, again, writing was canted out at the top.[90] Members of the congregation who saw the Imam on the *minbar*, saw him framed by Qurʾanic quotations, the real truths (*ḥaqāʾiq*) of which only he himself could fully reveal. In such a setting, the presence and authority of the Imam and obedience to him was visually linked with the words of God and obedience to them.[91] Yet despite this linkage of Imam and the Book, created by spatial proximity, the extraordinarily elaborated style of the writing of the Qurʾanic quotations even further distanced the direct relationship that traditionally existed between the Book hand and writing in sectarian spaces.

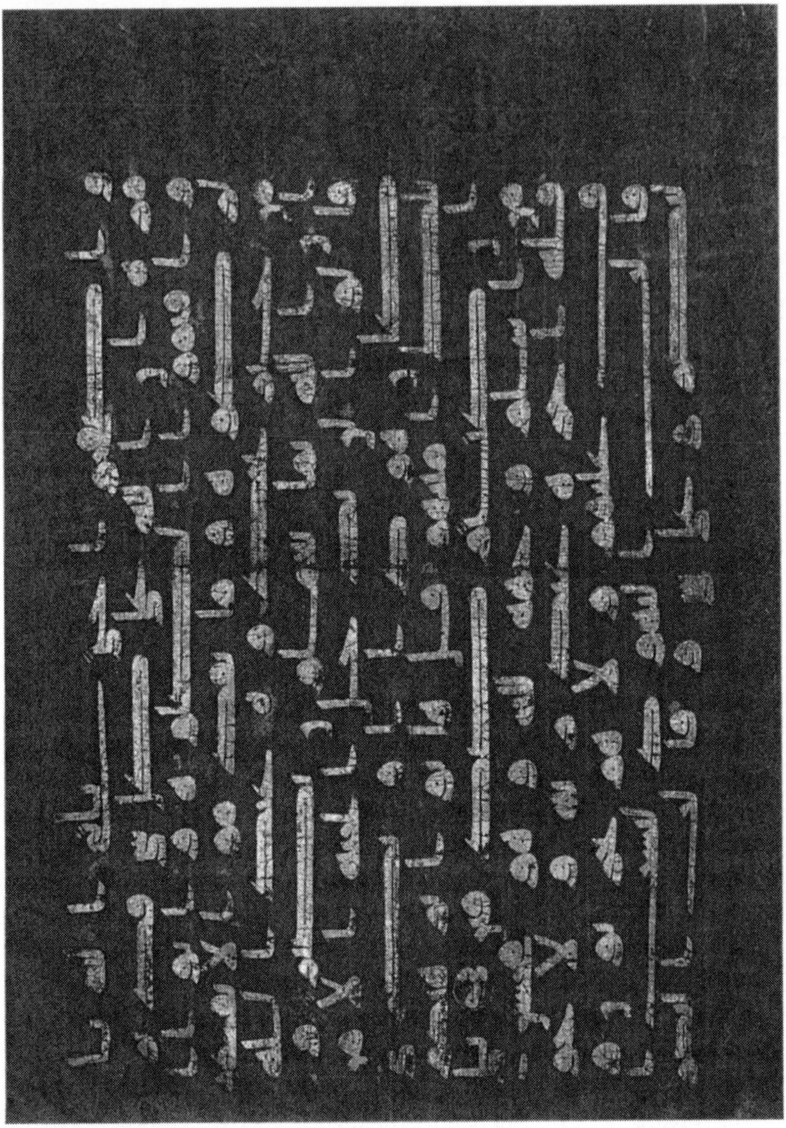

32. Qur'ān page, tenth century (courtesy of Seattle Art Museum, Eugene Fuller Memorial Collection)

It seems plausible to suggest that this distance created by the elaborated script style was intended to emphasize the role of the Ismāʿīlī Imam as sole knower of the fundamental truths of the Book. This message was directed at Ismāʿīlī Muslims. To non-Ismāʿīlī Muslims elaborated Kufic script was understood as a distinctive sign of the Fatimid Imam's patronage of this mosque.

As in the case of the golden curses, even these officially sponsored writings on the minarets of the mosque of al-Ḥākim were temporary signs of power. They were seen for barely seven years. In Ṣafar 401 (September–October 1010), bastions (*arkān*) were added around the minarets, completely covering the writing, and they remain in place today (figs. 22, 33).[92] They are composed of two stacked cubes, with the lower one the same height as the walls of the mosque. Why these bastions were added was not addressed directly by the medieval writers, nor by Creswell who undertook the architectural examination of the inner minarets. One obvious speculation is that the minarets themselves proved structurally unsound and the bastions were conducted to support them. Certainly the only reason that we today have any segments of these minarets is that the bastions protected them in the severe earthquake of 1303/702 which destroyed all the other minarets of the Fatimid mosques on this axis of Cairo.[93]

But whatever prompted Imam-Caliph al-Ḥākim to add these bastions, they added a more solid, almost military, aspect to this large structure. Moreover, what has occurred to me more than once in walking along the main north-south axis between the al-Ḥākim mosque and that of Aḥmad ibn Ṭūlūn, especially when approaching the latter from the southwest, is that the additions of these bastions brought the silhouettes of the minarets of al-Ḥākim's mosque more in conformity with that of the minaret of Aḥmad ibn Ṭūlūn's mosque, which was visited by the Imam on official occasions.

On these bastions officially sponsored writing was displayed much less innovatively and prominently than on the minarets which they surround. At least that is so on the western one, because only that writing and outer covering is the original. The northern bastion also originally displayed writing in the same manner as the western one, if Creswell is correct in suggesting that Badr al-Jamālī used the marble from the northern bastion for his inscription on the Bāb al-Futūḥ.[94] The bastions could have been left plain, or writing could have been carved into the stone itself as it had been on the minarets. But on the bastions the writing is carved in marble and in letters some 17 inches (43 cm.) high. The marble band is placed approximately halfway up and run around the bastions.[95]

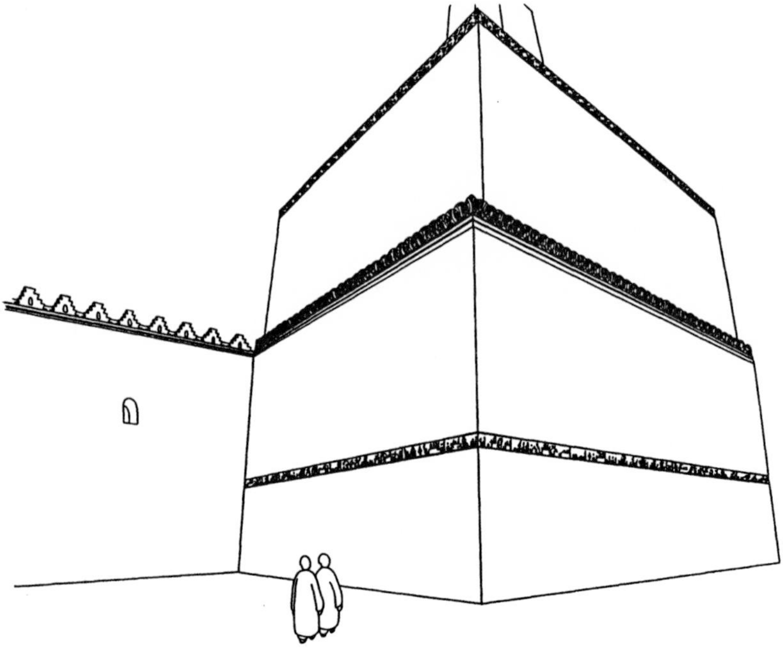

33. Bastion (*arkān*), al-Ḥākim mosque (drawn by Nasser Rabbat)

The difference between the marble bands and the stone bastion called attention to the writing, executed in an elaborated Kufic style. Certainly there is a clear distinction between the style of this writing and any of those on the minarets, and between this writing and that on the interior or on the top bands of the minarets. Still, vine and floral elaboration extrude from letters to fill blank background over horizontal letters. The writing itself was clearly legible to a beholder in the street, as it is today.

The semantic content of this writing was also addressed to a Muslim audience since it is based entirely in the Qurʾān. Yet the verses chosen are not used in Ismāʿīlī *taʾwīl*. It is difficult, by any interpretation, to understand most of these new quotations as particularly appropriate for indicating the functions of a mosque.[96] Only the short verse, displayed closest to the mosque, mentions Friday prayer (62:9). Still, writing with this semantic content was placed on the bastion of this mosque and addressed Muslim beholders in the public space. The question remains about the likely context of these quotations given the nature of the congregation of this mosque.

The connection of these verses with the Jarrāḥid revolt in Palestine is one that Sanders has made, although she has suggested that they respond to the original inscriptions on the minarets.[97] While fully agreeing with the importance of the context of the Jarrāḥid revolt, I would nonetheless suggest that they are better understood in the light of polemical uses of Qurʾanic quotations, which would account for the totally different tone of these quotations from the earlier ones on the minarets. Such polemical uses of the Qurʾān were at that time engaged in by al-Rashīd li-Dīn Allāh, the new Jarrāḥid anti-Caliph, an Alid *Sherīf* of Mecca, proclaimed leader of the Jarrāḥid movement. When he returned to Ramla, his new capital, the ***khatīb*** recited the first six verses of ***surāt al-Qaṣaṣ*** (The Narrative) in which Moses as prophet, and Pharaoh as overly exalted ruler, are compared, with favor, of course, to the former.[98]

The negative aspects of the comparison of Imam al-Ḥākim to Pharaoh cannot have escaped Imam al-Ḥākim who had barely recovered from Abū Rakwa's revolt (d. 1007), and who was engaged in a shake up of high and low officials within his immediate government.[99] The strident tones of the phrases of the bastion fit well with a situation in which such a revolt was underway in Palestine led by a non-Ismāʿīlī Shīʿī, and one in which ideological differences were being expressed in Qurʾanic words. The impact of this revolt was heightened by Imam-Caliph al-Ḥākim's reorganization of the personnel within his government, and the severe measures he addressed toward the Christians and Jews.[100] The official text on the bastion thus can be understood as a strong warning, couched in the words of God, to the Muslims of the ruling group in the northern sector of the city, to remain unified and committed to obedience to the Imam-Caliph. These phrases remained (and still remain) on the outside of the bastion as Imam succeeded Imam, and the audience and events changed. Because this original context was lost, scholars came to question the appropriateness of the semantic content of the inscription. What remained identifiable is the style of the inscription.

Flury, in the early twentieth century, identified the group responsible for the inscription by its style.[101] The aesthetic dimensions that were recognizable for him as group specific were the vine and leaf terminations. Yet eleventh century beholders would have been visually attuned to recognize that that specific style was not the only one in use at the time, and that the elaborated style had a specific use in terms of placement, for it was a style used only on the exterior of buildings.

Textiles and the Public Text

The writing on the portal and the bastions of the mosque of al-Ḥākim remained a public text in Cairo until the end of the dynasty, and beyond, until today. But it was not the only place people could be addressed by the public text.[102] In the rule of Imam-Caliph al-Mustanṣir (r. 1036–94/427–87) the accounts of Nāṣir-i Khusraw, the Ismāʿīlī traveler, indicate that writing was used prominently on textiles in the procession he saw for the opening of the canal. Imam-Caliph al-Mustanṣir processed to the head of the canal for the breaking of the dam. Nāṣir-i Khusraw described the procession of ten thousand horses with saddlecloths into which the name of the Imam was woven.[103] His report indicated a visually significant use of the written name of the Imam. If not actually ten thousand, at least many displayed it.

Although processions began in the rule of Imam-Caliph al-ʿAzīz (r. 975–96/365–86), and continued through the reign of al-Ẓāhir (r. 1021–36/411–27), the clothing worn by the Imam-Caliph and the court was singularly unornamented, especially during the reign of Imam-Caliph al-Ḥākim. Writing on clothing or animal trappings is not mentioned until the reign of Imam-Caliph al-Mustanṣir.

The official writing Nāṣir-i Khusraw described was embedded in the medium of official processions which the Fatimid Imams used in a systematized way. As Sanders has detailed, they made official progress from the royal city of Cairo to the mosque of Aḥmad ibn Ṭūlūn and that of ʿAmr ibn al-ʿĀṣ on certain occasions based on the Ismāʿīlī Muslim calendar and, as with the ceremony opening the canal, on occasions important in the economic life of Egypt.[104] Officially sponsored writing thus appeared in a new medium, and derived some of its meaning from the function of the processions themselves. Although the various Fatimid processions commemorated different events throughout the year, and thus had different immediate goals, fundamentally they were vehicles which connected the royal, Ismāʿīlī center in the north with the population centers of Miṣr in the south as Sanders has so ably argued. While more will be said on this point below,[105] these processions were all rituals that "set up [a range of] visible public definitions," fixing public meanings that classified the whole urban population as well as stabilized the relationships of various groups within it.[106]

These processions were structures linked to conscious social intentions of the ruling group. Thus while the processions fixed the connection between the northern and southern sectors of the city, they equally continually emphasized the separation between the participants and the audience; the rulers and the ruled. Those who watched knew their place in part through the location of their viewing position, where along the route they stood, and how close they could come to the Imam himself. Those riding and marching knew their place within the ruling group through their position in the ritual.[107] There is great concern, for example, to maintain proper position with respect to the Imam-Caliph.

Judging from Nāṣir-i Khusraw's effusive report, these ritual processions were highly effective because of their display of costly goods. In this context of fixing public meanings through ritual, officially sponsored writing played a role that associated the name of the Imam-Caliph with the ability to consume extravagant goods. It seems fair to assume that it was the medium in which the writing was embedded and not the style of the writing itself, or its specific semantic content, that evoked the primary meaning to Nāṣir-i Khusraw. Although he tells his readers about the content of the writing, he does not give the exact words, nor does he mention the style of the script. What he does discuss is the quality of the medium. Power to him was displayed by extravagant consumption. The choice of the goods displayed, as part of the continued ritual, created a pattern of discrimination that he recognized as making available to the Imam, and those who reinforced his rule, wealth in such prodigality that it invited quantitative and qualitative evaluation. The assemblage, rather than a specific discrete part, was what conveyed the meaning. Nāṣir-i Khusraw certainly engaged in the activity of evaluation and seems to have well understood the social purposes of the ritual.

He reported that ten thousand horses displayed "saddlecloths of Byzantine brocade and *būqalamūn* woven seamless to order.[108] In the borders of the saddlecloth are woven inscriptions bearing the name of the Sultan of Egypt."[109] By these words Nāṣir-i Khusraw conveyed to his readers very specific evaluations about the extraordinary abundance the Imam-Caliph commanded as his name label made clear. The horses of the ruling group were distinguished by the display not only of imported Byzantine brocade but Byzantine brocade that had been made to order and imported. Since Nāṣir-i Khusraw described the cloth as seamless, we can assume that was his way of noting that the size of the saddlecloths was wider than the standard loom width, so that without commanding special order, the requisite width for the saddlecloth could have been achieved only by sewing pieces together. This Imam's procession did not display goods that had to be pieced. Moreover, the special order included the weaving in of the Imam's name. The Fatimid Imam was able to command the Byzantine weavers, not only to weave the Imam's name, but to weave it in Arabic. By this description Nāṣir-i Khusraw distinguished what he viewed as the command of weaving in a foreign land, from the less masterful alternative of adding the Imam's name on an imported luxury fabric by embroidering it locally in Cairo.

Nāṣir-i Khusraw's evaluation did not stop there. The official writing on Byzantine brocade was itself embedded in still further extravagance. Camels, mules, and horses displayed reins studded with jewels and saddles of gold. Thousands upon thousands of soldiers walked or rode in rank, followed by contingents of princes from foreign lands and of scholars and literati who were maintained on stipends at court.[110] Jeweled weapons and musical instruments abounded. To Nāṣir-i Khusraw the meaning of this procession had less to do with the opening of the dam on the canal than with the evaluation of the Imam-Caliph al-Mustanṣir, who was the Imam of the Time (*Imām al-Zamān*) for him. He did, of course, describe the Imam throwing a spear at the dam, and the men who then quickly set to work breaking the dam so that the floodwaters of the Nile were opened into the fields, but he gave that part of the procession minimal treatment.

Nāṣir-i Khusraw was quick to understand how this display of abundance could be misunderstood by his readers. He carefully noted that the thousands upon thousands of soldiers beautifully outfitted were paid by the Imam and that no governmental agent or peasant was ever troubled by the army.[111] This is indicative of a refrain that is part of his description of Egypt. The Imam-Caliph who displayed his power through effective rituals involving material things did so even though he paid full measure to the weavers, the peasants, and the merchants. To Nāṣir-i Khusraw, Imam al-Mustanṣir, whose name he saw in procession passing to the head of the dam, was a beneficent ruler to all his subjects. Nāṣir-i Khusraw, of course, was a partisan, that is, an Ismāʿīlī. We can assume that his view was shared by many in the audience, and he notes the number of Ismāʿīlīs and Shīʿīs he saw. That other non-Ismāʿīlī members of the audience of these processions would have seen the goodness along with the power of the Imam from this display cannot be assumed.

The public text displayed on cloth in this manner was part of a more intensely social process than that displayed on buildings. It was an intensified spatial and temporal display that evoked meaning by its repetition rather than its permanence. That the name of the Imam-Caliph was associated again and again with such abundance conveyed to the beholders and reassured the participants that the social order or social boundaries were maintained despite the fluctuation in the categories of that order that were severely challenged at that time.

One further observation that Nāṣir-i Khusraw made about movement within the city of Cairo needs to be mentioned here. It relates not to writing directly so much as to a format for writing, namely, the sign of Ismaʿilism, and thus brings us full circle to where this chapter began. Nāṣir-i

Khusraw makes special reference to the one thousand guards that surround the palace of the Imam-Caliph (the Eastern Palace). Five hundred guards are mounted; five hundred on foot. They form two rings and continually circle the palace. After evening prayer while continuing this circular procession, they play trumpets and drums[112] until morning. We are left to wonder whether Nāṣir-i Khusraw recounted this circling because he recognized the relationship between the performance of concentric circles around the palace of the Imam and the concentric circle diagrams in Ismāʿīlī discourse. Nāṣir-i Khusraw himself contributed several volumes to Ismāʿīlī *taʾwīl*, in which he used concentric circle diagrams as memory devices.[113]

It is ironic that we are left Nāṣir-i Khusraw's report of harmonious social order and economic stability on the eve of the most severe economic crisis of Fatimid rule, which compelled the *wazīr* Badr al-Jamālī to stop these processions, and to alter the urban social and spatial order of Cairo-Miṣr drastically.

CHAPTER 4

The Fatimid Public Text in a Changing Political Climate

From the Rule of Wazīr *Badr al-Jamālī to the End of Fatimid Rule (1073–1171/466–567)*

It is not difficult to recognize that new and different messages dominated the public text during the last one hundred years of the Fatimid regime and, perhaps more important, that new formats became visually prominent both in public and in Muslim sectarian spaces. These changes appear directly related to a growing militarization within the ruling group as *wazīrs* and the troops that supported them gained power and authority. As these groups gained in power, they eroded the authority of the Fatimid ruler as Caliph.

This shift was recognized by all members of the population. The pages of Ibn al-Muqaffaʿ's *History of the Patriarchs* provides ample evidence of this awareness.[1] For the first one hundred years of Fatimid rule, events relating to the Christian community are told in relation to the actions of the Imam-Caliphs, as suggested by the anecdote related in chapter 3 concerning the actions of Imam-Caliph al-Muʿizz and the population of Miṣr. Over the course of the last one hundred years, almost without exception, the pages tell about the manner in which *wazīrs* and those troops who backed them shaped the lives of the population. Their rise and fall, and the troops who supported them, are intimately bound up with life in the Cairo urban area.

Concomitantly, the authority of the Fatimid ruler as Imam was reduced in scope. Two major succession disputes during this period reduced the number of Ismāʿīlīs in the Cairo urban area who recognized the Fatimid ruler as Imam. This reduced number of Ismāʿīlī Believers was not translated directly and consistently into a reduced display of signs of Ismaʿilism, or of processions in which cloth displayed Ismāʿīlī phrases. In some decades, what appears to be a bold use of these signs served, as the visual often does, to mask the weakness of the position of the Imam-Caliph in favor of supporting the social order as a whole, which in turn sustained the newly strengthened position of the *wazīr*. Those public texts which displayed the rank and title of the *wazīr* indicated strength where the real strength existed.

Cairo-Miṣr and *Wazīr* Badr al-Jamālī

New writing signs began to be displayed in Cairo-Miṣr in a physical and social environment which had changed significantly from the time, a mere two decades before, when Nāṣir-i Khusraw described the Imam-Caliph al-Mustanṣir's procession. This change in the former urban structure was accelerated in the mid-eleventh century by major socio-economic crises:[2] riots; administrative chaos between Turkish and Black army regiments; attacks by Berbers in the Delta; relentless famine caused by successive years of low Nile; epidemics and inflation; and Seljuk invasions in Syria and Palestine. These crises led Imam-Caliph al-Mustanṣir to summon Badr al-Jamālī, his commander of the army (*Amīr al-Juyūsh*), from Syria in 1073/465 to be *wazīr* and to restore social order.[3]

Badr al-Jamālī's measures to restore order in the capital area altered the composition and distribution of the urban population, particularly in Cairo. In the new urban social order his measures shaped, Badr al-Jamālī used officially sponsored writing actively to address new audiences with new messages.

The clashes between contingents of the Fatimid army and the actions Badr al-Jamālī undertook to curb the effects of the famine and plague all effectively blurred the distinctions between the northern and southern zones in Cairo-Miṣr.[4] Badr al-Jamālī allowed the Armenian Christian troops who came with him from Syria to establish themselves in a quarter within Cairo.[5] Because the plague had substantially reduced the entire population, Fusṭāṭ and al-Qaṭāʾiʿ being particularly devastated, Badr al-Jamālī permitted those living in these areas to take building materials from those southern zones to build in Cairo proper.[6] By these acts he opened Cairo to the whole society, even as he expanded and fortified its walls and gates to keep the common enemy out (map 3).[7] In time, notables from the Christian and Jewish populations also moved into Cairo. Other *wazīrs* followed and augmented this course, especially his son

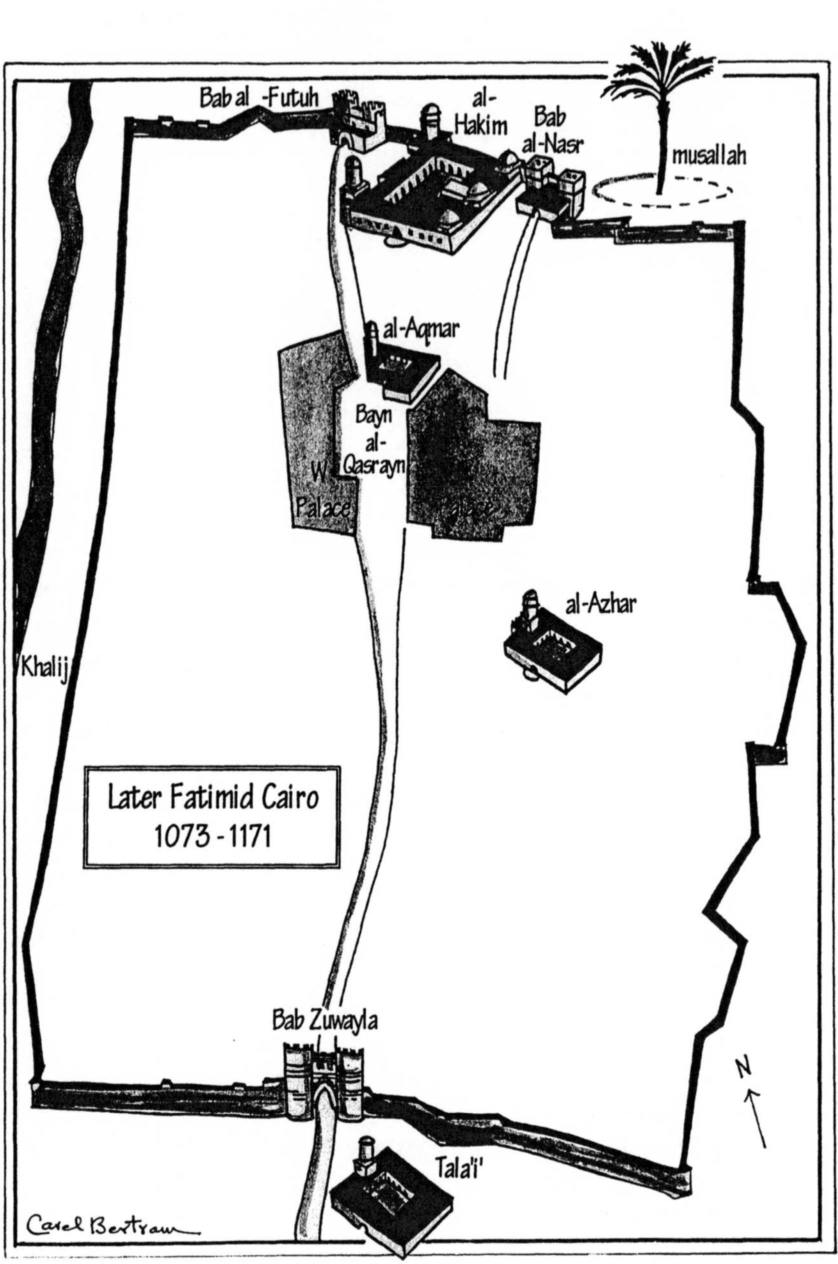

Map 3. Cairo, later Fatimid period 1073–1171 (drawn by Carel Bertram)

al-Afḍal, and the *wazīr* al-Maʾmūn. When conditions permitted, *wazīrs* also moved south to Miṣr, further blending the populations in the whole urban area.[8] As a result of these actions, Cairo no longer was simply an Ismāʿīlī royal enclosure.

While most areas of Cairo became mixed in population, and ordinary traffic on the Great Street increased, two areas were vested with special character. The northern half of Cairo retained its Fatimid Ismāʿīlī functions. The ruler still appeared in the *bayn al-qaṣrayn*, the area between the two palaces, before processions.[9] The mosque of al-Ḥākim was still visited on occasions that were part of the Ismāʿīlī and Muslim calendars, and the *muṣalla* outside the Bāb al-Naṣr still remained a destination for the Imam-Caliph, even to the last days of the dynasty. The Great Street, the common central north-south axis, was extended and given prominence, opening the urban zones into each other (map 4). In this changed urban context, it became the main thoroughfare along which merchants, as well as civilians, dignitaries, members of the ruling group, and official processions travelled.[10]

Later constructions on this street emphasized further its growing prominence as a thoroughfare linking both the northern and southern sections of the urban area, Cairo and Miṣr. It served as the spine along which important Muslim communal structures were built or restored (map 4).[11] In Cairo, facing the Great Street, just north of the Eastern Palace, the mosque known as al-Aqmar (moonlit), was built in 1125/519 by the *wazīr* al-Maʾmūn.[12] Outside the southern gate, the Bāb Zuwayla, a mosque was built in 1160/555 that was known after its patron al-Malik al-Ṣāliḥ Ṭalāʾiʿ.[13] Further south, still, on this road, in the area of the mosque of Ahmad ibn Ṭūlūn, tombs such as those of Sayyida Ruqayya and Sayyida Nafīsa were restored and enlarged by Badr al-Jamālī[14] and subsequent members of the ruling group (map 4).

These physical and social changes begun by Badr al-Jamālī were not the only changes effected by him. Within the ruling group itself, he drastically altered the site of power, appropriating it to himself, while maintaining the formal order of the ruling system and thus al-Mustanṣir as Imam-Caliph.[15] He acted, especially outside of Cairo, to maintain the officially sponsored writing signs that would signal a strong Fatimid ruler. For example, two years after becoming *wazīr* (1075/467), he exerted strong pressure, in the form of written messages and lavish presents, on the *sherīf* of Mecca to persuade him to display writing signs with the name of al-Mustanṣir on the Holy Sites in Mecca. The *sherīf* complied, erasing the titles of the Abbasid Caliph al-Qāʾim and the Seljuk Sultan at the

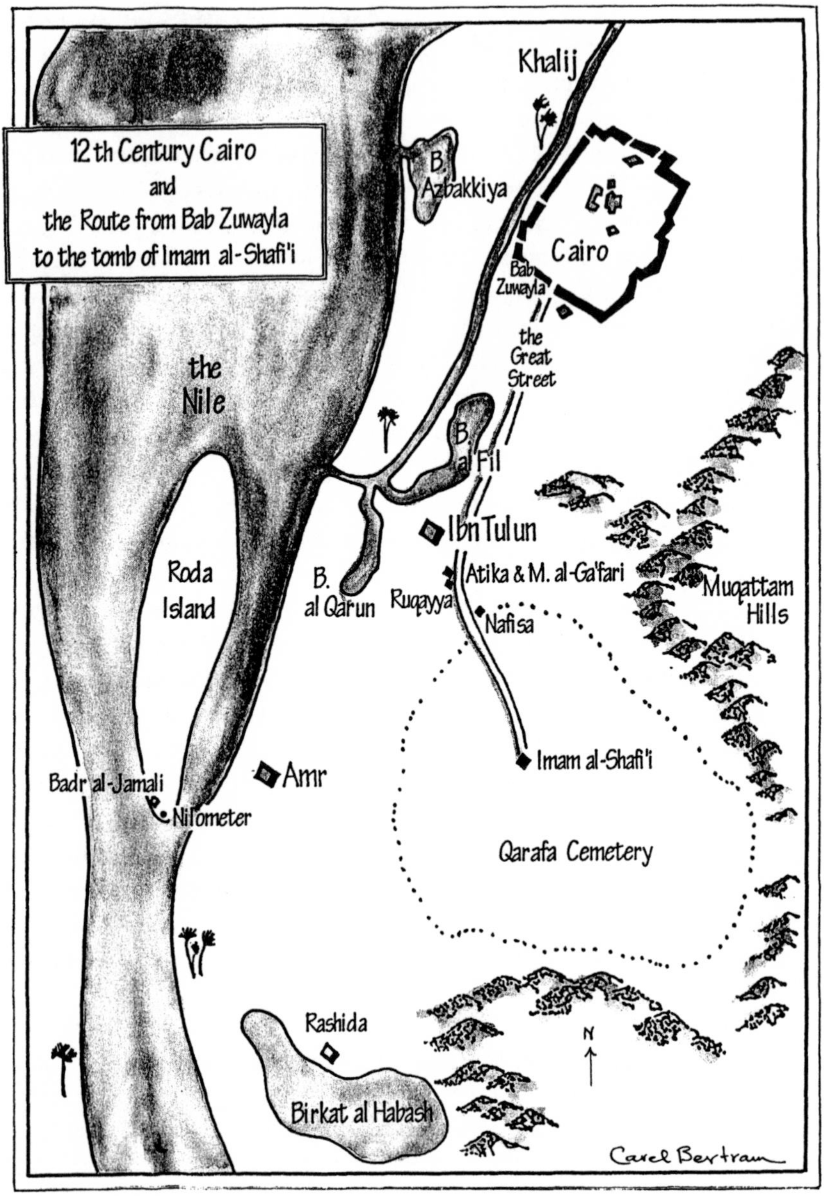

Map 4. Later Cairo and the route from Bāb Zuwayla to the tomb of Imam al-Shāfiʿi (drawn by Carel Bertram)

Zemzem, and removing the covering for the Kaʿba sent by the Abbasid Caliph, replacing it with the white *dābiqī* (linen) *kiswa* (covering) which displayed the names and titles of Imam-Caliph al-Mustanṣir.[16]

In Egypt, in the greater urban area of Cairo, however, Badr al-Jamālī used officially sponsored writing to proclaim the new power structure, with himself, the *wazīr*, as the possessor of power and authority within the social order. He did this by displaying his name and titles to the newly integrated urban audiences on the buildings he commissioned and reconstructed, a course of action paralleled by the change in formula in official petitions emphasizing his role.[17] Since he undertook a large program to restore the urban-infrastructure as a whole, as well as Muslim sectarian life, in specific, his name and titles appeared in many places; twenty-one have been identified to date.[18]

Those who passed saw his name and titles displayed on a plaque on the *ziyāda* (surrounding wall) of the mosque of Aḥmad ibn Ṭūlūn which he restored in 1077/470.[19] In addition to displaying his own name, he used this public text to comment on preceding events at the site, and, in only a lightly veiled manner, on the turbulence within the ruling group which caused his own rise to power. After his name and titles is the phrase, "He caused the restoration of this portal and what surrounds it [to take place] after the fire which destroyed it that the heretics let happen."[20] Wiet has plausibly suggested that the heretics (*māriq*) referred to were the Sunni Turkish troops who attacked the Black troops in 1062/454 and pillaged the treasures and the library, with the result that the area around the mosque of Aḥmad ibn Ṭūlūn fell into ruin until Badr began to revive it with his restoration of the mosque.[21]

A decade later, those passing into Cairo saw his name and titles displayed prominently in the writings on the new gateways he constructed as part of his effort to fortify the city of Cairo against its enemies (1087/440).[22] At the Bāb al-Futūḥ, if Creswell is correct, he used the marble slabs from the northern bastion of the mosque of al-Ḥākim to complete his inscription, thereby replacing what is presumed to have been a Qurʾanic inscription with one displaying names and titles and ranks of the *wazīr*. Shortly after, in 1089/482, he restored the mausoleum of Sayyida Nafīsa on the Great Street on which he also displayed his name and titles.[23]

With the completion of the fortification of Cairo, Badr al-Jamālī turned his attention to Roda Island. There he constructed a new mosque, on the exterior of which he prominently displayed his name. On this mosque, a large plaque on the western facade which faced directly onto the main boat channel of the Nile displayed Badr's name and titles in letters over two feet tall.[24] Aimed at the commercial boat traffic, it reminded viewers of his attention to the economic life of the area, and to his concern for the inundation of the Nile that supported it. An inscription with a similar message was placed over the entrance doorway, so that those on foot visiting the island and the mosque also viewed his name.[25] He also restored the adjacent Nilometer (*miqyās al-nīl*) and placed his name and titles inside it.

What predominates in all these inscriptions is the rank and titles of Badr al-Jamālī, although the Imam-Caliph's name is mentioned also. It is useful to explore these inscriptions in detail because they functioned as an *Ur*, or originary, text for subsequent powerful military leaders in Cairo—even those ruling after the Fatimid period. J. J. Marcel, in recording these structures on Roda Island for inclusion in the *Description de l'Egypte*, has left the only visual record of them.[26] He was primarily interested in the semantic content of the inscriptions for their value in dating the buildings. Consequently he simply recorded the content of the large inscription on the west wall of the mosque, and that over its portal, merely as variants of the inscription on the interior of the Nilometer (*miqyās al-nīl*).[27] Choosing to draw only the smallest and most compact of the inscriptions, that on the interior of the Nilometer (fig. 34), he merely gave a few details about the aesthetic aspects of the other inscriptions, especially that on the exterior of the mosque.

He noted that all these inscriptions were carved in white marble, a medium that seems to bind together all Badr al-Jamālī's extant public texts. He noted also that the form of the letters in the writing on the outside, western wall of the mosque were especially remarkable for their elegance, far greater than that of the other two inscriptions, especially that on the Nilometer, the only inscription he drew.[28] Marcel's comments leave us with some evidence to conclude that Badr al-Jamālī paid particular attention to public texts. Most attention was paid to the aesthetic qualities of the writing facing the traffic on the Nile, while less attention was paid to inscriptions on the interior of the Nilometer, or over the doorway into the mosque. But while Badr apparently made audience considerations the basis for aesthetic choices in the display of writing, the referential content remained basically the same.

It is well worth examining the inscription on the Nilometer in detail for its referential dimensions. The amount of space allocated to the component sections of the inscription remained stable in all his officially sponsored writing, even though they were not displayed in this manner—a

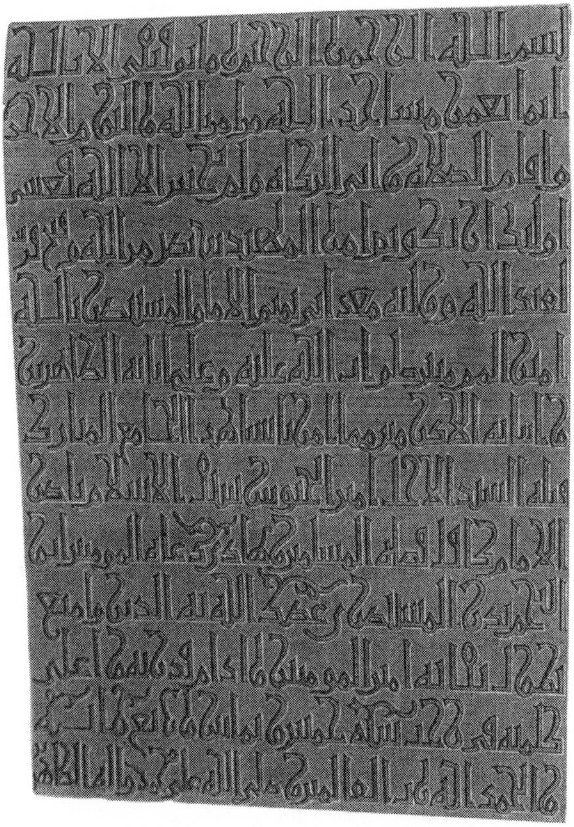

34. Inscription from Nilometer of Badr al-Jamālī, after Marcel, *Description de l'Egypte*

plaque of thirteen lines. The inscription begins in standard fashion with the formula, "In the Name of God, The Merciful, The Compassionate (*basmala*),[29] followed by verses from the Qur'ān which fill the first four of the thirteen lines.[30] The nine remaining lines give first the name of the Imam al-Mustanṣir, and then list in detail the names and titles of the Badr al-Jamālī, the person with the real power, along with the date of construction. Badr al-Jamālī is "the Prince Most Illustrious, the Commander of the Armies, Sword of Islam, Surety of the Judges of the Muslims, Guide of the Missionaries of the Believers." Further along, the inscription mentions his successes in the cause of religion, and wishes him a long life in the service of the Commander of the Faithful (*Amīr al-Mu'minīn*), that is, the Imam-al-Mustanṣir, whose power, according to the writing, Badr al-Jamālī affirms.

This visual display, and the others like it, of Badr al-Jamālī's name and titles in Cairo-Miṣr needs to be evaluated against the backdrop of the reduced visibility of the name of the Imam-Caliph and also of his person. While mentioned in all of Badr al-Jamālī's inscriptions, the names and titles of the Imam-Caliph are so abbreviated that they became almost a secondary dating device in addition to that given in the *hegira* calendar. Unlike in Mecca, where Badr al-Jamālī worked behind the scenes to support the display of the names and titles of only the Imam-Caliph, in Cairo not only did Badr minimize the display of the Imam's name but he stopped the processions. He stopped those like Nāṣir-i Khusraw described during which the ruler made himself visible to the whole population.[31] He also ended those in which the Imam led the Ismāʿīlī community in prayer at the *muṣalla*.[32] The succeeding *wazīr*, al-Afḍal, Badr's son, continued these policies. With the reduced visibility of the person and the names of the Imam, the public text became an especially effective visual instrument for the *wazīr*, and by extension the troops that maintained him in office, to display his power.

The Public Text and *Wazīr* al-Ma'mūn

Al-Ma'mūn[33] was *wazīr* for some four years, 1121–1125/515–519,[34] during the reign of Imam-Caliph al-Āmir (r. 1101–30/495–524).[35] An Ismāʿīlī,[36] he, like Badr al-Jamālī, had been a mamluk, and was an important Amir in the army when he was appointed *wazīr*. Like Badr al-Jamālī before him, he built and restored many structures on which he displayed his name. In 1122/516 he ordered the construction of the mosque of Kāfūrī in the Kāfūr Park west of the mosque of al-Aqmar.[37] In that same year, he repaired seven mausolea along the Great Street, and ordered marble plaques put on the outside of each, displaying his name, titles, and the date.[38] None of these examples of his officially sponsored writings survives. However, the mosque he built on the Great Street, just north of the Imam-Caliph's palace, known as al-Aqmar, displayed public texts in a layout that was brilliant for its subtle references to its contemporary visual contexts, and to al-Ma'mūn's own manner of functioning as a powerful *wazīr* in a governmental structure headed by an Imam whose position was highly contested (fig. 35).[39] These public texts combined *wazīr* al-Ma'mūn's rank and title information, in the tradition of Badr al-Jamālī,

35. Facade, al-Aqmar mosque

with a visually prominent display of the sign of Ismaʿilism, and with Qurʾanic quotations.

The facade of the al-Aqmar mosque is divided into three parts, a salient entrance portal with a large arch, and two recessed side sections with smaller arches.[40] This general layout is so remarkably like al-Mustanṣir's *kiswa* for the Kaʿba described by Nāṣir-i Khusraw that it is almost as if that covering were placed over the facade as a base. Nāṣir-i Khusraw described the covering in the following manner:

The covering with which the house [Kaʿba] was cloaked was a white covering which displayed two bands of embroidered ornaments, each a *gaz* wide. The distance between the two bands was about ten *gaz*. . . . On the four sides of the covering, colored mihrab were woven and embroidered and embellished with gold filigree. On each wall there were three mihrab, a big one in the middle and two small ones on either side.[41]

Nāṣir-i Khusraw is describing a *kiswa* he saw in 1050, some seventy years before al-Maʾmūn built the al-Aqmar mosque, but the three arch (or mihrab) elements of its design were even at that time present in stone and stucco on the Great Street.[42] The basic display of a central large arch and two smaller side arches was already present on the monumental entrance of the mosque of al-Ḥākim (fig. 29),[43] and in what is extant today of the Fatimid sections of al-Azhar, at the entrance to the prayer hall. It might also have been present in the "*muṣalla* with three mihrabs" that *wazīr* al-Afḍal built for the funeral service for those in Fusṭāṭ.[44] Obviously on each the spacing and placement differs. How they compared to the arches on the *kiswa* Nāṣir-i Khusraw saw is, of course, left to our imaginations. What the facade of al-Aqmar and the design on the *kiswa* share that the other arches apparently do not, is the bands that cut across them. On the *kiswa* we assume they displayed the names and titles of the Imam-Caliph. On the al-Aqmar mosque they display the names and titles of the *wazīr*, al-Ma'mūn.

Prominently—not once, but twice—across the entire facade, the two bands of writing display the name and all the titles of *wazīr* al-Ma'mūn, the date, and the name of the Imam-Caliph al-Āmir.[45] This is the referential base of the wide band of writing running along the entire facade under the cornice. The same information, in virtually the same words, but in smaller letters, runs the width of the facade at mid-point. This referential base is equivalent to that of the public texts of Badr al-Jamālī, even to the use of the Imam's name as a dating device. No viewer could have escaped knowing that Abū ʿAbd Allāh, "Commander of the Armies, Sword of Islam, Helper of the Imam, Surety of the Judges of the Muslims, and Guide of the Missionaries of the Believers," sponsored this structure in 519 (1125) in the reign of Caliph al-Āmir.

This is the writing sign most visually accessible to the viewer in the Great Street. The band format heightens its legibility against its background. The letter size in the top band (c. 18 in. high) ensured readability.[46] In the second band the letters are smaller, but they are half the distance from the ground.[47] Additional aesthetic properties aid the legibility of the rank and title information of these bands. The clearest and most elegant lettering, the one that is easiest to read, is in the top band. While the elaboration of the basic Kufic style lettering of each band on this facade differs from the other, the top band is further distinguished by a base line for the horizontal letters significantly above the bottom of the moulding of the band. In practical terms, letters like *rā* and *dāl* are thus differentiated by allowing the former to descend slightly below the line of the latter. In short, more basic letter forms are distinguishable from each other in this style of Kufic writing than in the other versions of that script on the facade. As mentioned above, in the Kufic style script, differentiation of letters aided in legibility.[48]

While these bands displaying the rank and title information of the *wazīr* are highly legible writing signs on this facade, the concentric circle medal-

36. Central concentric circle medallion, al-Aqmar mosque

lion over the entrance portal is also immediately recognizable by Ismāʿīlīs as the sign of Ismaʿilism (fig. 36). Its size, around 4½ feet (1.43 m.) in diameter, ensures its visual prominence to all beholders. A smaller concentric circle medallion is displayed over the flat arch on the left wing (fig. 37).[49] In form, the concentric circle medallion over the entrance portal replicates the sign of Ismaʿilism as we have come to expect it in terms of the placement of writing in its concentric circles. The outer circle displays a quotation from the Qurʾān, part of verse 33:33: "God only desires to take away uncleanness from you, Oh people of the house (*ahl al-bayt*)." In the center are the names "Muḥammad" and "ʿAlī." Some important differences exist, however, in the evocational base of the writing, which will be discussed below.

Under this concentric circle medallion is the only other substantial Qurʾanic quotation on the building facade. Over the salient doorway is a band stretching only the length of the doorway itself displaying two verses from the Qurʾān, 24:36–37. These two verses are appropriate to a mosque and to the obligations of Muslims:

It is in the houses which God has permitted to be exalted in His name to be remembered therein. Therein do glorify Him, in the mornings and in the evenings.

37. Small concentric circle medallion, side niche, al-Aqmar mosque

Men whom neither merchandise nor selling diverts from the remembrance of God and maintaining the *ṣalāt* and paying the *zakāt*, they fear a day in which the hearts and the eyes will turn around.

The writing signs on this facade at first glance might appear to be a highly ambiguous juxtaposition of referential dimensions aimed at unclearly defined audiences. Yet these public texts and their layout were astutely chosen for the intricately woven contexts in which they were embedded. Consider first the location of this mosque. Located on the Great Street, the facade was aligned to the street, which made it particularly highly visible to the multi-ethnic, multi-religious pedestrian traffic that passed. The highly legible bands displaying the names and titles of the *wazīr* were addressed to this broadly based public audience.[50] The titles awarded to *wazīrs* were both known, discussed, and evaluated by members of the Christian population of Cairo-Miṣr, and they concerned the Muslim population and members of the ruling group.

These writing signs were addressed to a Muslim audience, especially a Fatimid Ismāʿīlī one, when the space in front of the al-Aqmar mosque was used as a stopping place for processions and for viewing the Imam-Caliph on ceremonial occasions. These occasions were many at this time, more than a dozen throughout the year.[51] The al-Aqmar mosque, ***wazīr*** al-Maʾmūn's new construction, supplanted the structures of "forage merchants and the ***manzara***,"[52] or belvedere, where in earlier times the Imam-Caliph had shown himself to those assembled. In ***wazīr*** al-Maʾmūn's time, the space in front of the mosque, as a continuation from the Eastern Palace, became highly charged in these formal moments when the Imam al-Āmir appeared, and in which ***wazīr*** al-Maʾmūn was also highly visible. Here the processions stopped, so that al-Maʾmūn could escort the Imam-Caliph into his palace at the end of the procession. It was a stopping place where the ***wazīr*** saluted the Imam, and was in turn acknowledged. On the anniversary festivals for the Prophet, ʿAlī, and the Imam, Qurʾān reciters lined up in front of the neighboring palace and listened to the preacher of the al-Aqmar mosque deliver a sermon and prayers for the Imam. The preachers of the al-Ḥākim and al-Azhar mosques followed after.[53] On these occasions within the Ismāʿīlī calendar, it is hard to doubt that the Fatimid Ismāʿīlī audience perceived the sign of Ismaʿilism in the concentric circle medallion and all would notice the names and title of the ***wazīr*** who supported the construction.

In restoring and reinventing such ceremonies, ***wazīr*** al-Maʾmūn adopted a mode for operating within the ruling structure different from that of Badr al-Jamālī.[54] The times demanded such a change, and the specific selection of Qurʾanic verses on the facade suggests al-Maʾmūn's sensitivity in dealing with a doctrinal issue that came to be important in expressing the difference between the Fatimid and Nizārī Ismāʿīlīs.

We can probe further into the revolt that threatened the legitimacy, and thus the authority and stability of Fatimid rule at this time, by looking briefly at the dispute over the succession to the Imamate after the death of Imam al-Mustanṣir in 1094/487. The ***wazīr*** then ruling, al-Afḍal, Badr al-Jamālī's son, arranged to have Nizār, the son of Imam al-Mustanṣir, excluded from succession to the Imamate. Nizar had been designated by his father as having Divine Light, and thus the heir to succeed him. In his stead, ***wazīr*** al-Afḍal was able to have a younger son, Aḥmad, succeed to the Imamate with the ruling title al-Mustaʿlī (r. 1094–1101/487–95). Such a switch in the succession caused a major split in the Ismāʿīlī group, because succession and the passing on of the ***nūr*** (light) of the Imam were fundamental in establishing the authority of the Imam in the eyes of the Believers. In Fatimid Egypt, the al-Mustaʿlī line (or what this study calls the Fatimid Ismāʿīlīs) continued, but elsewhere, especially in Seljuk territories (Syria and Iraq), Ismāʿīlīs recognized Nizār as the Imam.[55]

In 1101, al-Āmir, at age five, succeeded his father al-Mustaʿlī as Fatimid

Ismāʿīlī Imam. He was helped in this succession by *wazīr* al-Afḍal, who, under the circumstances of the Imam's young age, ruled the Fatimid empire. When al-Maʾmūn became *wazīr*, after al-Afḍal was assassinated in 1121, Nizārī activity increased in Egypt. *Wazīr* al-Maʾmūn's actions of supporting public appearances of Imam al-Āmir made strategic sense both within the context of the Nizārī-Fatimid Ismāʿīlī dispute, and in terms of rallying the general population and the ruling group behind the Imam-Caliph, even as the number of Fatimid Ismāʿīlī Believers in Egypt was diminishing.

The subtlety of al-Maʾmūn's choice of Qurʾanic verses across the doorway of the al-Aqmar mosque indicates his sensitivity to excluding a verse that in fact at that time might have addressed doctrinal disputes among Ismāʿīlīs. The verses on the doorway—Qurʾān 24:36–37 quoted above—are certainly appropriate for a mosque, but they are not the only verses in the Qurʾān that mention such obligations, nor were they the only ones quoted on Fatimid buildings. But on the facade of the al-Aqmar mosque, these verses are taken from the *sūrat al-Nūr* (chap. 24, *sūra* of Light) which when displayed on Fatimid buildings usually included the immediately preceding verse (35) where God's light is likened to a lamp in a glass placed in a niche. This verse is on the al-Ḥākim mosque (see chapter 3), where God's light relates in the dimension of *taʾwīl* to the Imam himself. As Ismāʿīlīs, both the Nizārīs and the Fatimid Ismāʿīlīs shared a similar *taʾwīl* of verse 35, recognizing the Imam as an emanation of the Divine Light which passed from one Imam to another, linking them together. But an expanded Nizārī exegesis of this verse underscored a fundamental doctrinal difference. The *nūr* gave the Imam even greater spiritual power, manifesting the highest reality, a concept central to the doctrinal differences between these two groups of Ismāʿīlīs.[56]

Given such doctrinal differences, and their immediacy for the Ismāʿīlīs of the capital, it seems to me highly possible that verse 35, appropriate for public display on the outside of the mosque of al-Ḥākim in 1002/393 when Cairo and the northern zone was an Ismāʿīlī area, and the group of Believers was both larger and united behind the recognition of one Imam, was no longer appropriate in 1125/519.[57] At this later date, the population of Cairo and the ruling group were so diverse in composition, and the recent schism had exacerbated this diversity, that the presence of this verse might have led some Ismāʿīlī viewers to inopportune understandings and associations non-supportive of the Fatimid Ismāʿīlī Imam. The concerns for stability were real, for within five years after this mosque was completed, the Imam himself was assassinated, probably by Nizārī emissaries.[58] Given the context, I would argue that *wazīr* al-Maʾmūn would not choose to put a verse so religiously and politically charged on display.

Of course, that the verses that were displayed were chosen from the Qurʾanic chapter on Light (*sūrat al-nūr*) indicates a well-chosen allusion on al-Maʾmūn's part to the schism and the doctrinal dispute. It may even be that his allusion to light and the Imam was more clever than simply the act of excluding a verse. The large sign of Ismaʿilism over the entrance portal was aesthetically different from any other extant sign of Ismaʿilism in one significant structural respect. The names in the center, as well as the ring separating the center circle from the circle displaying the Qurʾanic verse, are pierced. Sunlight passes over them into the vestibule of the mosque. The results are that the sunlight daily "writes" the names "ʿAlī" and "Muḥammad" in shadow within a circle in the mosque's vestibule. That this sign of Ismaʿilism was consciously designed so that light passed over the names and caused them to appear in shadow as allusion to the Imam, emanation of Divine Light, is supported by the fact that a light screen is unnecessary in so small a mosque where the vestibule is well-lighted from the courtyard.

While this concentric circle medallion may have looked in all its formal aspects like a sign of Ismaʿilism, it is critical to understand that an important change had occurred in one of the functions of the writing it displayed (fig. 36). From the time Imam al-Muʿizz put the sign of Ismaʿilism on coins, to its appearance on the facade of al-Maʾmūn's mosque, the evocational field of the Qurʾanic quotation in the outer circle had been bivalent. The two evocational fields were the Qurʾān and Ismāʿīlī *taʾwīl*. While, of course, the whole Qurʾān is important to all Muslims, only some verses are directly related to Ismāʿīlī interpretation. The verse displayed in the outer ring of this sign of Ismaʿilism, Qurʾān 33:33, is not a text in *taʾwīl*. Its specific verse and the words *ahl al-bayt* (people of the household of the Prophet Muḥammad) are understood and honored by all Muslims. As I have argued elsewhere,[59] to Sunnis the *ahl al-bayt* are all of the progeny of the Prophet Muḥammad by all of his wives, thus all four of his daughters. In contrast, to all Shīʿī groups, the concept is more focused, referring only to the descendants of the Prophet's daughter Fāṭima, her husband ʿAlī, and their two sons, Ḥassan and Ḥusayn.

This change in the evocational base of the text in the outer ring of the concentric circle medallion was made difficult for any literate viewer to discover. Fixed in place over the portal, what the pedestrian can readily read in the outer ring is *basmala*, which begins at the 3 o'clock position and runs counterclockwise. The Qurʾanic verse, starting in the 11 o'clock position, is mostly upside down to the pedestrian. The gestalt of this sign of Isma'ilism, its formal or aesthetic qualities, and not the evocational base of its writing is what conveys meaning to those who recognize it. To all others, as argued above, the concentric circle medallion is one format for writing signs used by the Fatimid ruling group.

The Text and *Wazīrs* Bahrām al-Armanī and Riḍwān ibn al-Walakshī

It is worth recounting in brief the strategy that defeated *wazīr* Bahrām al-Armanī (Bahrām, the Armenian) because it not only tells of the nature of the power struggles in the ruling establishment, it also reinforces one of the recurring themes of this study.[60] That is, it shows that the Qur'ān was the only emblem that could predictably bring all Muslims together, in this case opposing the power of non-Muslims, mainly Armenian Christians. Moreover, it shows that Muslims were consciously using the Qur'ān in the public spaces as such a sectarian emblem. The incident in question reportedly occurred in 1137–38/532. But understanding the issues at stake requires a return to a brief discussion of the serious level the political instability in Cairo had reached.

Another succession crisis that further split the Fatimid Ismā'īlī group occurred in 1130/524 after the murder of Imam-Caliph al-Āmir. From this schism, the Ṭayyibī Ismā'īlīs split from those Fatimid Ismā'īlīs who recognized al-Ḥāfiẓ as the new Imam.[61] This matter is somewhat more complex than the earlier crises. This new crisis illustrates how the diversity of players and groups in the power relations of the ruling elite led to a fragility in the ruling system—and ultimately to the overthrow of Fatimid Ismā'īlī rule. Coming little more than three decades after the Nizārī schism, this Ṭayyibī crisis involved the murder of an infant heir (al-Ṭayyib), and reached a climax when the *wazīr* Abū 'Alī Kutayfāt (related to both Badr al-Jamālī and Imam al-Mustanṣir) abolished the Fatimid Ismā'īlī Imamate. He took the power in the name of the authority of the Expected Imam of the Imāmī Shī'ī (or Twelver Shī'ism).

Ultimately, within a year, *wazīr* Kutayfāt was himself killed by Fatimid Ismā'īlī adherents, and Abū al-Majīd was proclaimed Imam with the ruling title al-Ḥāfiz, even though he was not a son of the previous Imam. The Fatimid Ismā'īlī Imamate and Caliphate, more specifically the Ḥāfiẓ-Fatimid Ismā'īlī Imamate, was thus restored, although, of course, the Ḥāfiẓ-Fatimid Ismā'īlī group was quite small. The Ṭayyibī schism reduced the Ismā'īlīs in Egypt almost solely to adherents based in the palace in Cairo. Even after this schism, the Fatimid Imam-Caliph was, of course, still head of the Fatimid ruling system. But he retained that position in even more palpable ways than before solely because the interests of all the groups were best served by maintaining the form of Imam-Caliphal rule, rather than because the Fatimid Ismāʿīlīs had the power to enforce the ruler's position.[62]

Now, to return to the incident where this section began—the struggle between *wazīr* Bahrām al-Armanī and the contender for that position, Riḍwān ibn al-Walakshī. In the ensuing disturbances after Imam al-Ḥāfiẓ assumed the throne, the army brought Bahrām al-Armanī to be confirmed as the *wazīr*.[63] As Ibn al-Muqaffaʿ notes, as a direct result of *wazīr* Bahrām's policies the Christians gained influence and positions in the important *dīwāns* of the kingdom.[64] When "the word of the Muslims weakened," as he describes it, the Muslims sought to remove Bahrām from office of *wazīr*. Muslim groups within the army turned to one of their own, an *amīr* and a Sunni Muslim, Riḍwān ibn al-Walakshī, who declared a *jihād* against the Christian *wazīr* Bahrām and his troops.[65] The issues in this struggle involving various Muslim and Christian groups were ones of economic and political power in the Fatimid government. Riḍwān, however, visually emblematized them in a Muslim sectarian reference that brought the Muslim groups together. In the thick of the battle, his troops raised the Qurʾān on their lances as a battle standard.[66]

It was a genuinely brilliant choice. The Muslims understood the message conveyed by using the Qurʾān as emblem, and left the army of Bahrām, who fled with only his Christian troops.[67] Riḍwān's raising of the Qurʾān as a battle standard recalled the Battle of Ṣiffīn (657 C.E.) where Muʿāwiya in fighting ʿAlī originally employed the same tactic. Of course, for Sunni Muslims it recalled an action that led ultimately to Muʿāwiya's gaining the title Caliph, but the initial arbitration at the end of the fighting did not take the title away from ʿAlī. Thus all Muslim army contingents, Sunni (Mālikī, Shāfiʿī and Ḥanbalī) and Shīʿī (Ismāʿīlī and Imāmī), could rally around that emblem—the Qurʾān hoisted on a lance. Christians, of course, if we are to believe this widely reported story, did not. At the approach of the fourth decade of the twelfth century, the Qurʾān was being actively used to rally all Muslims in the military elements of the ruling group, and to exclude Christians.

Wazīr al-Malik al-Ṣāliḥ Ṭalāʾiʿ and the Public Text

Ṭalāʾiʿ ibn Ruzzīk, an Imāmī,[68] was invested as *wazīr* with the title *al-malik al-ṣāliḥ* in 1154/549 during yet another time of trouble, when the Imam-Caliph al-Ẓāfir had been murdered and al-Fāʾiz became the new Imam-Caliph. Ṭalāʾiʿ held the position of *wazīr* through the six years of Imam al-Fāʾiz's reign into the early days of the reign of the last Fatimid Imam, al-ʿĀḍid (r. 1160–71/555–67).[69] Known as avaricious, *wazīr* Ṭalāʾiʿ nevertheless, as the *wazīrs* before him, was generous in supporting Muslim communal life, and used public texts to display his name and messages.

He built his mosque on the Great Street, like *wazīr* al-Maʾmūn before him, only he constructed it outside the Bāb Zuwayla (map 3).[70] He is said to have regretted choosing this location because in the unrest in the capital area his mosque was used by insurgents attacking the southern gates of Cairo proper.[71] This mosque, finished in 1159/555 a few months before Ṭalāʾiʿ died, has three articulated facades, on the north, south, and west. The west facade facing the Great Street is the main facade and main entrance. The basic layout of these facades share with that of the al-Aqmar mosque important elements: bands of writing that divide a ground of arches in three places (fig. 38). On the Ṭalāʾiʿ mosque multiple arches of the same height articulate the facades vertically, rather than as on the al-Aqmar mosque, where the arches were of differing heights. The three bands of writing run the full lengths of the three sides. Like on the facade of the al-Aqmar mosque, the widest one is under the cornice. One is placed about midway, and one at door height. The second band from the top is best preserved, and like the one on the facade of al-Aqmar, displays the name of the Imam, here al-Fāʾiz, and the date. The major portion of the inscription displays the names and titles of the *wazīr* Ṭalāʾiʿ.[72]

What is important to note is that the public text on these three facades consists of rank and title information, with quotations from the Qurʾān over the doors and windows, and in the upper band. This balance underscores and focuses attention on the very real power of this *wazīr* who ruled Fatimid lands. He served two Imams. Imam-al-Fāʾiz was a child, and Ṭalāʾiʿ kept Imam al-ʿĀḍid as virtual prisoner in the palace.[73] The sign of Ismaʿilism is not present on any of the facades of the Ṭalāʾiʿ mosque.

Rather, the sign of Ismaʿilism, so closely related to communal memory devices from Ismāʿīlī discourses, is transformed on the facades of the mosque of Ṭalāʾiʿ into roundels elaborately filled with geometric forms based on sixty degree angles. These roundels are placed in the spandrels between the arches on the three facades. On the west facade, the blind arches with the articulated hoods so reminiscent of those on the al-Aqmar mosque, also display roundels in their center. At this late date, the only sign of Ismaʿilism continually reissued and displayed is that on coins (fig. 39) where the concentric circle format and writing in circles is main-

38. Exterior, mosque of Ṭalāʾiʿ

tained. Even the Qurʾanic quotation in the outer ring, 9:33, with its bivalent evocational field, was maintained. This continuance has much to do with the conservative nature of coinage, and its gold fineness, rather than a recognition of the ideological referents of its concentric circle format.[74] The coin with its recognizable format had come to be recognized and valued for its purity.

It is understandable that the sign of Ismaʿilism disappeared as a component format for the public text on Muslim sectarian buildings at this time. For approximately four decades, since al-Maʾmūn, no *wazīr* had been an Ismāʿīlī,[75] while at the same time the number of Fatimid Ismāʿīlīs in the capital area was drastically reduced by schisms. Support for Sunni Islam was on the increase. There was neither patronage to know and to support, nor audience to perceive such a writing sign, especially one placed a distance from the immediate Eastern Palace area. That the concentric circle form, the sign of Ismaʿilism, should be transformed into a roundel displaying geometric designs is in keeping with the history of forms that develop, as the sign of Ismaʿilism did, with specific referents in a social context. Art Deco forms, for instance, in the early twentieth century related to issues of streamlining and speed. In their transformed appearance today, they have lost those specific connotations for most of their

39. Dinar, Imam al-Fā'iz (1002.1.890 Collection of the University of Pennsylvania Museum in the Cabinet of the American Numismatic Society)

audience, and with those connotations aspects of the original form are altered.

Processions and the Public Text

On the urban stage of Cairo-Miṣr, the other use of officially sponsored writing was on cloth displayed in the public ceremonies and processions. Our knowledge stems mainly from Ibn al-Ṭuwayr (d. 1220/617), the late-Fatimid- and early-Ayyubid-period historian whose writings are lost, but whose accounts were cited by al-Maqrīzī.[76] Although I suspect that more writing was displayed on cloth than we can reconstruct with the limited citations al-Maqrīzī uses from Ibn al-Ṭuwayr's work, these are, nonetheless, sufficient to give some sense of the various functions of writing on cloth displayed in the public space.

In recording the Imam-Caliph's entrance into the Anwar mosque (al-Ḥākim's mosque) during Ramadan, Ibn al-Ṭuwayr described the white silk curtains displaying *sūras* from the Qur'ān rendered in red silk pointed writing (i.e., with diacritical marks) that hung on either side of the mihrab. This description, mentioned in chapter 1, was part of a longer record of the Imam's entrance into the mosque, a ceremony celebrated by elaborate display in which mihrab curtains were part of the outfitting of the mihrab area where he sat. Three white silk *farāsh* (mattresses or spread out cloths) with writing on them were spread on the floor in this area, completing its appropriate dressing in Fatimid official colors.[77] These lavish displays are in the main hard to date, but are part of the restoration of the processions of the Imam-Caliph in the northern part of Cairo begun under *wazīr* al-Ma'mūn.

Ibn al-Ṭuwayr is also responsible for details about writing in official processions. Describing the New Year's ceremonial,[78] he records that the banners twenty-one of the Troops of the Stirrup (*ṣibyān al-rikāb*) carried in the official procession displayed the phrase *naṣr min allah fatḥ qarīb* (Help from God and Victory Near at Hand), part of Qurʾān 61:13.[79] This writing was variegated in color, and fashioned in silk. Each banner had three *tirāz* bands placed on the lances of the horsemen.[80] They helped provide a colorful procession, predominantly red and yellow in color.

In a different context, al-Qalqashandī, in a lengthy description of the arms of the infantry, mentioned that they carried a (one) narrow banner of variegated (*malawna*) colored silk upon which was written *naṣr min allah wa fatḥ qarīb* (Help from God and Victory Near at Hand).[81] This single banner was part of the trooping of colors and followed behind two riders from the Special Troops (*ṣibyān al-khāṣṣ*), who carried lances each with eight banners of red and yellow *dībāj*.[82] These two descriptions seem to be of different instances, different troops and somewhat different banner, although displaying the same semantic content. In fact, a Treasury of Banners (*khizānat al-bunūd*) existed in Cairo, employing 3,000 artisans in Imam al-Ẓāhir's reign which would have been responsible for fashioning all these banners.[83] Although it is not specifically recorded, presumably the *amīr*s who headed this treasury (and a similar one for armor and parade adornment) were responsible for the maintenance, provision, and collection of the banners which were taken out and used as the occasion demanded. Fabrication of all of the banners may not have actually occurred in the treasury, yet the officials must have been responsible to procure them. If they were not embellished by these 3,000 artisans, then these various banners must have been procured on special order from weaving establishments, many probably in the Delta.[84]

These banners or, more likely, some related cloth, might possibly be represented in the archaeological textile fragments from this period. Fragments of textiles, mainly decorated bands, displaying *naṣr min allah* (Help from God) in red silk with yellow lattice design on a linen ground are relatively common in museum collections throughout the world (fig. 40). In fact, the embellished area on these textiles is usually woven in what could be described as a tripartite composition. While these textile fragments display part of the semantic content described in the history texts, and also the red and yellow colors mentioned as dominating almost all ceremonies and processions, to our contemporary eyes, they do not fully coincide with the descriptions of the banners bearing this message. Certainly none of the fragments I am aware of displays gold threads.

40. Textile fragment, with ***nasr min allah***, later Fatimid period (courtesy of Seattle Art Museum, Eugene Fuller Memorial Collection)

These instances are to my knowledge the only ones that describe cloth used in public official ceremonies as displaying writing.[85] Hundreds of robes and turbans with elaborate borders are described as being handed out to various members of the ruling group during official distribution of the *kiswa*.[86] These distributions were extraordinarily lavish in the reign of Imam-Caliph al-Āmir, as one might imagine in such a period of socio-political instability, although they existed in the earlier Fatimid period, too.[87] These same reports even record that the cloth for this distribution was stored in Cairo in the Treasury of the Wardrobe (*khizānat al-kiswa*) which housed both the clothing for the troops as well as the costly robes for the Imam and other dignitaries.[88]

But no description I am aware of, no matter how lengthy and detailed the record, or how often borders of turbans and robes are mentioned, or even how frequently linen is noted as the ground fabric states specifically that any of this cloth displayed writing. The word most frequently used to describe borders of cloth and clothing is *manqūsh*. Many scholars have translated this word as "inscribed." But its medieval meaning, substantiated by medieval dictionaries and the Geniza records, is "embellished," and I have now come to favor this as the proper translation of the word.[89] *Manqūsh*, or "embellished," should probably be seen as an umbrella term that could include written borders, but is not limited to them. Thousands of fragments displaying writing remain today from this period, some from very beautiful and fine cloth, yet we need more evidence than exists currently before they can be attached to these official clothing distributions. Historical accounts thus help us only to a limited extent in understanding the official use of textiles with writing on them and the extant archaeological fragments. Evidence absent is not proof of absent practice, of course. We are simply reminded that written documents and remains of visual culture do not explain each other but function in interrelated ways, in separate tracks, in society.

What is clear is that quotations taken from the Qurʾān were displayed on cloth and elsewhere in ever-increasing numbers in the last two or three decades of Fatimid rule. Such quotations were addressed even more urgently to all Muslims, for their cohesion was the underpinning of the ruling system headed by the Fatimid Ismāʿīlī Imam-Caliph. The curtains on the sides of the mihrab in the Anwar mosque (al-Ḥākim's mosque) are a good example of this practice. Both curtains displayed the *basmala* and then the *sūrat al-fātiḥa* (the opening *sūra* of the Qurʾān). Then on the right one the *sūrat al-jumʿa* (62, The Gathering or Congregation) was written, and, on the left, the *sūrat al-munāfiqūn* (63, The Hypocrites). The former *sūra* was also displayed in the writing on the western salient outside this very mosque. This *sūra* is most appropriate for the location of its display because it refers to Friday prayers. Its placement in the mihrab of this Friday mosque then would have been comfortable for all Muslims. Likewise, *sūra* 63 discusses the role of the Messenger of God and those who do not believe in his mission. This chapter, too, had relevance for all Muslims especially in the social circumstances of the late Fatimid period, when those who did not recognize the message or the Messenger (namely, the Christians), so dominated the ruling group.

These same kinds of associations and audiences were evoked by the semantic content of the writing on the banners, ***naṣr min allāh wa fatḥ qarīb*** (Help from God and Victory Near at Hand). On one level it was a battle cry for all Muslims against their enemies. Yet, on another level, this phrase and the words from it were important in Fatimid Ismāʿīlī practice. Qāḍī al-Nuʿmān, for example, understand them to refer to the Qāʾim and to the resurrection.[90] Also, these were (and are) the names of the two main gates of Cairo. Outside the Bāb al-Naṣr the ***muṣalla*** was located where the Imam and ruling group and Believers processes on ʿĪd celebrations. In the later Fatimid period, processions for the New Year exited from the Bāb al-Naṣr and re-entered Cairo through the Bāb al-Futūḥ, the site of the Anwar mosque (al-Ḥākim's mosque). These two words, as mentioned above, were also part of the quotations from the Qurʾān placed under the dome before the mihrab where these curtains hung in the mosque of al-Ḥākim.

The accounts described above also give details about the aesthetic and territorial functions or meanings of these same writings. As in the earlier period, the lavishness of the display in which the writing on textiles was embedded was intended to convey to the participants, as well as to the beholders, the power and thus the stability of the ruling group; they were increased in number over time as the government grew more unstable and, predictably, ***wazīrs*** turned over rapidly. The more the personnel in powerful positions changed, the greater was the need for processions which continually re-hierarchized (to themselves and to the urban audience) the members of the ruling group by their order in the processional ranks.[91] If the number of processions and ceremonies was in reverse proportion to the stability of the government, so, too, was the amount of display in terms of the drain on available governmental resources to support it.[92]

While Ibn al-Ṭuwayr's description of the lavish display of gold and jeweled fabrics and trappings rivals that of Nāṣir-i Khusraw, the changing taxation and troop payment systems meant that the Imam-Caliph and the palace establishment had less monetary resources than earlier to support such lavishness. In addition, the ***wazīrs*** had their own processions and sections of the processions. Thus the display of gold and jewels and colors represented a greater distance between the display of power and its actuality in the later Fatimid period than it did in the former.

In each of these descriptions of writing, we are told that the writing was in silk—usually on silk or brocade cloth. These comments on the aesthetics of the writing conveyed to the reader information both about the quality of the writing and the cost of production. Silk, of course, was probably imported and thus expensive. Mentioning silk as a medium distinguished the fibre in which the writing was rendered from the dominant fibre in the processions, namely linen, which was locally produced. By noting inscriptions and other elements, especially when they were red or yellow, Ibn al-Ṭuwayr was probably also signalling a quality distinction to his readers. To mention red and yellow was to note two very expensive colors produced from dye substances obtainable only on the international market.[93] By contrast, for example, to have commented on blue as a textile color would not have evoked such connotations of luxury, because blue was produced from indigo, a common local dye.

In short, what might appear from the descriptions of the aesthetic and territorial functions of writing on cloth to be the "same" display of power in terms of the consumption of expensive commodities by the ruling group in both the early and late Fatimid period was in fact something quite different. Neither the meaning of the medium nor the message of the writing in these processions was the same.

We could ask when the writings we do know about were included in these ceremonies and what we might infer from this timing. The ceremonies in which writing on cloth was reported were those broadly based in the Muslim calendar. The historical accounts that record them, however, are all undated. But considering that Ibn al-Ṭuwayr was the source, and noting where these stories were placed in the sequence of al-Maqrīzī's recounting of Fatimid practice, the earliest moment that this writing on cloth could have appeared was probably late in the reign of Imam-Caliph al-Ḥāfiẓ (r. 1131–49/525–44). Al-Ḥāfiẓ might well have been the Imam that Ibn al-Ṭuwayr described as entering the Anwar mosque during Ramadan; and his troops might well have been the ones displaying the phrase ***naṣr min allah wa fatḥ qarīb*** (Help from God and Victory Near at Hand). Whether the moment was then, or later, knowledge about the shifts in the composition of the army and within the ruling group as a whole, as well as about the audience addressed, helps us understand more clearly the full import of the writing.

The reports of cloth with writing on it described above specifically refer to the semantic content of the writing. These displayed words from the Qur'ān, and thus obviously were taken from a Muslim referential field—a clearly different evocational base from that of the writing displayed in the procession described by Nāṣir-i Khusraw in chapter 3. Those who were in the Anwar mosque at the time the Imam entered during Ramadan, and those who displayed the banners in the processions, were, by late in the reign of al-Ḥāfiẓ, mainly Muslims who had just engaged in a struggle to reduce the Christian influence in the ruling establishment. They had succeeded in defeating *wazīr* Bahrām al-Armanī and his troops.[94] The semantic message of all of this writing publicized triumph and victory in Muslim sectarian terms.

Exterior, Interior, and Writing Signs

Thus far in this chapter the considerations of the Fatimid use of writing signs have focused on writing in the public space, public texts, beginning with the writing signs of Badr al-Jamālī. The referential dimensions of writing in the public space were used by him and by succeeding *wazīrs* to disseminate specific kinds of information about the changing social order, namely the growth of the power of the wazirate and the military as indicated by the elaborate titularity of the *wazīr*. The aesthetic and territorial dimensions of those writing signs functioned both to distinguish Muslim sectarian practices of displaying writing signs from those of other sectarian groups, and within Muslim sectarian practices, to blur the distinction between the practices of displaying writing on the inside and outside of structures.

While it is difficult to reconstruct the visual practices of the medieval Coptic community in relation to writing signs with any certainty, most historians agree that Coptic churches and monasteries remained unarticulated by the display of writing on the exterior.[95] The display of officially sponsored writing was reserved for the interior, and there it was used in a traditional manner: a secondary sign framing images, with references to the Book and community, in the script style of the Book. Thus, beginning with Imam-Caliph al-Ḥākim's golden curses and the writing placed on the exterior of the mosque outside the Bāb al-Futūḥ and continuing to the mosque Ṭalā'iʿ built outside the Bāb Zuwayla, the display of writing on the outside of Muslim sectarian structures built by the Fatimid ruling group distinguished them from other sectarian structures. They displayed public texts.

The aesthetic dimensions of displaying writing signs on the interior of Muslim communal structures also underwent a change at the same time. In the al-Ḥākim mosque, as noted above, writing became a primary sign for elaborating the interior. It no longer framed depictions as in traditional practice, or as in the contemporary practice of using writing signs inside Christian space. This new display of writing on the interior was maintained in the later Fatimid period in both extant mosques, the al-Aqmar (fig. 35) and that built by Ṭalāʾiʿ (fig. 38). It also characterized the gifts or additions that *wazīrs* of this period made to the interior of existing structures: for example, the mihrab al-Afḍal added to the mosque of Aḥmad ibn Ṭūlūn around 1094/487 (fig. 41),[96] and the restorations to the mausoleum of Sayyida Ruqayya, 1130–60 (fig. 42). Of course, it was not simply the display of writing but writing in Kufic script in a variety of ornamented styles that became a primary visual sign on the interior of Muslim communal spaces. Medium also served as a visual link. Carved and incised stucco was the primary medium for the display of writing on the interior surfaces of both mosques and mausolea. Writing signs in Kufic script incised in stucco bound together and identified those structures supported by the Fatimid ruling group. Displaying writing, and seeing the display of writing, became a visual convention in Muslim communal spaces, mosque and mausolea, and for Muslim audiences throughout the capital area.

One aesthetic practice of displaying writing on Muslim communal buildings in this later period blurred what centuries of tradition had maintained, namely, a distinction between the uses of writing signs on the exterior and the interior of communal structures. The layout of a central large arch flanked by two smaller arches with bands of writing first described by Nāṣir-i Khusraw on the *kiswa* of the Kaʿba in Mecca in 1050/441 was used for both the exterior and interior of Muslim sectarian spaces, primarily those sponsored by *wazīrs*. It is found in structures throughout the Cairo-Miṣr urban area and in the Qarafa cemetery[97]—for example, on the outside of the al-Aqmar mosque in Cairo, on the *qibla* wall inside the mausoleum of Ikhwat Yusuf in the Qarafa,[98] and on both the *qibla* wall and on the portico of the mausoleum of Sayyida Ruqayya on the Great Street near Aḥmad ibn Ṭūlūn.[99] This basic layout is rendered in different media: carved stucco in the mausoleums, and stone on the outside of the mosque. In this difference in medium it is possible to read a hierarchy of materials, as well as, perhaps, in the social status of the structures within the society. While differences exist in the details of the specific variations of the layout of the arches and bands in every structure, most of these arched layouts also include roundels.

The basic aesthetic similarities of these arched layouts providing the framework for officially sponsored writing mask the referential differences in the writing displayed on the interior and exterior of these Muslim communal structures. The components of the evocational fields of the writing, and in tandem with that, the allocation of space to each component,

41. Mihrab donated by *wazīr* al-Afḍal in mosque of Aḥmad ibn Ṭūlūn

42. Interior, central arch, mausoleum of Sayyida Ruqayya, after Creswell, *Muslim Architecture of Egypt*, vol. 1

on the interior and exterior of structures are seemingly mirror opposites of each other. On the outside, rank and title information is detailed and lengthy, while quotations from the Qur'ān are limited relative to these social references.[100] On the interior, the Qur'ān is the main evocational field, although the donor's name and minimal titles may appear.

Roundels were a part of this arched layout, and the appearance of this form on buildings brings us to the important consideration of what happened to the sign of Isma'ilism as a component of officially sponsored writing in this later period. As part of the public text, its appearance remains constant on coinage in this period. Even the Qur'anic quotation (9:33) chosen at the time of Imam-Caliph al-Mu'izz is maintained in the outer ring of the coin (fig. 39). Obviously, as the number of Ismā'īlīs in the Cairo urban area decreased substantially, the specific meaning of this concentric circle format was perceived by only a very small audience trained to recognize its referents. Yet maintaining the sign of Isma'ilism on coinage is explicable by the conservative nature of coinage itself, the strong linkage between its aesthetic form and its material value, particularly with the gold dinar, and the fact that many are struck. The situation in regard to coinage then is not unlike that now what with the Masonic signs on the back of the U.S. one-dollar bill. These signs were imbued with a particular meaning in relation to the Masonic ceremonies important to the founding fathers of the U.S. Today these Masonic signs are maintained on the dollar to validate the "realness" of the dollar, even though the audience who understands their original referent is limited.

In contrast, however, the form and content (or semantic referent) of the sign of Isma'ilism dissolves both as part of the public text on the exterior of buildings, and as part of an Islamic sectarian one on the interior. This dissolution results in a semi-autonomy of form and content enabling the form and its content (or referents) to have separate trajectories. Naturally, the form or format lasts longest in the visual culture. It is like an empty shell left by a creature on the beach. The referent, like the creature who inhabits the shell, is most fragile, depending on complex social relations and the configuration of a certain kind of discourse, here Ismā'īlī discourse.

This dissolution of form and content did not happen sequentially or evenly in Fatimid society. Look at the round form in the central arch on the facade of the al-Aqmar mosque (fig. 36) and that in the central arch in the mausoleum of Sayyida Ruqayya (fig. 42). Both these displays of writing in a round form are products of the last fifty years of Fatimid patronage. Seeing the play and slippage between the form and content of these two round forms helps us understand the complex ways form and content are layered.

On the portal of the al-Aqmar mosque, the roundel preserved the form of the sign of Isma'ilism: the al-Ḥākim period variant, lines of writing displayed in a central core surrounded by outer, concentric circles which included writing. The center displays the names "Muḥammad" and "'Alī," both appropriate to both Ismāʿīlī and general Muslim discourses. The outer ring displays Qur'ān 33:33, "God only desires to take away uncleanness from you, Oh people of the household." While meaningful to all Muslims, this verse is not cited in Ismāʿīlī *ta'wīl*. Until this time, the reference base of the writing in signs of Isma'ilism, whether on buildings or on coins, has been bi-valent and included reference within Ismāʿīlī *ta'wīl*. Contemporary coins maintain this bi-valent reference. Here, on the al-Aqmar mosque, the form of the sign of Isma'ilism is preserved, but not the full range of the content.

In the mausoleum of Sayyida Ruqayya, restored within thirty years of the construction of the al-Aqmar mosque, the form and content (referent) of the roundel have dissolved even more. The writing displays the same semantic content as that in the roundel of the al-Aqmar mosque, yet not in the same round form. Rather, it is displayed within the arch and roundel format together. The round form is preserved, but the center is expanded so as to be almost coterminus with its perimeter. In this center, the names "Muḥammad" and "'Alī" appear, but the writing is displayed in an interlocked geometric pattern. This interlocked pattern is not at all related to the conventions for the presentation of writing in either the sign of Isma'ilism or in the diagrams in Ismāʿīlī discourse. While the content, or evocational field, of the writing in the center is the same as that on the facade of al-Aqmar, the form in which the writing is displayed dissolves the visual relationship between this writing and that on al-Aqmar and the diagrams in Ismāʿīlī discourse.

No concentric circle of writing surrounds these names in the center. The band of writing above the roundel, on the mihrab itself, displays the same part of Qur'ān 33:33 as displayed in the outer ring on the al-Aqmar roundel. The round form in this mausoleum is the shell left behind by a creature on the beach. It becomes a vehicle for other uses. Those uses include the display of writing, as well as the display of geometric forms and other devices, like on the facade of the mosque of Ṭalā'iʿ. The Ismāʿīlī content has left this shell—perhaps to another form.

In the last one hundred years of Fatimid rule, knowledge of Ismāʿīlī discourses reached fewer and fewer people as avenues of Sunni learning increased. The audience who knew and could perceive signs of Ismaʿilism became very circumscribed, a condition affecting both patrons and viewers. In this later period of Fatimid rule, Muslim communal structures, especially mausolea, were rebuilt and restored by non-Ismāʿīlī *wazīrs* as a means of fostering a type of religious piety and devotion among all Muslims, separating them from the substantial Christian minority within the population and ruling group.[101] This was essentially a conservative action supporting the status quo in the government—a ruling system that was headed by a Fatimid Ismāʿīlī Imam but which was otherwise composed predominantly of non-Ismāʿīlī Muslims.[102] The support of such buildings was facilitated during this period by the presence of the Crusaders in Palestine. Muslim pilgrims preferred to skirt some of the shrines in that area and visit the Egyptian capital instead.[103] The appearance of pilgrimage guidebooks gives evidence to the relevance of these structures to Muslims of all *madhhab*s (law traditions). It is not surprising, then, that in these structures, the writing, officially sponsored by non-Ismāʿīlī *wazīrs* and addressed to a primarily non-Ismāʿīlī audience referred to the Qurʾān and individuals important in the collective general Islamic memory, and not to referents in Ismāʿīlī sectarian discourse.

Indeed, the use of writing by various members of the Fatimid ruling group, especially in the public space, turned the capital area into a more obvious text. The issue of using a city as "text" when applied to social practice of this period, involved the population attending to different but co-existent meanings implicit in a single text. Messages could be read, as we have above, in the semantic content of the words. They could be read in the long expanses of writing in expensive materials, and in the multiplicity of styles of script and formats of writing placed on buildings. Such readings also entailed attending to subtle nuances given to existing texts as new texts were added to the visual environment, when successive mosques were added southward along the Great Street, or dropped, as when writing was no longer displayed in concentric circle formats. To the beholder who walked this road, the writing on the mosque (as well as the buildings themselves) presented an extraordinarily diverse display: differences in scale, nuances in style, and plurality of messages.

Afterword

The caution with which I began, reminding myself and my readers, was that writing serves a society in many complex ways. That writing signs was a practice of ruling persons and groups in societies for a long time. That the Fatimid phenomenon needed to be seen in the full context of the uses of writing signs among Christian, Jewish, and other Muslim groups in the eastern Mediterranean. That the Fatimid writing of signs, of making a public text, was unique. Stated either way, my intention was to confront two notions: that *only* Muslim rulers used officially sponsored writing, and that all Muslim rulers used it in the same way. That is why so much of this study has focused on explicating the conditions that supported, the people who sponsored, and the audiences who saw the written signs in the years of Fatimid rule.

Beyond this in-depth discussion and analysis of the signs the Fatimids wrote—those public texts that were raised—we can weigh the Fatimid achievement by a brief record of how long it endured, especially in the Cairene area its signs dominated. In very real ways Fatimid practice became part of the Cairene tradition of writing signs. For at least the next two centuries, Ayyubid (1171–1250/567–648) and Baḥrī Mamluk (1250–1389/648–791) military rulers used public texts in specific locations in ways similar to those of the Fatimid *wazīrs* before them. If we consider the social uses that the military leaders, the *wazīrs*, made of officially sponsored writing signs during the last decades of Fatimid rule, the continuation of such practices is almost predictable. The termination of support for the Fatimid Ismāʿīlī Caliph did not alter many of the social conditions in which the practices of writing signs were embedded. The first of the Ayyubid dynasty to rule in Egypt, Ṣalāḥ al-Dīn Yūsuf ibn Ayyūb (d. 1193/589) was also the last Fatimid *wazīr*. He became *wazīr* in 1168/564, Sultan in 1171/567. By this act he accomplished the task of terminating Fatimid rule that several *wazīrs* before him had considered.[1] He signalled this change as Muslim rulers traditionally did, by having the *khutba* delivered in Cairo in a new ruler's name—the Abbasid Caliph al-Mustaḍī (r. 1170–80/566–75).

His coins maintained the Fatimid format of concentric circles with lines of writing in the center circle (fig. 43). They also maintained Qur'ān 9:33, which was present on Fatimid coins. But he and the Ayyubid Sultans that followed him maintained this format for only a few decades, as part of the transition to their new rule in Egypt which required economic stability. The Fatimid dinar, format and material, was a known and valued part of international exchange. Once Ayyubid rule was stabilized, the Fatimid concentric circle format was abandoned, and the Umayyad-Abbasid traditional format was again adopted.

Ṣalāḥ al-Dīn's use of writing signs is known also from the plaque he placed on the Burg al-Imam at the citadel, a use of public texts on thresholds known for centuries in the eastern Mediterranean.[2] This writing sign displays Ṣalāḥ al-Dīn's titles and the year 576 (1180–81), and like the plaque Badr al-Jamālī had displayed on the mosque of Aḥmad ibn Ṭūlūn, the writing refers directly to the political circumstances. Ṣalāḥ al-Dīn is "he who has unified the language of belief and crushed the servants of the Cross [referring to the Crusaders] . . . who has revived the empire of the [Abbasid] Caliph." While the referential dimensions of the writing here are equivalent to those found in the later Fatimid period, an aesthetic link with the past is broken. The script style is *naskh*, a cursive script that breaks the visual link with the writing signs from the Fatimid period. A pedestrian can readily link this writing style with the other inscriptions of the new ruler and rule—for example, the foundation inscription at the citadel, recording its construction, under the order of Ṣalāḥ al-Dīn and his *wazīr* Qarāqaush in 579 (1183–84).[3]

Later Ayyubid and then Baḥrī Mamluk rulers changed the script style of their writing signs, but they maintained a reference base equivalent to those of the Fatimid *wazīrs* before them. The placement of Ayyubid and then Mamluk public texts, both on the facades of Muslim communal structures, and the location of these structures in the Cairo urban area, play visually and semantically with those of existing Fatimid texts.

Four sites formed the topography of rule in the Fatimid period: the Bayn al-Qaṣrayn—the palaces flanking it and the al-Aqmar mosque; the

43. Dinar, Ṣalāh al-Dīn (1002.1.1027 Collection of the University of Pennsylvania Museum in the Cabinet of the American Numismatic Society)

Anwar or al-Ḥākim mosque at the Bāb al-Futūḥ; the *musalla* at the Bāb al-Naṣr; and the al-Azhar mosque (map 3).[4] The Ayyubid and then the Baḥrī Mamluk rulers maintained three of these sites as part of their own topography of rule—the Bayn al-Qaṣrayn, and the al-Azhar and al-Ḥākim mosques—but effectively inscribed them within different aesthetic, social, and structural networks. In this manner the sites became historically layered in their associations with rule. One of these sites, the Bayn al-Qaṣrayn and the two palaces along with the al-Aqmar mosque, is especially relevant here.[5]

The area of the Fatimid palaces and the al-Aqmar mosque remained important in the new hierarchies within both Ayyubid and Mamluk Cairo. The Fatimid palaces may have continued to be inhabited in the early Ayyubid period, but on both sides of the street, complexes were built over and with materials from these demolished palaces. On the east side, the Fatimid Imam's residence and the mausoleum of the Ismāʿīlī Imams were replaced by the *madrasa* and mausoleum complex of Najim al-Dīn Ayyūb,[6] and in the Mamluk period, by the *madrasa* built by al-Zahir Baybars in 1262.[7] On the west side, the overlay of the Western Palace was completed in the Baḥrī Mamluk period with the construction of the complexes and mausolea of Sultan Qalāʾūn and Sultan al-Nāṣr Muḥammad (map 5).[8] Thus the area remained residential in character, as it had been, but in the Ayyubid and Mamluk times the residents were students, professors, and other functionaries at the great academic, medical, and commemorative structures that shaped the space. The area also remained the burial site of the rulers; Ayyubid and then Mamluk rulers were interred there.

Najim al-Dīn Ayyūb (r. 1240–49/637–47), the last of Ṣalāḥ al-Dīn's dynasty to rule, and then Mamluk Sultans Qalāʾūn (r. 1280–90/678–89) and al-Nāṣr Muḥammad[9] used public texts on the outside of the complexes

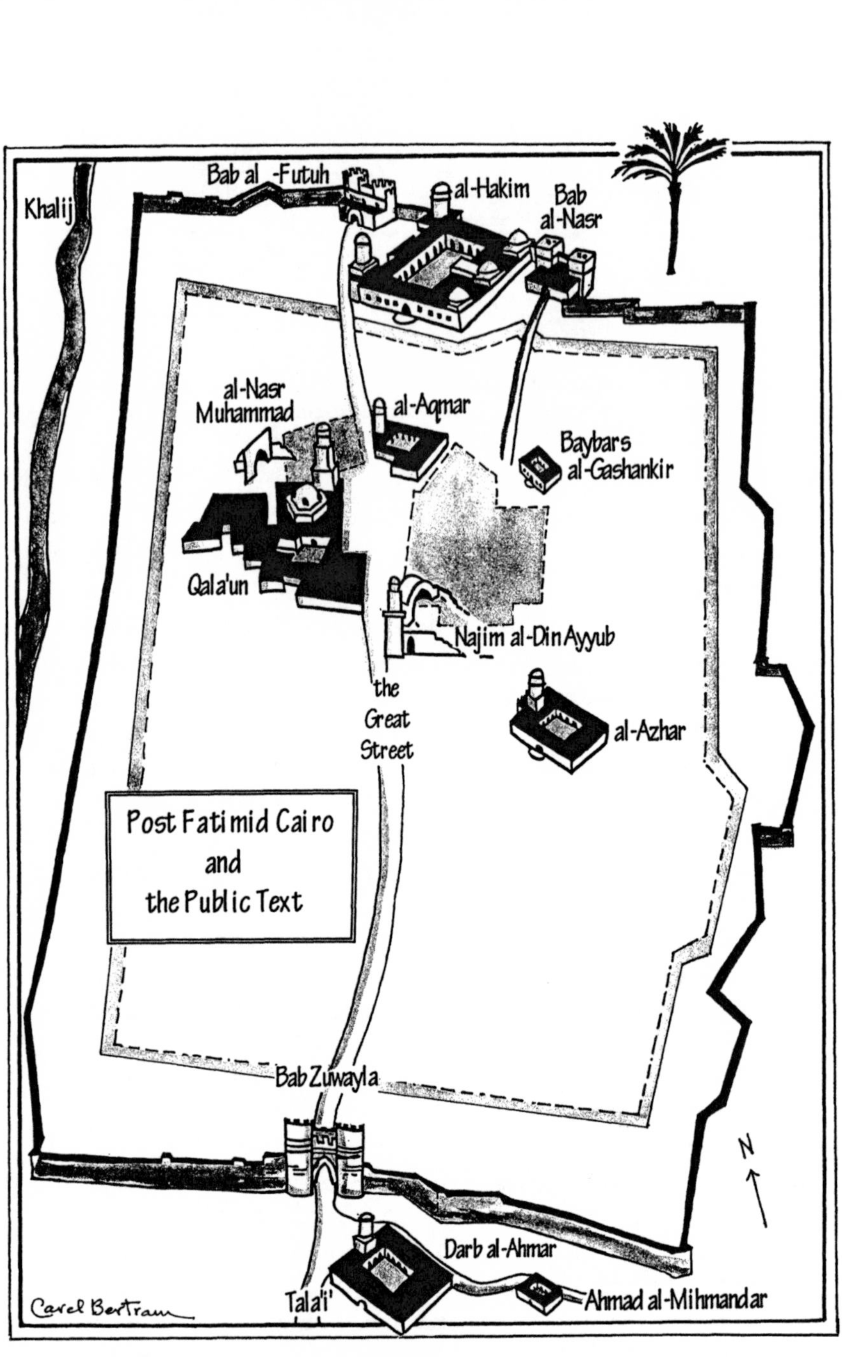

Map 5. Post-Fatimid Cairo (drawn by Carel Bertram)

they built in this area. In the mid-thirteenth century, Najim al-Dīn Ayyūb built a *madrasa* on the site of the Eastern Palace, an act that replaced the Fatimid Imams' residence and mausolea with a teaching institution for the four Sunni schools of law. After the Sultan's death, his widow inserted a tomb for her husband into the *madrasa* by building into the main teaching hall of the Mālikī law school.[10] The facade of the *madrasa* resonates strongly with that of the mosque of Ṭalā'iʿ located to the south, along the Great Street (map 5), and its entrance portal relates directly to that of the al-Aqmar mosque, almost immediately to the north, on the same side of the Great Street (fig.44).[11] The band of inscription on the portal displays the names and titles of the Sultan. In the arched hood over the portal, where in the al-Aqmar mosque a large concentric circle medallion is displayed, a plaque with lines of writing displays in a different format the names and titles of the Sultan. Although these public texts on the *madrasa* share an equivalent evocational base with those on the al-Aqmar mosque and that of Ṭalā'iʿ, the *naskh* script distinguishes them visually from those on the Fatimid structures. At the same time, the *naskh* script links them with the other Ayyubid public texts in the city.

Within the next five decades, three more major complexes were constructed in this area, two across the street on the site of the Western Palace. On the order of Mamluk Sultans Qalā'ūn and al-Naṣr Muḥammad major *madrasa*-mausoleum complexes were built on this site.[12] On the facades of both of these complexes the Sultans displayed writing signs in visually prominent bands running the length of the facade (fig. 45).[13] The semantic content of each of the bands is the names and titles of the Sultan. Sultan Qalā'ūn's titles are especially elaborated twice on the facade of his complex, following the practice on the al-Aqmar mosque. In addition to the usual range of titles, Sultan Qalā'ūn is: "the King of Kings of Arabs and Persians, the Possessor of Two *Qibla*s, the Killer of Infidels and Polytheists."

The other complex in this location, the *khanqah* (dervish lodge) and mausoleum of Sultan Baybars al-Gashankīr built in 1309, displays public texts similar in form, in placement, and in content to the two Mamluk complexes mentioned above. This *khanqah* and mausoleum were built over the palace used by the very last Fatimid *wazīr*s located on the northern side of the Eastern Palace, on the road from the Bāb al-Naṣr (map 5, fig. 46).[14]

These Mamluk public texts, in placement on structures, location within the city, and referential base, continue the Fatimid Cairene tradition of using writing signs on Muslim communal structures. However, they were

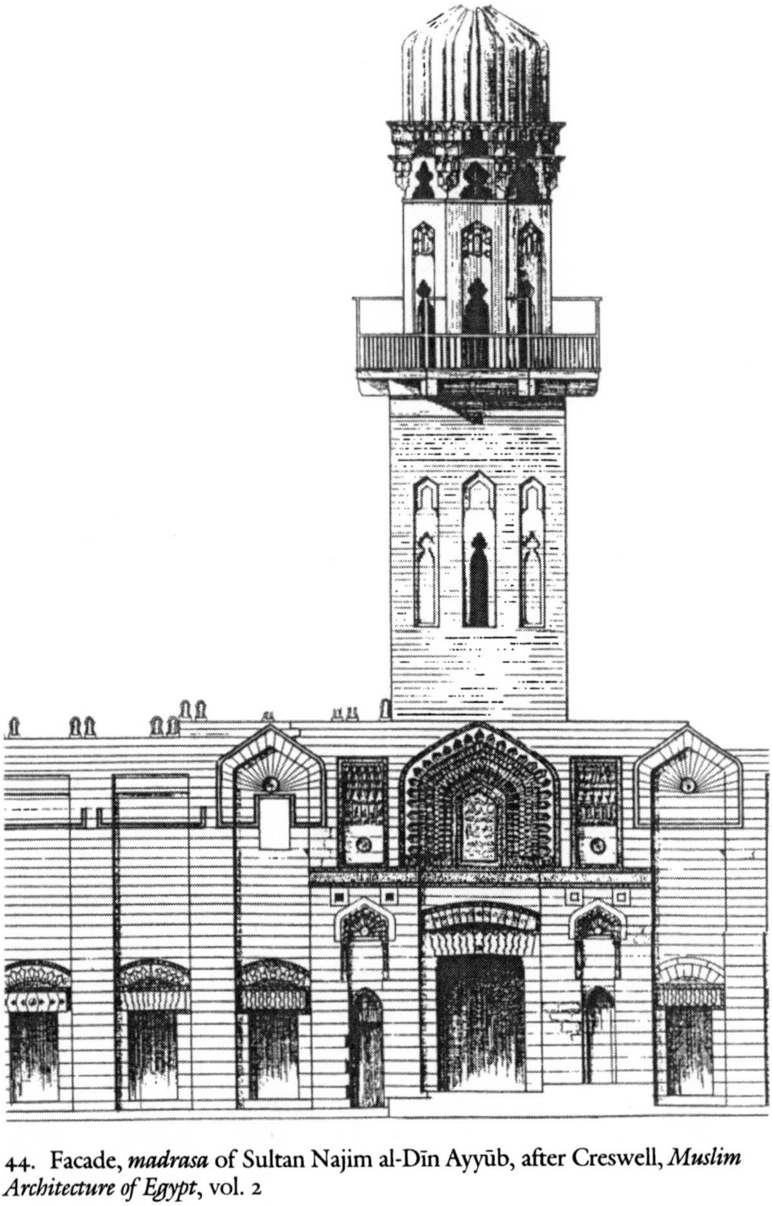

44. Facade, *madrasa* of Sultan Najim al-Dīn Ayyūb, after Creswell, *Muslim Architecture of Egypt*, vol. 2

45. Facade, *madrasa*-mausoleum of Sultan Qalā'ūn

made readily distinguishable from those of both the Fatimid *wazīrs* and the Ayyubid Sultans by the style of the script, *naskh*. While *naskh* script was used by the Ayyubids, the proportions of Mamluk *naskh* are recognizably different from the Ayyubid writing signs. The upright letters are much taller in relation to the horizontal lines. In addition, the Mamluk writing signs themselves are much larger than those of the Ayyubids.

This practice of displaying public texts created a dense network of texts in the area where the Fatimid palaces were built and where the al-Aqmar mosque was preserved. The addition to the Fatimid base, the Ayyubid, and Mamluk public texts created (and create) a richly textured network of signs. When all these structures were completed, audiences could easily perceive the differences in writing styles. But seeing a hierarchy among those visual differences was a social function, and belongs to the ways each of these structures was inscribed in the social use of the day.[15] How the structure itself was used in the social order, its privilege of place, formed part of the judgment the audiences made when perceiving these writing signs. To the beholder of all these writing signs, medium was a less relevant aesthetic dimension for conveying meaning than it was, for example, in the Dome of the Rock, because all of these inscriptions were in either marble or finely finished stone.

46. Facade, *khanqah*-mausoleum of Sultan Baybars al-Gashankīr

Relevant to this study also is the area of the Ṭalāʾiʿ mosque just outside the Bāb Zuwayla. While not important within the topography of Fatimid rule, the Darb al-Aḥmar, the new street running southeast from the Bāb Zuwayla, became the main thoroughfare in the Mamluk period (map 5). It supplanted the extension of the Great Street in importance and along it members of the Mamluk ruling group built communal structures. The importance of this street in the Mamluk period focused attention on the Ṭalāʾiʿ mosque.

This site lacks the dense association with rule of the Fatimid palace and mosque of al-Aqmar area, but the visual impact of the Ṭalāʾiʿ mosque, and the public texts on it, undoubtedly accounts for the Mamluk response in the form of writing signs. The orientation of the Ṭalāʾiʿ mosque toward the *qibla* assures that the main facade of the structure is fully in the view of a pedestrian exiting the Bāb Zuwayla. In addition, the structure gives definition to the street patterns outside this gate. It creates the corner where the Great Street and the Darb al-Aḥmar meet, so that anyone proceeding down either street must pass the full length of one of its facades. The long north side of this mosque creates the beginning of the Darb al-Aḥmar, just as the west facade does for the Great Street. The bands of public texts on the Ṭalāʾiʿ mosque were a highly visible feature of the facades (fig. 38).[16] It is not at all surprising, then, that the first mosque built by a Mamluk nearby on the Darb al-Aḥmar responded with the display of public texts in bands (fig. 47). Amīr Aḥmad al-Mihmandar, Sultan al-Nāṣr Muḥammad's chief of protocol, built the first Muslim communal structure on that street in 1325. It was a mosque located on the same side of the Darb al-Aḥmar as the mosque of Ṭalāʾiʿ, and just shortly beyond it (map 5).[17] As expected, the bands of public text display his name and titles and also provide some indication as to why he was chosen chief of protocol. The text of the inscription is an astute presentation of the Amīr as a good Muslim who works gratefully within the social order under Sultan al-Naṣr Muḥammad. The *naskh* style of the writing links it visually with those writing signs within the walled city sponsored by the Mamluk Sultans.

The post-Fatimid Cairo map (map 5) is especially designed to highlight the juxtaposition of the extant structures that display prominent public texts along their facades, and their locations are easy to apprehend. In no other locations within the urban area of Cairo-Miṣr did military leaders use public texts to the same degree of density. This assessment of the practice of writing signs is based, of course, on an examination of extant buildings. Fortunately, numerous buildings of the Mamluk period sur-

47. Facade, mosque of Amīr Aḥmad al-Mihmandar

vive, and provide ample evidence to support this contention, as do the few remaining from the Ayyubid period. Sultan al-Naṣr Muḥammad's practices of using writing signs are indicative of the more general practice. He displayed public texts along the facade only on the complex he built over the Fatimid palace. No bands of inscriptions articulate the exterior walls of the large mosque he built on the citadel. In other parts of the city, the Mamluks developed a different practice for the display of writing on the exterior.

One element of Fatimid practice, that of displaying writing signs on the interior of Muslim communal structures, was maintained by the succeeding rulers. These writing signs were maintained as the prominent visual sign in the articulation of the interior. This practice was applied to interiors of communal structures throughout the entire urban area, and is readily apparent from any brief survey. In mausolea, like those of Najim al-Dīn Ayyūb, Sultan Qalā'ūn at the Bayn al-Qaṣrayn, Sultan Haṣan at the foot of the citadel, or Imam al-Shāfi'ī in the Qarafa cemetery, writing signs were prominently displayed on the interior. As in the Fatimid period, this practice was applied in mosques and in *madrasas* in the Ayyubid and Mamluk periods as well. Although in mosques, whether courtyard or *iwan* (three-sided chamber) style, writing signs were placed most consistently only in the *qibla* area, and not, as in Fatimid practice, throughout the interior. The reference base of the inscriptions remained primarily the Qur'ān, although, as before, patron information did appear. The style of script used for these writing signs was varied, even within structures, especially in Mamluk practice, again a contrast with Fatimid practice in which writing signs were always presented in a variant of Kufic script.

The intent here is to point to the most salient aspects of the continuation of the Fatimid public text and practices of writing signs. The social uses of officially sponsored writing addressed to a group audience in the Ayyubid, and especially in the Mamluk period where much evidence remains, require their own serious analysis.

In drawing this study to a close, it is useful to bring the continuation of the Fatimid public text into the twentieth century, and to do so requires returning to an issue taken up in the previous chapter. There the issue of the dissolution of form and content was discussed in relation to practices in the later Fatimid period in which the round form of the sign of Isma'ilism was maintained, but its Ismā'īlī content dissolved. The dissolution of form and content of the sign of Isma'ilism was part of the process by which a publicly visible architectural element was appropriated and assigned a new meaning or connotation. Such appropriation is a continuous process in a city, and is linked to a related, but distinct, process in which old forms are a conscious model for new forms. Newly created old forms are used to fabricate a past and make linkages with it.[18] Naturally, here, too, new meanings and new uses are assigned to the old forms. The facade of the al-Aqmar mosque, with its striking format for public texts, is an old form that in the twentieth century has been newly made and appropriated.

Earlier this century, the Coptic community fabricated a new version of the facade of the al-Aqmar mosque, using it as the facade for the new Coptic Museum (fig. 48). The formal aspects of the new facade closely resonate with those of the al-Aqmar mosque (fig. 35): its tripartite division, salient portal, roundel within the portal, and three bands cutting the facade. But the alterations present in the new old form are part of a twentieth-century connotative system that is Cairene, and serve to highlight for us how architectural forms can become modern emblems of the historical past of an urban area.

The writing on the facade of the museum is in two languages, and is more limited in its display than on the earlier form. In the center of the facade, under the cornice of the salient portal of the museum, the band of writing is in Coptic, alphabet and language. It names the place. On

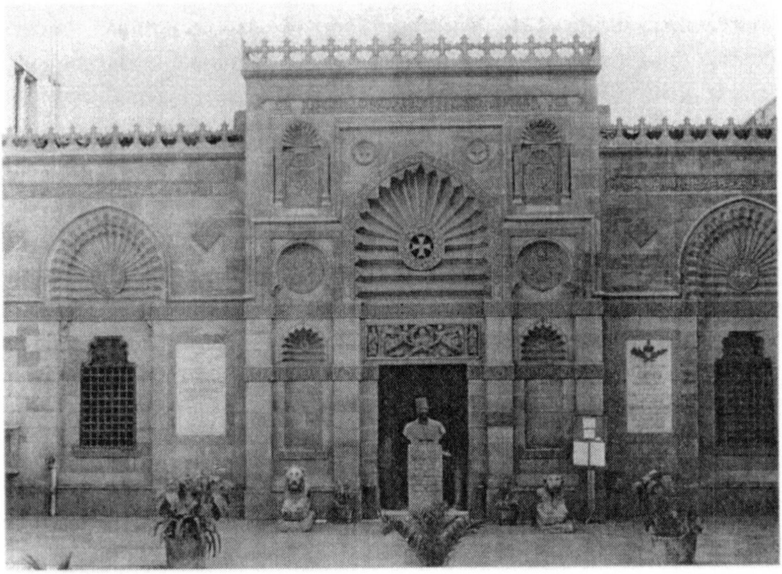

48. Facade, Coptic Museum

the two side wings, the top band displays writing in Arabic, language and alphabet. It also names and dates the place. The alphabets and languages, as well as their placement on the facade, relate directly to the community, society, and local audience of this museum.

The two other bands, the intermediate one running the full length of the facade, and the third and lowest one running only on the portal, which on the facade of the al-Aqmar mosque were spaces for writing signs, on the facade of the Coptic Museum are filled with geometric designs. The other format for writing on the facade of the al-Aqmar mosque, the concentric circle medallions above the entrance portal and in the niches on the side, is maintained, but not as a space for writing. Instead, on the facade of the Coptic Museum, the center of each circle displays the form of the Coptic cross. For those beholders who visit the museum and cannot read, and perhaps even identify either writing sign, the form of the Coptic cross marks the building as belonging to the Coptic community. There are, of course, many beholders for whom the writing signs are not public texts because they do not recognize the presence of writing. The Coptic Museum is visited by many foreign tours yearly.

The relationship of the new old form of the facade of this museum to its surrounding area provides a confirmation in the twentieth century of the contention of this study, namely, that Fatimid practice of the public text was different in its day from the traditional practice of writing signs. The Coptic Museum is located in what today is known as Miṣr al-Qadīmah (old Miṣr), or Fusṭāṭ, to use the other medieval term, just south of the mosque of ʿAmr. The imposition of this new version of the al-Aqmar facade in the oldest part of the Cairo urban area juxtaposes the form for the display of Fatimid public texts to the facades of medieval Coptic churches, the mosque of ʿAmr, and the synagogue which neighbor it.[19] No writing signs appear on the exterior of those Muslim, Jewish, or Christian sectarian structures. The only building belonging to the Coptic community in this area that displays public texts is the facade of the museum, which displays those texts in the framework of the old Fatimid form. In this juxtaposition, this new old form is the thread connecting the modern beholder to other parts of the city and to Fatimid practices of writing signs.

I end with a line perhaps familiar to all who see writing signs everywhere: "The waterskater, that is an insect and dumb, traces the name of God on the surface of ponds—or so the Arabians say" (J. M. Coetzee, *Foe*). Taking a cue from a passage from the same author cited in my Preface, I could add that this tracery is endless.

Appendix

Fatimid Imam-Caliphs (reign dates)

al-Muʿizz	953–75/341–65
al-ʿAzīz	975–96/365–86
al-Ḥākim	996–1021/386–411
al-Ẓāhir	1021–36/411–27
al-Mustanṣir	1036–94/427–87
al-Mustaʿlī	1094–1101/487–95
al-Āmir	1101–1130/495–524
al-Ḥāfiẓ	1131–49/525–44
al-Ẓāfir	1149–54/544–49
al-Fāʾiz	1154–60/549–55
al-ʿĀḍid	1160–71/555–67

Wazīrs mentioned

Badr al-Jamālī (al-Mustanṣir)	1073–94/466–87
al-Afḍal (al-Mustaʿlī, al-Āmir)	1094–1121/487–515
al-Maʾmūn (al-Āmir)	1121–25/515–19
Bahrām al-Armanī (al-Ḥāfiẓ)	1134–37/529–32
Riḍwān ibn al-Walakshī (al-Ḥāfiẓ)	1137–39/532–34
Ṭalāʾiʿ ibn Ruzzīk (al-Fāʾiz, al-ʿĀḍid)	1149–60/549–56
Ṣalāḥ al-Dīn al-Ayyūbī (al-ʿĀḍid)	1168–71/564–67

Glossary

Abbasid	Dynasty that ruled from Iraq 749–1258/132–656.
ādhān	Call to prayer.
asās	Foundation.
asbāb al-nuzūl	Literally, "the causes for the coming down." It is the collection of accounts that documents the conditions or reasons that caused God's messages to be given to the Prophet Muḥammad.
āya	Verse of the Qur'ān.
Ayyubid	Dynasty that ruled in Egypt 1169–1250/564–648.
basmala	The formula, "In the name of God, the Merciful, the Compassionate."
bāṭin	Esoteric (or hidden) dimension.
bayn al-qaṣrayn	Literally, between the two palaces. The name given to the open area in Cairo that was between the Imam's palace on the east side of the street and the palace on the west side of the street.
dābiqī	Term for fine linen.
dār al-ḥikma	Literally, House of Wisdom. Place in Fatimid Cairo where Isma'ili studies took place (see *dār al-ʿilm*).
dār al-ʿilm	Literally, House of Knowledge. Place in Fatimid Cairo where Ismāʿīlī studies took place (see *dār al-ḥikma*).
daʿwa	Organization of religious dignataries in Ismāʿīlī practice.
dinar	Gold coin.
dirham	Silver coin.

dīwān Literally, a collection or group. As used in the text, it means council.

ḥajj Pilgrimage to Mecca.

hegira Emigration of the Prophet Muḥammad from Mecca to Medina in July 622. The term also refers to the Muslim calendar which is reckoned from that event and is designated "A.H."

iwan Three-sided space or room, open on the fourth side.

khalīj Channel; in this text it refers to the channel flowing from the Nile.

khutba Sermon delivered in the mosque during the Friday noon prayer.

kiswa Covering(s). It is the term used for the covering of the Kaʿba and in the medieval period refers to coverings in general and gifts of textiles.

madhhab School or rite of (Islamic) law. Mālikī, Shāfiʿī, Ḥanbalī, Hanafī are the four main Sunni schools. Ismāʿīlī and Imāmī (or Twelvers) are two Shīʿī schools.

maghariba Literally, "westerners." Berber North African forces.

Mamluk Dynasty that ruled in Egypt 1250–1517/648–922.

manẓara Place commanding a view, a look out. No specific form is denoted by this term.

mashriqiya Literally, "easterners." Newly recruited forces into the Fatimid armies mainly composed of Turks and Daylami and others from the east.

mihrab Niche in the wall of a mosque or other place of prayer indicating the direction of Mecca.

Miṣr In the medieval period the term referred to Fusṭāṭ and those urban areas south of the royal city of Cairo. In the modern period the term refers to the urban area of greater Cairo and often to Egypt as a whole.

muṣalla Delineated (but not enclosed) space for prayer, usually outside the city walls. It was customarily used on special days in the Muslim calendar when many Muslims gathered for prayer. Located outside Bāb al-Naṣr.

naskh A cursive script style.

nātiq Speaker-Prophet.

qāḍī Judge.

qibla Direction (of Mecca). In prayer spaces, the *qibla* wall is the one oriented to Mecca.

raḥba Open area.

Ramadan — The ninth month of the Muslim calendar. The month of fasting.

Safavid — Dynasty that ruled from Iran 1501–1786/907–1200.

ṣāmit — Silent One.

Seljuk — Rulers in what is today Iraq, Syria, Iran, and Turkey from 1037–1307/429–707. Length of rule varied by area.

shahāda — The formula "No god but The God and Muḥammad is the prophet of God."

shāriʿa al-aʿẓam — Literally, the Great Street. As applied to medieval Cairo it indicates the main street forming the central spine running from the Bāb al-Futūḥ in the north through the city and out the southern central gate and beyond to the population areas south of the walled city of Cairo.

sikka — The right to strike coins.

sūra — Chapter, of the Qurʾān.

tafsīr — Exegesis.

taʾwīl — Interpretation.

tirāz — Technically means embroidery. In many art historical writings the term is applied to the bands of writing in Arabic on textiles whether or not they were embroidered. By extension, from the early nineteenth century on, the term has been applied to bands of writing on buildings.

Umayyad — Dynasty that ruled from Syria 661–750/41–132.

waṣī — Spiritual Legatee.

ẓāhir — The literal (or obvious) dimension.

ziyāda — Extension; term applied to an enclosure added to a mosque—either surrounding it or on one side.

Notes

Abbreviations

CIA/MCIA	*Matériaux Pour un Corpus Inscriptionum Arabicarum*
EMA	Creswell, *Early Muslim Architecture*
MAE	Creswell, *The Muslim Architecture of Egypt*
RCEA	Institut français d'archéologie orientale du Caire, *Répertoire Chronologique d'Épigraphie Arabe*

Notes to Chapter 1

1. I have used this phrase "public text" before, defined in a less circumscribed manner. See Irene A. Bierman, "The Art of the Public Text: Medieval Rule," in *World Art Themes of Unity in Diversity, Acts of the 26th International Congress of the History of Art*, ed. Irving Lavin, 3 vols. (Philadelphia: Penn State University Press, 1989), 2:283–91. I also used the term as part of a title for a session "Public Text and Style: Writing and Identity in the Islamic World" at the 1988 Annual College Art Association Meetings in Houston.

2. Writing, its uses and effects on society, is discussed by a number of scholars in a variety of disciplines. Some of the more general works that have informed this study are: M. T. Clanchy, *From Memory to Written Record, 1066–1307* (London: Arnold, 1979); Jacques Derrida, *Writing and Difference*, translated and with an introduction by Alan Bass (London: Routledge, Kegan Paul, 1978); Jack Goody, *The Logic of Writing and the Organization of Society* (Cambridge: Cambridge University Press, 1986); Jack Goody, *The Interface Between the Written and the Oral* (Cambridge: Cambridge University Press, 1987); Geoffrey Sampson, *Writing Systems* (Stanford: Stanford University Press, 1985); Sylvia Scribner and Michael Cole, *The Psychology of Literacy* (Cambridge: MIT Press, 1981); Brian Stock, *The Implications of Literacy* (Princeton: Princeton University Press, 1983);

and Brian V. Street, *Literacy in Theory and Practice* (Cambridge: Cambridge University Press, 1984).

3. A recent article on aspects of the symbolic in Roman use of writing is, Calle Williamson, "Monuments of Bronze: Roman Legal Documents on Bronze Tablets," *Classical Antiquity* 6, no. 1 (April 1987): 160–83. Susan Downey drew my attention to this article.

4. See chap. 2 for an elaboration of pre-public text practice.

5. Nāṣir-i Khusraw, *Safar-nāma*, edited and annotated by Muhammad Dabir Siyaqi (Tehran: Zuvvar, 1956), 82.

6. See chap. 2.

7. Omitted here is consideration of *muṣalla*s because they appear to have been minimally delineated spaces. Early ones have been found that are simply rows of stones like that adjoining the mosque at Jabal Says in southern Syria (Klaus Brish, "Das Omayyadische Schloss in Usais," *Mitteilungen des Deutschen Archaologischen Instituts Abteilung Kairo* 19 (1963): 147–49) and two undated ones found next to camp sites in the Negev (G. Avni and S. Rosen, "Negev Emergency Survey —1983/1985," *Excavations and Surveys in Israel* 4 (1985): 86–87). Judging from al-Maqrīzī's lack of substantive descriptive comments about the *muṣalla* outside the Bāb al-Naṣr of Cairo, it, too, was simply a large delineated space.

8. At least one Fatimid structure is known through J. J. Marcel, *Description de l'Egypte, état moderne, II, IIe part* (Paris: n.p., 1822). See chap. 4.

9. Some of the interior walls from the Eastern Palace have recently been discovered. They were found under the direction of Nairi Hampikian who heads the restoration of the mausoleum and part of the *madrasa* of al-Ṣālih Najm al-Dīn Ayyūb by the German Institute of Archaeology. Under a part of the *madrasa* demolished in late 1992 to make way for an entreprenurial complex, the Fatimid walls emerged. They are angled to the street in ways quite different from the walls of the overlaying Ayyubid structure, suggesting a somewhat different street alignment than presently assumed. But the month long salvage archaeology permitted on the site will not add to our knowledge about the facade of the palace.

10. Most major museums have some Fatimid *tirāz*. The largest collections in North America are in The Textile Museum, Washington, D.C.; the Metropolitan Museum of Art, NYC; the Museum of Fine Arts, Boston; the Cleveland Art Museum, Cleveland; and the Royal Ontario Museum, Toronto. In Western Europe, the major collections are held by the Victoria and Albert Museum, London, and the Benaki Museum, Athens. In the Middle East, the Islamic Museum in Cairo has the most extensive holdings.

The major catalogues or publications of the museum holdings are the following: Nancy Pence Britton, *A Study of Some Early Islamic Textiles in the Museum of Fine Arts* (Boston: Museum of Fine Arts, 1938); E(tienne) Combe, "Tissus Fatimides du Musée Benaki," in *Mélanges Maspero*, 3 vols. (Cairo: L'Institut français d'archaéologie orientale, 1934), 1:259–72; Florence E. Day, "Dated Tiraz in the Collection of the University of Michigan," *Ars Islamica* 4 (1937): 420–26; M. S. Dimand, in various of *The Metropolitan Museum of Art Bulletin* numbers, notes additions of *tirāz* to the MMA's collections; Lisa Golombek and Veronica Gervers, "*Tiraz* Fabrics in the Royal Ontario Museum," in *Studies of Textile History in Memory of Harold B. Burnham*, ed. Veronica Gervers (Toronto: Royal Ontario Museum, 1977), 82–126; A. F. Kendrick, *Catalogue of the Textiles from the Burying-Grounds in Egypt*, 3 vols. (London: Victoria and Albert Museum, 1924); A. F. Kendrick, *Catalogue of Muhammadan Textiles of the Medieval Period* (London: Victoria and Albert Museum, 1924); Ernst Kuhnel, *Islamische Stoffe* (Berlin: Ernst Wasmuth, 1927); Ernst Kuhnel, with textile analysis by Louise Bellinger, *Catalogue of Dated Tiraz Fabrics* (Washington, D.C.: The Textile Museum, 1952); and Carl Johan Lamm, "Dated or Datable Tiraz in Sweden," *Le Monde Oriental* 32 (1938): 103.

11. Some of the implications of the state of the textile remains for the study of textiles have been discussed by Golombek and Gervers, "*Tiraz* Fabrics," 82–86, and their burial context has been shown in Jochen A. Sokoly, "Between Life and Death: The Funerary Context of Ṭirāz Textiles," in *Islamisch Textilkunst des Mittelalters: Aktuelle Problem* (Riggisberg: Abegg-Stiftung, 1996): 71–76.

12. Bierman, "Art of the Public Text," 283–90.

13. Al-Maqrīzī, *Al-Khitat*, 2 vols. (Cairo: Būlāq, 1853), 2:281.

14. Ibid. 1:147–48. The text mentions the fabric as Tustar, a fabric identified with the province of Khuzistan.

15. The "veil of St. Anne" is one such textile. Some fragments in museum holdings indicate by their lavishness that the original textile when it was whole must have been sumptuous.

16. This textile was first published in G. Marçais and G. Wiet, "Le voile de Sainte Anne d'Apt," *Académie des Inscriptions des Belles-Lettres, Fondation Eugène Piot, Monuments et Mémoires* 34 (1934): 65–72. Most recently it was exhibited in London, 1976, and published by the Arts Council of Great Britain in the catalogue, *The Arts of Islam* (London: Westerham Press, Ltd. Council of Great Britain, 1976), 76.

17. Few excavations in the area of Egypt and the Sudan have been careful to record their textile findings in detail. A notable recent exception: Ingrid Bergman, *Late Nubian Textiles*, vol. 8 of *The Scandinavian Joint Expedition to Sudanese Nubia* (Stockholm: Esselte Studium, 1975). More usual is the publication of fragments, like that of the pile fragment with the writing on it specifically discussed by Ali Ibrahim Pasha in the *Bulletin de l'Institut d'Egypte* (1935), published with a photograph but no information about where in Fusṭāṭ (or even if in Fusṭāṭ) it was found.

18. We are tempted to make guesses of course about the sectarian identity of the persons buried in the graveyards, but we need to take care. By regulation, of course, Muslims and Jews should not be buried in clothing, and we are tempted thus to assume that the graves were Christian. But we know that the practice did not always follow regulation. For example, the Jewish man from the lower middle class, who provides for an "austere" funeral for himself. He directs his survivors to bury his body clothed in "two cloaks, three robes, a turban, new underpants and a new waist band." S. D. Goitein, *A Mediterranean Society*, vol. 4, *Daily Life* (Berkeley, Los Angeles, London: University of California Press, 1983), 160.

19. Several fragments of similar cloth exist in the collections of these museums. Interestingly, the layout remains roughly constant on all of the pieces, but the quality of the execution of the design varies as does the weight of the cloth and quality of the weaving. The Metropolitan Museum pieces are nos. 1974.113.14a, 1974.113.14b, 29.136.4, published in the *Bulletin of the Metropolitan Museum of Art*

25 (1930): 129. Those in the Textile Museum are nos. 73.367, 73.228, 73.229, 73.79, 73.164. All of the fragments are either blue or green linen. I thank Marilyn Jenkins for introducing me to these textiles.

20. What is not considered here is official writing on weights. The inclusion of the writing on coins and exclusion of that on weights is basically a decision based on audience. What is assumed here is that many buyers in the markets experienced the effects of the use of weights, but only a limited group handled them, saw them and the writing on them. Other weights, like those used to set the weights of coins, had even more limited circulation.

21. Goitein, *Mediterranean Society* 1:236.

22. For Armenian, Georgian, and Latin inscriptions, see Michael E. Stone, ed., *The Armenian Inscriptions from the Sinai* (Cambridge: Harvard University Press, 1982); for Greek and Nabatean, Avrahm Negev, *The Inscriptions of the Wadi Haqqaq, Sinai* (Jerusalem: Institute of Archaeology, 1977); and C. W. Wilson and H. S. Palmer, *Ordnance Survey of the Peninsula of Sinai* (Southampton: Ordnance Survey Office, 1869). Numerous other articles and books mention these inscriptions, many simply in passing; others like I. Svecenko, "The Early Period of the Sinai Monastery in the Light of Its Inscriptions," *Dumbarton Oaks Papers* 2 (1966), use inscriptions to recreate history.

23. For examples of these and graffiti at other locations see: Abū al-Faraj al-ʿUsh, "Kitābāt ʿarabiyya ghayr mansūra fī Jabal Says," *Al-Abḥāth* 17 (1964): 227–316; D. Baramki, "Al-nuqush al-ʿarabiyya fī al-bādiya al-sūriyya," *Al-Abḥāth* 17 (1964): 317–46; Janine Sourdel-Thomine, "Inscriptions et graffiti Arabes d'époque Umayyade à propos de quelques publications récentes," *Revue des Études Islamiques* 32 (1964): 115–20; and the section on inscriptions in Arabic, in Oleg Grabar, R. Holod, J. Knustad, and W. Trousdale, *City in the Desert, Qasr al-Hayr East*, 2 vols. (Cambridge: Harvard University Press, 1978), 1:191–93.

24. Many examples of glass vessels with writing on them exist in most glass collections throughout the world. The range of quality of the glass is from very fine to rather coarse. Most of the writing on glass vessels, whether in Latin, Greek, or Arabic, is mold blown. Some is engraved. The types of messages range from good wishes to the names of artists (perhaps workshops) to the labeling of images. A few examples from the eastern Mediterranean will serve to indicate the range of the whole. Specific examples, rather than generic types, when given, refer to the collection at the Corning Museum, in Corning, New York.

Drinking vessels displaying good wishes in Greek, dated to the first centuries C.E., commonly display such sentiments as, "Be happy so long as you are here," "Success to you," "Rejoice and be Merry," and "Cheers." Similar messages appear in Arabic on glass vessels, although sometimes the format is more formal, as in the case of a small cup with Arabic dated to the eighth or ninth century (69.1.1), where the message is: "In the Name of God the Merciful, the Compassionate, Blessings on him who drinks from this cup which was made in Damascus under the supervision of Sunbat in the year 1. . . . "

Other vessels displayed scenes or figures which were identified by writing, such as the "gladiator bowls." On others, writing identified biblical figures, or geographical sites represented on the vessel. Sometimes writing was used simply to label contents, like the glass vials made to contain Jerusalem earth and labeled as such.

25. Ibn ʿAbd Rabbihi and al-Washshā are two well known and frequently quoted authors who described the Baghdad and Samarra court passion for wearing and giving textiles with verses of poetry embroidered on them. Both sources quote several examples of the verses found on textiles, belts, hair decorations, and sashes of the people at court. This was a lyrical fashion for the literate to enjoy privately. Ibn ʿAbd Rabbihi, *Al-ʿIqd al-Farīd*, 7 vols. (Cairo: Būlāq, 1332H), 4:223–26; and al-Washshā, *Kitāb al-Muwashshā*, ed. R. E. Brunnow (Leiden: E. J. Brill, 1886), 167–73. Chaps. 37–56 are especially full of short verses that appeared on the dress of court.

26. Muhammad Abdel Aziz Marzouk, "The Turban of Samuel ibn Musa, The Earliest Dated Islamic Textile," *Bulletin of the Faculty of Arts, Cairo University* 16 (December, 1954): 143–51.

27. Al-Qalqashandī, *Ṣubḥ al-aʿsha fī sināʿat al-inshāʾ*, 14 vols. (Cairo: al-Muʾassasah al-Miṣriyya, al-ʿĀmma, 1964), 3:485–88.

28. Al-Ṭabarī, *Taʾrīkh*, vol. 5 (Cairo: Maṭbaʿat al-Istiqāma, 1939), 2752–53. The Arabic phrase transliterated is "ḥābisūn fī sabīl Allah." Michael Morony drew my attention to this mention of the use of writing.

29. I am paraphrasing here because Gombrich in his attack on essentialism was talking about markings or lines or form in painting. E. H. Gombrich, *Art and Illusion: A Study in the Psychology of Pictorial Representation, The A. W. Mellon Lectures in the Fine Arts, 1956*, Bollingen Series 35 (Princeton: Princeton University Press, 1956), 28–32; "On Physiognomic Perception," in *Meditations on a Hobby Horse and Other Essays on the Theory of Art* (London: Phaidon Publishers, 1963), 45–56; and "Raphael's Madonna della Sedia," in *Norm and Form: Studies in the Art of the Renaissance I* (London: Phaidon Publishers, 1966), 64–80.

30. Boundary formation has been studied by a wide range of disciplines. See Fredrik Barth, ed., *Ethnic Groups and Boundaries, The Social Organization of Difference* (London: George Allen Unwin, 1969); Gregory Bateson, "The Logical Categories of Learning and Communication," in *Steps to an Ecology of the Mind* (New York: Ballantine Books, 1972), 279–308; Heather Lechtman, "Style in Technology —Some Early Thoughts," in *Material Culture, Style, Organization, and Dynamics of Technology*, ed. Heather Lechtman and Robert S. Merrill (Cambridge, Mass.: West Publishing, 1976), 3–20; and Margaret Conkey, "Boundedness in Art and Society," in *Symbolic and Structural Archaeology*, ed. Ian Hodder (Cambridge: Cambridge University Press, 1982), 115–28.

31. A detailed history of the creation of the Armenian alphabet is A. G. Perizanyan, "Concerning the Origin of Armenian Writing" (in Russian), *Peredneaziatskij sbornik II* (Moscow: Izd-vo vostochnoi literatury, 1966), 103–33. A more abbreviated account of the history, but one which focuses on the morphology, is the two part series of articles by Serge N. Mouraviev, "Les caractères danieliens (identification et reconstruction)" and "Les caractères mesropiens (leur gènes reconstituée)," both in *Revue des Études Arméniennes* 14 (1980): 55–85, 87–111.

One can see in the historical circumstances and in the rationales for this alphabetic change direct parallels to those that led to the change by Ataturk from the Arabic alphabet and Ottoman language to the modified Latin alphabet and Turkish language. More contemporary examples abound. In the former Soviet Union Rumanian and Maldavian were distinguished by different alphabets although they were the "same" language. And, now, with the breakup of the Soviet Union, the Turkic-speaking republics are engaged in deciding the serious issue of which alphabet is the appropriate emblem of their new nations.

32. Of course, the new alphabet also distinguished Armenian from other neighboring Indo-European languages and writing systems: e.g., Pahlavi and Avestian, used primarily by non-Christians.

33. What is specifically referred to here is that the difference in beliefs, dogma, or ritual among the various Christian groups usually did not leave traces in the communal buildings of these groups. Churches usually can be distinguished from synagogues and mosques, but, for example, Armenian, Byzantine, and Syriac churches of this period are currently archaeologically indistinguishable, unless, of course, writing appears. See chap. 2.

34. See chap. 2.

35. While this issue will be taken up in chap. 2 in detail, Greek inscriptions in synagogues appear in areas where the community spoke Greek. In the coastal city of Caesarea, for example, the synagogue displayed three inscriptions in Greek: see Moses Schwabe, "The Synagogue of Caesarea and Its Inscriptions," in *Alexander Marx: Jubilee Volume on the Occasion of His Seventieth Birthday* (New York: Jewish Theological Seminary, 1950), 433–49; E. L. Sukenik, "More about the Ancient Synagogue of Caesarea," *Bulletin Rabinowitz* 2 (June 1951): 28–30. The synagogue in the coastal city of Apollonia has two inscriptions in Greek (and one in Samaritan): see Marilyn Joyce Segal Chiat, *Handbook of Synagogue Architecture*, Brown University Judaic Studies, no. 29 (Chico: Scholars Press, 1982), 166–67. In Ascalon there are two Greek inscriptions and one in Hebrew: see E. L. Sukenik, *The Ancient Synagogue of el-Hammeh*, 62–67. In Tiberias, one inscription in Greek: see E. L. Sukenik, *Ancient Synagogues in Palestine and Greece* (London: Oxford University Press, 1934), 7–21 and 52; and Chiat, *Handbook of Synagogue Architecture*, 95. For certain of these issues, the discussions in chaps. 2 and 4 of Walter J. Ong, S.J., *The Presence of the Word* (Minneapolis: University of Minnesota Press, 1967) are especially relevant.

36. See Joseph Dan, "Midrash and the Dawn of Kabbalah," in *Midrash and Literature*, ed. Geoffrey H. Hartman and Sanford Budick (New Haven: Yale University Press, 1986), 127–39, for a provocative discussion of the trajectory of the role of writing among the Jews and reasons for the difference in contrast with medieval Christian practice.

37. Clearly, this reality conjoined elements of the referential and territorial functions of officially sponsored writing. Referential dimensions thus did, at times, have territorial functions.

38. C. B. Welles, "Inscriptions," in *Gerasa City of the Decapolis*, ed. Carl H. Kraeling (New Haven: American Schools of Oriental Research, 1938), 355–493. This study is especially effective in demonstrating the longevity of Greek as the language of official use.

39. As more groups of people adopted the Greek language they also became part of the acculturation whereby pagan images and institutions were becoming adopted and adapted into the newly emerging culture of the fifth and sixth centuries. For examples of this process: Speros Vryonis, Jr., "Panegyris of the Byzantine Saint: A Study in the Nature of a Medieval Institution, Its Origin and Fate,"

Sobornost (1981): 196–228, esp. 209 ff.; Michael Avi-Yonah, "Ancient Synagogues," *Ariel* 32 (1973): 29–43, and "La mosaïque juive dans les relations avec la mosaïque classique," in *La mosaïque greco-romaine*, colloque international sur "La mosaïque greco-romaine," Paris, 1963 (Paris: Editions du Centre National de la Recherche Scientifique, 1965), 325–31.

40. For a series of discussions about the presence of Greek and Latin on buildings, see: S. Thomas Parker, *Romans and Saracens: A History of the Arabian Frontier*, American School of Oriental Research Dissertation Series, no. 6 (Winona Lake: American Schools of Oriental Research, 1986), chaps. 1–5; and Welles, "Inscriptions," 355–493. For a detailed analysis of Christian practices of public texts into the late eighth century in the area of the Byzantine provinces of Palestine Prima, Secunda, and Tertra, parts of Arabia and Phoenicia Maritima, or the Umayyad Junds of al-Urdun and Filastin, see Robert Schick, "The Fate of the Christians in Palestine during the Byzantine-Umayyad Transition, A.D. 600–750" (Ph.D. diss., University of Chicago, 1987), esp. 12–38.

41. For all these examples see the sources indicated in note 33 above. In the oral practice, of course, we know that the vernacular was used to summarize what was being read in Hebrew, so that orally versus visually Greek was used to communicate essential beliefs.

42. This kind of relationship of Hebrew to the other languages exists in other synagogues where the community, for instance, spoke Aramaic—and some members of some synagogues knew Greek. See, for instance, the inscriptions in the six synagogues in Beth She'an (Scytholoplis) in the Galilee where Aramaic inscriptions appear along with Greek.

Beth Alpha: two inscriptions, one in Aramaic—partially destroyed—gives the date and lists the in-kind donations of the congregation. The Greek inscription gives the names of the craftsmen (father and son) who did the work. An inscription with the same content (bearing the names of the father and son) appears in another synagogue of the city, Beth She'an A: see E. L. Sukenik, *The Ancient Synagogues of Beth Alpha* (London: Oxford University Press, 1932); and Chiat, *Handbook of Synagogue Architecture*, 126–27. In Beth She'an A, three Greek and one Aramaic inscriptions appear: see Nehum Tsori, "The Ancient Synagogue at Beth She'an," *Eretz Israel: Archaeological, Historical and Geographical Studies* 8 (1967): 149–67. Beth She'an B has two Greek and one Aramaic inscriptions: see Chiat, *Handbook of Synagogue Architecture*, 134–35. At Rehov the archaeological work is not complete.

43. Style here has an extended meaning (adopting one offered by Lechtman, "Style in Technology," 4–5) which includes the activities which produce the formal, physical characteristics of writing.

44. Al-Maqrīzī, *Al-Khitat* 2:281. The weaving displayed the *basmala*, and *sūras al-fātiḥa, al-jumʿa*, and *al-munāfiqūn*.

45. The date of this incident is unclear because Ibn al-Ṭuwayr did not mention the name of a specific Imam-Caliph. But judging from where this incident was reported in the *al-Khitat*, he is probably reporting an incident from the first half of the twelfth century. Most of the mausoleums displaying elaborate Kufic on the interior would have been built by this time, and probably, too, the mosque of al-Aqmar.

46. See chap. 3 for detailed information on this subject.

47. Roman Jakobson, "Closing Statement: Linguistics and Poetics," in *Style in Language*, ed. Thomas A. Sebeok (Cambridge: MIT Press, 1960), 350–77, esp. 353. He lists here six functional perspectives: emotive, referential, poetic, phatic, metalingual, and conative. These perspectives applied to various communication functions of poetry. While in the analysis of the Fatimid public text the label "referential" has been adopted, it is here defined somewhat differently than in Jakobson.

48. For a critique of Jakobson's paradigm, see Donald Preziosi, *Rethinking Art History: Meditations on a Coy Science* (New Haven and London: Yale University Press, 1989), esp. chap. 5. A thorough list of scholars influenced, directly or indirectly, by Jakobson's work is impossible and unnecessary here. The following list will give a range of the scholars and the fields where his issues were taken up: Frederic Jameson, *The Prison-House of Language* (Princeton: Princeton University Press, 1972), chap. 3; Hayden White, *Tropics of Discourse: Essays in Cultural Criticism* (Baltimore: Johns Hopkins University Press, 1978), chap. 3; and Terence Hawkes, *Structuralism and Semiotics* (Berkeley and Los Angeles: University of California Press, 1977), 76–86. See also Michael Baxandall, *Painting and Experience in Fifteenth-Century Italy* (Oxford: Oxford University Press, 1972); and Oleg Grabar, "Symbols and Signs in Islamic Architecture," in *Architecture as Symbol and Self-Identity*, Proceedings of Seminar Four in the Series Architectural Transformations in the Islamic World, Fez, Morocco, October 9–12, 1979 (Philadelphia: The Aga Khan Award for Architecture, c. 1980), 12–17.

49. Oleg Grabar delivered a paper, "Grafitti or Proclamations: Why Write on Buildings?" (Annual Meeting of the College Art Association, Philadelphia, 1983) in which he proposed in a very tentative manner a five-modal paradigm (indicative, commemorative, semantic, iconic, and formal) which shared some of the limitations of Jakobson's on which it, too, was modeled. Yet, the literature on the social function of signs, in which the beholder, reader, user is present is not large. The text edited by Marshall Blonsky, *On Signs* (Baltimore: The Johns Hopkins University Press, 1985) contains more articles addressed to this issue than most volumes of this sort. See also Hedge and Gunther Kress, *Social Semiotics* (Ithaca: Cornell University Press, 1988).

50. A. I. Sabra, *Optics, Astronomy and Logic Studies in Arabic Science and Philosophy* (Variorum, 1994); Alhazen, *The Optics of Ibn al Haytham*, trans. A. I. Sabra, 2 vols. (London: Warburg Institute, University of London, 1989); A. I. Sabra, "Sensation and Inference in Alhazen's Theory of Visual Perception," in *Studies in Perception: Interrelations in the History of Philosophy and Science*, ed. Peter K. Machamer and Robert G. Turnbull (Columbus: Ohio State University, 1978).

51. Aspects of these issues that pertain to shaping the interpretation of the configuration one sees are termed by Baxandall, "the period eye" (*Painting and Experience*, 29–103). Baxandall presents the beholding audience as homogeneous.

52. Most studies mentioned in note 2 understand writing and literacy from the same theoretical perspective as adopted in this study. The notable exception, of course, is the work of the social anthropologist, Jack Goody. Goody, in most, but not all, of his studies, argues that writing brings with it inherent qualities replicated in all societies. For an exposition of the problems of Goody's approach, see Street, *Literacy in Theory and Practice*, chap. 12.

53. J. M. Rogers, in his review of *Calligraphy and Islamic Culture* by Annemarie Schimmel, in *Art International* 27, no. 4 (1984): 68, where he calls for a re-evaluation of the practice within the Islamic field of seeing a direct relationship between chancery handwriting and writing on buildings and other objects.

54. Priscilla P. Soucek, "The Arts of Calligraphy," in *The Arts of the Book in Central Asia*, ed. Basil Gray (Paris: UNESCO-Shambala Publications, 1979), 7–34, where she defines her topic as calligraphy within court circles and outlines questions which remain unanswerable.

55. Richard Ettinghausen, "Arabic Epigraphy: Communication or Symbolic Affirmation," in *Near Eastern Numismatics, Iconography, Epigraphy and History: Studies in Honor of George C. Miles*, ed. Dickran K. Kouymijian (Beirut: American University of Beirut, 1974), 297–311; Oleg Grabar, "The Umayyad Dome of the Rock in Jerusalem, " *Ars Orientalis* 3 (1959): 51–84; of the writings of Janine Sourdel-Thomine, those taking up issues similar to "L'ecriture Arabe et son évolution ornamentale," in *Ecriture et la psychologie des peuples, XXIIe semaine de synthèse* (Paris: A Colin, 1963), 249–61.

56. These include A. H. Christie, "The Development of Ornament from Arabic Script," *Burlington Magazine* 40 (1922): 287–92; Samuel Flury, "Le décor épigraphique des monuments Fatimides du Caire," *Syrie* 17 (1936): 365–76; Adolph Grohmannn, "The Origin and Development of Floriated Kufic," *Ars Orientalis* 2 (1957): 183–213; Muhammad Abdel Aziz Marzouk, "The Evolution of Inscriptions on Fatimid Textiles," *Ars Islamica* 10 (1942): 164–66; and Lisa Volov-Golombek, "Plaited Kufic on Samanid Epigraphic Pottery," *Ars Orientalis* 6 (1966): 107–33.

Franz Rosenthal, "Significant Uses of Arabic Writing," *Ars Orientalis* 4 (1961): 15–23, where the basis for the development of use is religion. Erica Cruikshank Dodd, "The Image of the Word," *Berytus* 18 (1969): 35–73, esp. 49, 54; Anthony Welch, "Epigraphs as Icons: The Role of the Written Word in Islamic Art," in *The Image and the Word: Confrontations in Judaism, Christianity and Islam*, ed. J. Gutman, American Academy of Religion and Society of Biblical Literature, Religion and The Arts, Series 4 (Missoula, Mont.: Scholars Press for the American Academy of Religion, 1977), 63–74, where he augments Dodd's position by discussing the role of the Caliph ʿAbd al-Malik.

Obviously excluded here are the compendiums that document the use of inscriptions and which provide the records of praxis that are essential to scholarly work: e.g., the *Corpus inscriptionum Arabicorum*, the *RCEA*, and various works of Sourdel-Thomine, such as "Inscriptions et grafitti Arabes."

57. R. Bulliet, *Conversion to Islam in the Medieval Period, An Essay in Quantitative History* (Cambridge & London: Harvard University Press, 1979), 117–31, where in discussing the entire western area of Islam he sets the date for the conversion process (when most non-Muslims would have become Muslim) in Egypt at 1010, a date that coincides almost precisely with the Fatimid public text. Other scholars (such as D. Dennett, *Conversion and Poll Tax in Early Islam* [Cambridge: Harvard University Press, 1950] and I. Lapidus, "The Conversion of Egypt to Islam," *Israel Oriental Studies* 2 [1972]: 256–57, among others) set the date for this conversion some two hundred years earlier.

Michael Morony, in "The Age of Conversions: A Reassessment," in *Conver-*

sion and Continuity, Indigenous Christian Communities in Islamic Lands Eighth to Eighteenth Centuries, Papers in Medieval Studies 9, ed. Michael Gervers and Ramzi Jibran Bikhazi (Toronto: Pontifical Institute of Medieval Studies, 1990), 135–50, reviewed the evidence for conversions within Islamic societies and assessed some of the purposes to which conversion hypothesis have been applied in scholarly writings. He cautioned against using conversion as a "cause" for developments especially when relationships are asserted rather than demonstrated.

58. Michael Carter, "Language, Truth and Power in Classical Islam" (paper delivered at American Research Center in Egypt, February, 1993), and notes from this lecture which he kindly made available to me. The fourth/tenth and especially the fifth/eleventh centuries saw the publication of teaching grammars for *faṣīḥa* as the standardization of what constituted pure and proper Arabic became established.

59. Many kinds of comments in Abū Ṣāliḥ, al-Armani, *The Churches and Monasteries of Egypt and Some Neighbouring Countries*, trans. B. T. A. Evetts (Oxford: The Clarendon Press, 1895) suggest the level at which the leaders of the various Christian (mainly Coptic, Armenian, and Nestorian communities) interacted with the upper echelons of the Fatimid governing group and thus presumably interacted in Arabic language. Almost every page of this text reports incidents of conversations between leaders of the Christian communities and members of the Fatimid ruling groups.

60. Robert N. Nelson, "An Icon at Mt. Sinai and Christian Painting in Muslim Egypt during the 13th and 14th Centuries," *Art Bulletin* 65, no. 2 (1983): 201–18, discusses an illustrated mid-thirteenth century gospel where Arabic is used. For the use of Arabic in the Jewish communities one need only consult the various scholarly works of, among others, Goitein, especially *Mediterranean Society*, vols. 1–4. It should be noted here that the Jewish community wrote Arabic primarily in Hebrew characters.

61. Sampson, *Writing Systems*, 11–45, where he supports this position.

62. Stock, *The Implications of Literacy*, esp. 3–11. He wrote a cogent summary of this monograph, including these points, in "Texts, Readers and Enacted Narratives," *Visible Language* 20, no. 3 (1986): 194–301.

63. Reading phrases within a context was an issue raised by Ettinghausen, "Arabic Epigraphy," 297–302. He pointed out that beholders often could comprehend the content of an inscription regardless of (serious, and often hilarious) spelling errors. On a broader base, Sampson, *Writing Systems*, 77–98, raises these issues. Scribner and Cole, *The Psychology of Literacy*, published a contemporary ethnographic study with results that are directly relevant to this definition of "literacy." I have raised this question before in speaking of the Fatimids in "Art of the Public Text."

64. Scribner and Cole, *The Psychology of Literacy*.

65. Sampson, *Writing Systems*, 74–75, 92–93, where he discusses incomplete scripts and their readability. This issue is also considered in Bierman, "Art of the Public Text."

66. Clearly the appearance of Kufic writing on the walls of buildings in the Fatimid period was not an invitation to beholders to participate in an elegant game of decipherment where graphic shapes of letters could represent innumerable

words. It is the knowledge of the context, as Sampson's work explains, that, for example, enables today's researchers accustomed to reading medieval inscriptions of the Fatimid period to more easily read the lines of Kufic writing on the facade of the al-Aqmar mosque, than fully literate speakers and readers of Arabic, the person on the street, so to speak, who is not savvy about the Fatimid context.

Notes to Chapter 2

1. A good text to consult is Schick, "The Fate of Christians in Palestine."

2. See *EMA*, vol. 1, pt. 2, 483–84.

3. The location of the Nea cathedral and its complex are known and have been excavated, although they are minimally published. Nahman Avigad, *Discovering Jerusalem* (Nashville, Camden, New York: Thomas Nelson Publishers, 1980); Meir Ben-Dov, *In the Shadow of the Temple*, trans. Ina Friedman (New York: Harper & Row, 1982). Reconstructions of the Nea have been drawn from the foundation remains, but we cannot reconstruct its ornamentation. The Nea was described by Procopius in general laudatory terms without the kind of specificity needed for this study. A *tabula ansate* containing an inscription in Greek was found, Avigad, *Discovering Jerusalem*, 242–45 with plates.

4. Jere L. Bacharach, "Administrative Complexes, Palaces, and Citadels: Changes in the Loci of Medieval Muslim Rule," in *The Ottoman City and Its Parts*, ed. Irene A. Bierman, Rifaʿat A. Abou-El-Haj, and Donald Preziosi (New Rochelle: A. D. Caratzas, 1991), 111–28.

5. The walls of most churches that continued in use, for instance, were significantly altered in the Crusader period or later.

6. Berton De Vries, "Urbanization in the Basalt Region of North Jordan in Late Antiquity: The Case of Umm el-Jimal," in *Studies in the History and Archaeology of Jordan II*, ed. Adnan Hadidi (Amman: Department of Antiquities Jordan, 1985), 249–56, where he points to this need for explanation; Robert A. Coughenour, "The Fifteen Churches of Umm el-Jimal," in *The Umm el-Jimal Excavations*, ed. Berton De Vries (Oxford: British Archaeological Reports, forthcoming), where he postulates that the Ghassanids were the tribe most likely to be the sponsors of these churches and, in fact, to be the occupants in Umm al-Jimal in the sixth century. Umm al-Raṣṣās is another town with almost as many churches.

7. Many of these small mosques still exist. The most accessible overview is Geoffrey King, C. J. Lenzen, and Gary O. Rollefson, "Survey of Byzantine and Islamic Sites in Jordan Second Season Report," *Annual of the Department of Antiquities Jordan* 27 (1983): 385–436. The mosque at Umm al-Walīd, which had a minaret, is the type of early mosque where the mihrab projected from the *qibla* wall (like the mosque at Khān al-Zāhid, now vanished but published by Brunnow and von Domaszewski, one at Qaṣr Jabal Says, one east of Qaṣr Hallabat, and one, still unpublished, north of Hammām al-Sarakh).

8. Syro-Palestinian Aramaic (also variously called Christian Palestinian Aramaic and Christian Palestinian Syriac) is a form of Western Aramaic in Syriac type characters that appears to have served a Christian community—that is, the place-

ment and content of inscriptions on Christian sectarian buildings plus the existence of a gospel lectionary and various parchment documents in that alphabet and language indicate its use by a Christian community. For an article discussing the various sites where inscriptions are found, and map of the sites, see A. Desreumaus, "The Birth of a New Aramaic Script in the Bilad al-Sham at the end of the Byzantine Period," in *The History of the Bilad al-Sham during the Umayyad Period*, ed. M. Adnan Bakhit and Robert Schick, 4th International Conference of the History of Bilad al-Sham, 1987 (Amman: University of Jordan and Yarmouk University, 1989), 26–36.

9. Many texts catalogue the milestones along the Roman roads. One that offers interesting interpretations of the social practices is Benjamin Isaac and Israel Roll, *Roman Roads in Judea I: The Legio-Scythopolis Road*, BAR International Series 141 (BAR: Oxford, 1982).

10. The two, possibly three, milestones known from the Umayyad period are reviewed by G. Rex Smith, "Some Umayyad Inscriptions of Bilad al-Sham—Palaeographic Notes," in *The History of the Bilad al-Sham*, ed. Bakhit and Schick, 185–94. A few have been found in Arabia.

11. Although somewhat outside the geographical area covered here, Abbasid rulers put writing on the gates of the capital, Baghdad. No communal structure directly sponsored by the Abbasids from the eighth through the tenth centuries is extant in the eastern Mediterranean. They did, however, maintain and repair earlier important structures like the Dome of the Rock. We include them here because they ruled a significant portion of the territory we are discussing.

12. For Constantinople consult C. Mango, "The Byzantine Inscriptions of Constantinople: A Bibliographic Survey," *American Journal of Archaeology* 55 (1951): 52–66; for Aqaba, Donald Whitcomb, "Evidence of the Umayyad Period from the Aqaba Excavations," in *History of the Bilad al-Sham*, ed. Bakhit and Schick, 164–84.

13. Two scholarly works supply easy access to the sequencing of inscriptions of the Byzantine period: Parker, *Romans and Saracens;* and Mango, "The Byzantine Inscriptions of Constantinople."

14. The most recent study of these forts in the eastern Mediterranean is Parker, *Romans and Saracens*, where he details the uses of these forts into the reign of Justinian. Of particular interest are chaps. 1–5, where Parker notes the care taken to update the inscriptions from Roman to Byzantine use.

15. Philip D. Curtin, *Cross-Cultural Trade in World History* (Cambridge and New York: Cambridge University Press, 1984), where he suggests that trade in kind prevailed over payment in coin.

16. The first solely epigraphic dinar or gold coin was minted in 696–97 C.E.; the first silver coin, or dirham, in 698–99. Many interpretations of the early coinage of Muslim rulers have been advanced over the years, but the most persuasive was detailed by George C. Miles, "Mihrab and ʿAnazah: A Study in Early Islamic Iconography," in *Archaeologica Orientalia in Memoriam Ernst Herzfeld*, ed. George C. Miles (Locust Valley: J. J. Augustin, Inc., 1952), 33–49. More recent studies have analyzed the early changes in light of the specific historical changes within the empire. In particular, the studies of P. Grierson, "The Monetary Reforms of ʿAbd al-Malik," *Journal of the Economic and Social History of the Orient* 3 (1960): 241–64;

Michael Bates, "Islamic Numismatics," *Middle East Studies Association Bulletin* 12, no. 2 (1978): 1–6; 12, no. 3 (1978): 2–18; 13, no. 1 (1979): 3–21; 13, no. 2 (1979): 1–9; and Michael L. Bates, "History, Geography and Numismatics in the First Century of Islamic Coinage," *Revue Suisse de Numismatique* 65 (1986): 231–63, have suggested more historically specific studies of coins and mints and an understanding that coins are more than the depictions on their surface. Part of their meaning lies in their weight and the system of which that weight is a part. Emiko Terasaki, "The Lack of Animal and Human Figural Imagery in the Public Art of the Umayyad Period," (Master's thesis, UCLA, 1987), suggested understanding certain of the iconographic changes in the Umayyad period as related to intra-Muslim politics.

I want to thank especially Jere Bacharach and Michael Bates who, while not responsible for my interpretation, have patiently answered my questions and freely shared the insights of their numismatic research.

17. For the issue of weights of these reform coins, see Grierson, "Monetary Reforms," 247–50.

18. Much has been written about ʿAbd al-Malik's putting writing on textiles (A. Grohmann, "Tiraz," *Encyclopaedia of Islam*, 1st ed. (Leiden: E. J. Brill, 1913–36); Irene A. Bierman, "Art and Politics: The Impact of Fatimid Uses of *Tiraz* Fabrics," [Ph.D. diss., University of Chicago, 1980]), but these textiles had no official use that is traceable. If one looks carefully at the writing on the few textiles that do remain from the Umayyad or early Abbasid period one can understand why the ceremonial impact of the writing (its form and materiality) on these textiles could not be great. The aesthetic dimensions of the writing were undeveloped. In Abbasid practice, the Caliph and those surrounding him wore plain unpatterned black. See Hilāl ibn al-Muḥassin al-Ṣābiʾ, *Rusūm dār al-khilāfah* (Baghdad: Matbaʾat al-ʿAni, 1964), 73–84.

19. Eusebius even commented on the plainness of the outside of Byzantine structures. J. W. Crowfoot, *Early Churches in Palestine* (London: Oxford University Press, 1941), 108–10, quoting Eusebius.

20. This practice is in contrast with how groups within U.S. society often use the presence of specific alphabets today where writing on the outside of structures is a sign of the socio-religious nature of the communal functions taking place in the interior. A building near UCLA displays a sign that reads Malinow and Silverman Funeral Home above an image of a flame in which Hebrew writing appears. What confirms or re-marks for the viewer the group-specific or sectarian adherence of the funeral services performed within the building is the presence of Hebrew letters in the sign. To those who can identify the letters they see as Hebrew letters (and many within the society can do that—maybe most people who would pass by at this location), the mere presence of those letters conveys sufficient meaning to indicate that this is a Jewish funeral home because writing in Hebrew letters is used mainly by this group. We wager that most people who pass by this sign cannot read the content of the message in Hebrew, yet the main message of this sign has been conveyed—Jewish funeral home.

21. These inscriptions, their history and bibliography, were detailed in *EMA*, vols. 1 and 2.

22. For Achtamar see Sirarpie Der Nersessian, *Armenian Art* (London:

Thames and Hudson, 1977), 80–81. For the Three Door Mosque, see *EMA* 2: 325–26.

23. The tenth-century Byzantine Book of Ceremonies, which contains prescriptions and descriptions of ceremonies, has been preserved. J. J. Reiske, *Corpus Scriptorum Historicum Byzantinorum*, 2 vols. (Bonn: 1829–30). See also A. Toynbee, *Constantine Porphryogennetos and His World* (Oxford: Oxford University Press, 1973). Secondary analysis of Byzantine ceremonial is extensive; see particularly Averil Cameron, "The Construction of Court Ritual: The Byzantine Book of Ceremonies," in *Rituals of Royalty: Power and Ceremonial in Traditional Societies*, ed. David Cannadine and Simon Price (Cambridge and London: Cambridge University Press, 1987), 106–36; C. Mango and I. Sevcenko, "A New Manuscript of the De Cerimoniis," *Dumbarton Oaks Papers* 14 (1960): 247–49; R. L. Nelson, "Symbols in Context," *Studies in Church History* 13 (1976): 97–119; and P. Magdalino and R. Nelson, "The Emperor in Byzantine Art of the Twelfth Century," *Byzantinische Forschungen* 8 (1982): 123–83. Also, Sabine MacCormack, *Art and Ceremony in Late Antiquity* (Berkeley: University of California Press, 1981).

During the many centuries in which extensive ceremonial was developed and used, writing did not play a systematic and extensive role in the display. I am almost tempted to suggest that oral utterances dominated. Abbasid ceremonial is detailed in Hilāl ibn al-Muḥassin, *Rusūm dār al-khilāfah*. One edited edition (from the Baghdad ms.) has been published, ed. Mikhā'il ʿAwad (Cairo: al-Aini Press, 1964). An English translation with notes (of the Cairo ms.) has been published by Elie A. Salem, *Rusūm dār al-khilāfah, The Rules and Regulations of the ʿAbbasid Court* (Beirut: American University Press, 1977). Al-Ma'mūn wore green when he entered Baghdad in 819/204, but restored black as the color following suggestions of his advisors. Al-Ṣābi', *Rusūm dār al-khilāfah*, 73. Umayyad ceremonial—such as it was—can only be viewed through an aggregate of accounts, all of which suggest that no formal ceremonial existed in the sense meant here. Also see Oleg Grabar, "Notes sur les cérémonies Umayyades," in *Studies in Memory of Gaston Wiet*, ed. Myriam Rosen-Ayalon (Jerusalem: Institute of Asian and African Studies, Hebrew University of Jerusalem, 1977), 51–60. Fatimid ceremonial is detailed by Paula Sanders, *Ritual, Politics, and the City in Fatimid Cairo* (New York: SUNY Press, 1994).

24. Hugh G. E. White, *The Monasteries of the Wadi ʿN Natrun*, Metropolitan Museum Expedition, 8 vols. (New York: The Metropolitan Museum of Art, 1933), vol. 8.

25. These floors are usually published in distinct categories: Jewish Art, Armenian Art, or Christian Art. Only one article, by Avi-Yonah, brings them all together: Michael Avi-Yonah, "Une école de mosaïque à Gaza au sixième siècle," *La mosaïque greco-romaine II*, IIe Colloque International pour l'étude de la mosaïque antique, Vienna, 1971 (Paris: A. & J. Picard, 1975), 377–83, and republished in *Art in Ancient Palestine*, collected papers (Jerusalem: Magnes Press—Hebrew University, 1981), 389–395. Avi-Yonah argues that a school of mosaicists existed in the area of Palestine because of the formal and technical similarities in these mosaics. He does not take up the issue of the presence of writing in these mosaics, and in fact, the plate he uses of the floor in the Armenian Church is so cropped as to eliminate the writing.

More recent studies that treat "inhabited vine" depictions and which offer interesting hypotheses contradicting (in part) traditional notions about presentational formats and traditional notions of center and periphery are: Claudine Dauphin, "New Method of Studying Early Byzantine Mosaic Pavements (coding and a computed cluster analysis) with Special Reference to the Levant," *Levant* 8 (1976): 113–49, esp. 120–23, 130–31; and Claudine Dauphin, "Development of the Inhabited Scroll, Architectural Sculpture and Mosaic Art from Late Imperial Times to the Seventh Century A.D.," *Levant* 19 (1987): 183–212.

26. Some of these formal features are present in other mosaics, although they are often smaller in format. The mosaic of one of the synagogues displays in addition a menorah flanked by two lions.

27. See A. Grabar, "Un thème de l'iconographie Chrétienne: L'oiseau dans le cage," *Cahiers Archéologiques* 16 (1966): 9–16; A. Grabar, "Recherches sur les sources juives de l'art Paléochrétien," *Cahiers Archéologiques* 12, no. 5 (1962): 124, 125, and fig. 8; O. Hjort, "L'oiseau dans le cage: Exemples mediévaux à Rome," *Cahiers Archéologiques* 18 (1968): 21–31; Gabrielle Sed-Rajna, *Ancient Jewish Art* (Seacaucus, N.J.: Chartwell Books, n.d.): 117–18.

28. The standard work on coins of this period has been John Walker, *A Catalogue of Muhammadan Coins in the British Museum*, vol.1, *Arab-Sassanian Coins* (London: British Museum, 1941), and vol. 2, *Arab-Byzantine and Post Reform Coins* (London: British Museum, 1965). Recent understandings of early coinage—and thus new categorizations—have been put forward especially in the following works: Michael G. Morony, *Iraq after the Muslim Conquest* (Princeton: Princeton University Press, 1984), esp. 38–51; Bates, "History, Geography and Numismatics," 231–63. The coins specifically mentioned here are discussed especially on pp. 243–54.

29. *EMA* 1:69.

30. Ettinghausen, "Arabic Epigraphy," 297–311.

31. For a cogent syntactic exposition of these issues, Umberto Eco, "Function and Sign: The Semiotics of Architecture," in *Signs, Symbols and Architecture*, ed. Geoffrey Broadbent, Richard Bunt, and Charles Jenks (Chichester and New York: John Wiley & Sons, 1980), 11–70.

32. Crowfoot, *Early Churches in Palestine*, esp. chap. 4; *EMA*, vols. 1 and 2; Grabar, "Umayyad Dome of the Rock."

33. Alexander Van Milligen, *Byzantine Churches in Constantinople, Their History and Architecture* (London: MacMillan, 1912), 94–101. The mosaic section completed during the reign of Justinian is detailed on pp. 94–95.

34. Van Milligen, *Byzantine Churches*, 62–74. The mosaic program is no longer extant, but the writing exists.

35. Charles Diehl, M. Tourneau, and H. Saladin, *Les monuments Chrétiens de Salonique* (Paris: Ernest Leroux, 1918), 136–43; and Charles Diehl, "Les mosaïques de Sainte-Sophie de Salonique," in *Académie des inscriptions et belles-lettres mnuments and mémoires* (Paris: Fondation Piot, 1909), 39–60.

36. *EMA*, vol. 1, chaps. 4 and 5.

37. *EMA*, vol. 1, chaps. 7 and 8 (buildings); Margaret van Berchem, *EMA*, vol. 1, chap. 10 (mosaics).

38. *MAE*, vol. 1, chap. 4.

39. See details in van Berchem, *EMA*, vol. 1.

40. C. Mango, *Byzantine Architecture* (New York: Abrams, 1976), 98, fig. 106.

41. Crowfoot, *Early Churches in Palestine*, 116–45.

42. Ibid., 116.

43. Myriam Rosen-Ayalon in a salvage expedition in Ramla found a mosaic floor depicting an arch with writing in Arabic. She evaluated the remains of the structure as a house. How the specific area where the mosaic was found functioned in the use pattern of the whole structure is unclear. "The First Mosaic Discovered in Ramla," *Israel Expedition Journal* 26 (1976): 104–11.

44. This unique bronze polycandelon is shown in Frowald Huettenmeister and Gottfried Reeg, *Die Antiken Synagogen in Israel*, 2 vols. (Wiesbaden: Reichert, 1977), 1:256–58; and in Steven Fine, "Synagogue and Sanctity: The Late Antique Palestinian Synagogue as a 'Holy Place'" (Ph.D. diss., Hebrew University, 1993), 146.

45. Charles Diehl, *Constantinople* (Paris: H. Laurens, 1924), 242–342.

46. Al-Maqrīzī, *Al-Khitat*, 1:507, where he quotes al-Fākihī and lists the latter's record of inscriptions he had seen in Mecca on parts of various fragments of old Kaʿba coverings; more generalized material can be found in R. B. Serjeant, "Material for a History of Islamic Textiles up to the Mongol Conquest," *Ars Islamica* 9 (1942): 54–92; 10 (1943): 71–104; 11–12 (1946): 98–145; 13–14 (1948): 75–117; 15–16 (1951): 29–86.

47. Meyer Schapiro, "Style," *Anthropology Today* (1969): 279–303; and Lechtman, "Style in Technology," 3–20.

48. An exception can be found in the orthography of the word "Allah" where the dagger *alif* of the word *ilāhun* is written above, which in certain Kufic scripts fashioned in stone and stucco is represented as an ornamental graph in the center. For further details, see Bierman, "Art of the Public Text," esp. 285.

49. See especially Joseph Naveh, *Early History of the Alphabet, An Introduction to West Semitic Epigraphy and Paleography* (Jerusalem and Leiden: Magnes Press, Hebrew University and E. J. Brill, 1982), where he shows that this use of a single formal alphabet was not peculiar to the centuries studied here as the "community" stage, but that such practice was common for an extended period in the eastern Mediterranean before the centuries under discussion here.

50. In the instance of the groups issuing coins, this formal association included the coins and sometimes official seals.

51. These terms for the script in which the Hebrew language was written are taken from Naveh, *Early History of the Alphabet*, 162–70, who distinguishes the Aramaic-based medieval formal script from older Hebrew letters for Hebrew language. By the Middle Ages the use of the old Hebrew alphabet for the Hebrew language had stopped.

52. The studies of manuscript writing styles and officially sponsored writing scripts are quite copious for writing in Greek. Many of the works, like those detailed above for Arabic, are compendiums, but some are synthetic and take up issues of the relationships of styles to the political situation mainly between the Eastern and Latin Churches. Most notable of these studies is Stanley Morison, *Politics and Script* (Oxford: Oxford University Press, 1972).

53. Cristel Kessler, "ʿAbd al-Malik's Inscription in the Dome of the Rock: A Reconsideration," *Journal of the Royal Asiatic Society* (1970): 1–14, esp. 10, and n. 16.

54. Ibid., 13. Here she notes that the inscriptions on the Umayyad milestones had similar characteristics.

55. Not all writing in this period followed a linear format. In fact the formats for displaying writing are most inventive when the writing is not officially sponsored. For example, on what are known as "incantation bowls," writing sometimes spirals inward from the rim, sometimes outward from the center, sometimes in radiating patterns. I want to thank Michael Morony for sharing his continuing research on these bowls.

56. All of the topics of Morison, *Politics and Script*, the collection of the Lyell Lectures Morison delivered in 1957, concern authority and script style, but chaps. 1–3 are where he suggests theological and historical implications for the styles of Latin and Greek writing.

57. Naveh, *Early History of the Alphabet*, 165–70.

58. These kinds of changes in officially sponsored writing seem in tandem with changes in the manuscript hand in which the communal text was written. Yet, as we mentioned above, the evidence is far too inconclusive to expand these general observations. We do not possess, for example, communal texts from each sectarian group that represent the same date, place, and sponsorship as the officially sponsored writing in the sectarian space. With the discovery of the Qur'ān manuscripts in Sana'a we are seeing a greater range of writing styles and qualities than previously. These pages are beginning to be published: *Kuwait National Museum, Masahif Sana'* (Kuwait, 1985); Hans-Caspar Graf von Bothmer, "Meisterwerke islamischer Buchkunst: Koranische Kalligraphie und Illumination im Handschriftenfund aus der Grosse Moschee in Sanaa," *Jemen, 3000 Jahre Kunst und Kultur des glücklichen Arabien*, 177–83. I wish to thank Ursala Drebholz and Marilyn Jenkins for sharing their knowledge and slides of these pages.

59. Crowfoot, *Early Churches in Palestine*, 118, quoting the codex of Theodosius. Such laws began to be promulgated as early as the fifth century.

60. Muḥammad ibn Bahadur Zarkashī, *I'lām al-sājid bi-aḥkām al-masājid* (Cairo: n.p., 1384H), was against the writing on the *qibla*, and adornment in general, 335–38; Yūsuf ibn 'Abd al-Hadī, *Thimār al-masājid fī dhikr al-masājid*, ed. As'ad Talas (Beirut: n.p., 1943), 166, 170.

61. *EMA*, vols. 1 and 2.

62. Some recent papers by Oleg Grabar and Sheila Blair are suggesting an alteration of this date, but the precise date is not germane for this argument.

63. Of this latter building program substantial Umayyad material remains only in the Great Mosque in Damascus, and of that extensive mosaic work less than 15 percent of the original is extant.

64. This conversation is reported in Ali ibn 'Abd Allah al-Samhudi, *Khulāṣat al-wafā' bi-akhbār al-muṣtafa* (al-Qāhira: 1392H), 370.

65. The arguments of where the workmen who completed the mosaics came from are most accessible in van Berchem (*EMA*, vol. 1) whose work relied heavily on al-Balādhurī (*Futūḥ al-Buldān)*, al-Ya'qūbī (*Tārīkh*), and al-Ṭabarī (*al-Tārīkh*). Wide expanses of mosaics represented al-Walīd's command of money and resources, including the skills of the best workmen whether they were Copt or Syrian or possibly from within Byzantine territory.

66. The text through which these kinds of details are most readily available is

Chiat, *Handbook of Synagogue Architecture*, where the synagogues in the ten cities of the coastal region are detailed on pp. 149–94. Detailed bibliographies are included.

67. 'Isfiya is southeast of Haifa. Chiat, *Handbook of Synagogue Architecture*, 158–61; M. Avi-Yonah and M. Makhouly, "A Sixth-Century Synagogue at 'Isfiya," *Quarterly Department of Antiquities Palestine* III (1933): 118–31; Rachel Hachlili, "The Zodiac in Ancient Jewish Art: Representations and Signification," *Bulletin of the American School of Oriental Research* 228 (December 1977): 61–77.

68. Chiat, *Handbook of Synagogue Architecture*, 153–58; M. Avi-Yonah, "The Ancient Synagogue at Caesarea: Preliminary Report," *Bulletin Rabinowitz* 3 (1960): 44–48; and especially Schwabe, "Synagogue of Caesarea," 433–49.

69. See note 67 above.

70. Similar patterns in the display of officially sponsored writing are found in the synagogues in other areas, e.g., the Galilee, where Samaritan is often present. Chiat, *Handbook of Synagogue Architecture*, 19–148.

71. For a discussion of the role of Greek among Christian communities see Schick, "The Fate of Christians in Palestine," 15–16, 698–702.

72. These types of issues are taken up by modern linguistic studies usually in the framework of oral-written diglossia, but these same studies provide data for understanding the link between performance in writing and class structure. A synthetic work that takes up these issues in particular is Goody, *The Interface*, esp. chap. 11. More specific studies that inform these questions are Clanchy, *From Memory to Written Record;* and Scribner and Cole, *The Psychology of Literacy*.

73. See chap. 1 and relevant notes for further explication of the role of Greek.

74. Naveh, *Early History of the Alphabet*, 112–24.

75. Oleg Grabar, "Pictures on Commentaries: The Illustrations of the *Maqamat* of al-Hariri," in *Studies in the Art and Literature of the Near East in Honor of Richard Ettinghausen*, ed. Peter J. Chelkowski (Salt Lake City: Middle East Center, University of Utah, 1974), 85–104.

76. Chiat, *Handbook of Synagogue Architecture*, 176.

77. White, *Monasteries* 3:187, plates 58, 59.

78. Max van Berchem, *CIA*, part 2, *Syrie du Sud;* vol. 2, *Jerusalem: Haram*, 224–28, 248–51.

79. Chiat, *Handbook of Synagogue Architecture*, 185.

80. RCEA, vol. 1, no. 87.

81. Van Milligan, *Byzantine Churches*, 73–74.

82. Grabar, "Umayyad Dome of the Rock," 76–77.

83. White, *Monasteries*, 194. This inscription is partially damaged so that the name of the second person who died is no longer extant.

84. Peter R. L. Brown, "Art and Society in Late Antiquity," in *The Age of Spirituality*, ed. Kurt Weitzmann (Metropolitan Museum of Art and Princeton University Press, 1980), 17–28.

Notes to Chapter 3

1. Proclaimed in the *khutba* on Friday, 21 Rabīʿ II 297, January 910.
2. Mainly Mālikī in North Africa and Shāfiʿī in Egypt.

3. On this issue see: Farhad Daftary, *The Ismaʿilis: Their History and Doctrine* (Cambridge: Cambridge University Press, 1990), esp. chap. 4, "Fatimid Ismaʿilism"; S. M. Stern, "Cairo as the Centre of the Ismaʿili Movement," Colloque International sur l'histoire du Caire (Cairo: Ministry of Culture of the Arab Republic of Egypt, n.d.), 437–50.

4. S. M. Stern, "Ismaʿili Propaganda and Fatimid Rule in Sind," *Islamic Culture* 23 (1949): 298–307.

5. The issues revolving around the social uses of writing—what kinds of messages were published in what ways in the society—have not *per se* been discussed for the medieval Islamic period, but the issue of writing, mainly in books, and its social effects has been provocatively considered by Jack Goody and Ian Watt, "The Consequences of Literacy," *Comparative Studies in Society and History* 5, no. 3 (1963): 304–45, esp. 311–26; and Jack Goody, "Writing, Religion and Revolt in Bahia," *Visible Language* 20, no. 3 (1986): 318–43, where he discusses the role of (contextual) literacy in Arabic in the Yoruba Muslim slave revolt in Brazil in the first half of the nineteenth century.

6. A readily available reference for this coinage is George C. Miles, *Fatimid Coins in the Collection of the University Museum, Philadelphia, and the American Numismatic Society* (New York: American Numismatic Society, 1951). Michael Bates discussed the changes in Fatimid coinage in, "Shiʿi Inscriptions on Buyid and Fatimid Coins" (paper delivered at the Annual Meeting of the Middle East Studies Association, Chicago, November 1983). He generously has sent me this unpublished paper, in which he tentatively suggests that the format might have related to the Ismāʿīlī cyclical world view. Doug Nichol, whose major catalogue of Fatimid coinage is forthcoming, has guided me in understanding the changes in Fatimid coinage over time. See also Stanley Lane-Poole, *Catalogue of Arabic Glass Weights in the British Museum* (Paris: Rollin, 1891), for coin weights with a similar format.

7. Personal communication from Dr. Mourad Rammah. Consult also the forthcoming study by Dr. Ibrahim Chabbouh on "The Three Fatimid Cities."

8. For the reign of al-Muʿizz, see: al-Qāḍī Abū Ḥanīfah al-Nuʿmān ibn Muḥammad, *Al-Majālis wa'l-musāyarāt*, ed. Al-Ḥabīb al-Fāqī, I. Shabbūḥ, and M. al-Yaʿlawī (Tunis: n.p., 1978); ʿArif Tāmir, *al-Muʿizz li-Dīn Allah al-Fātimī* (Beirut: Dār al-Afāq al-Jadīda, 1982); and Farhat Dachraoui, *Califat Fatimide au Maghreb* (Tunis: n.p., 1981).

9. Michael Bates generously shared his research notes with me on this topic. The writing on the first stage coins included such phrases as: *wa ʿAli ibn Abī Ṭālib waṣiyy al-rasūl wa al-nā'ib al-faḍūl wa-zawj al-zahrā' al-batāl* (ʿAlī is the designee of the Prophet and the representative of the most radiant virgin) and *muḥā sunnat Muḥammad sayyid al-murṣalīn wa-wārith majd al-aʿimma al-mahdiyyin* (Revivifier of the *sunna* of Muḥammad, pre-eminent of the messengers, and heir of the rightly guided imams.) See also A. Launois, "Catalogue des monaies Fatimites entrées au Cabinet des Médailles depuis 1896," *Bulletin d'Études Orientales* 24 (1971): 19–53.

10. The date of al-Sijistānī's death is still a matter of discussion. See especially Paul Walker, *The Wellsprings of Wisdom* (Salt Lake City: University of Utah Press, 1994), 15–16.

11. For both Qāḍī al-Nuʿmān and al-Sijistānī, see the individual entries in Ismail Poonawala, *Biobibliography of Ismaʿili Literature* (Malibu: Undena Publications, 1977).

12. For al-Sijistānī's contributions to Ismāʿīlī thought, see: Husain F. al-Hamdani, "Some Unknown Ismaʿili Authors and Their Works," *Journal of the Royal Asiatic Society* (1933): 359–78; Henry Corbin's introduction (in French) to his edition of al-Sijistānī's *Kashf al-maḥjūb* (Tehran: Institut Franco-Iranien, 1949): 5–25; and more recently, Walker, *The Wellsprings of Wisdom*, where he discusses the writing of al-Sijistānī, and offers an annotated translation of *Kitāb al-yanābīʿ*, which he translates as "Wellsprings of Wisdom." Earlier authors, such as Corbin, translated the title as "The Roots of Wisdom" or "The Book of Sources."

13. On the use of al-Nuʿmān's texts in teaching, see Stern, "Cairo as the Centre," 437–50.

14. For issues relating to the plurality of Ismāʿīlī discourse, see Azim Nanji, "Between Metaphor and Context: The Nature of Fatimid Ismaʿili Discourse on Justice and Injustice," *Arabica* 37 (1990): 234–39.

15. On the role of memory devices in the Latin language-based Middle Ages, see Mary Carruthers, *The Book of Memory, A Study of Memory in Medieval Culture* (Cambridge: Cambridge University Press, 1990).

16. The Fatimid *dāʿī* Ḥamīd al-Dīn Aḥmad ibn ʿAbd Allah al-Kirmānī, philosopher and prolific writer, died c. 1021/ 422. He was most active during the reign of the Fatimid ruler al-Ḥākim.

17. Nāṣir-i Khusraw lived and travelled in the mid-eleventh century. Perhaps best known for his *Safar-nāma*, his treatise, *Kitāb-i Khvān al-Ikhvān* (Tehran: n.p., 1929), is most relevant here. It relates in significant ways to the writings of al-Sijistānī a century earlier.

18. See Irene A. Bierman, "Cairo: A Parallax of Judgment," in *Identities in Medieval Cairo*, ed. Irene. A. Bierman, Working Papers, Gustav E. von Grunebaum Center for Near Eastern Studies (Los Angeles: Gustav E. von Grunebaum Center for Near Eastern Studies, 1995).

19. Walker, *The Wellsprings of Wisdom*, reproduces the one such diagram that is present in some of the manuscripts, and recreates the diagrams that are called for in the manuscripts and for which space has been left. H. Corbin, *Trilogie Ismaélienne* (Tehran-Paris: Department of Iranology, Institute Franco-Iranian, 1961), 5–127, describes the diagrams, but reproduces only the one from Nāṣir-i Khusraw's *Khvān al-Ikhvān* as an example, esp. pp. 64, 105–6.

20. The creation of the world is likened to God's imperative "Be" (*kun*). The two letters—*kaf* and *nun*—forming this word result in two principles, the words *kūnī* and *qadar*. Wilfred Madelung, "Aspects of Ismaʿili Theology: The Prophet Chain and the God Beyond Being," in *Ismaʿili Contributions to Islamic Culture*, ed. Seyyed Hossein Nasr (Tehran: Imperial Iranian Academy of Philosophy, 1398 /1977), 51–55. S. M. Stern, *Studies in Early Ismaʿilism* (Jerusalem: Magnes Press, Hebrew University, 1983), esp. chap. 1, "The Earliest Cosmological Doctrines of Ismaʿilism," 1–29; and Heinz Halm, *Kosmologie und Heilslehre der frühen Ismaʿiliya* (Weisbaden: Franz Steiner, 1978).

21. In al-Sijistānī, *Kitāb al-yanābīʿ*, "Allah" is an important word. It is discussed both as an isolated word, and as part of the *shahāda* (the profession of Faith).

22. Walker, *The Wellsprings of Wisdom*, 45–49.

23. Ibid., 98–99.

24. The counterclockwise direction is not dictated by the fact that Arabic is written from right to left. It would have been possible to have the writing "face" the outside. Then, the stance for reading the writing would be outside the circles.

25. Walker, *The Wellsprings of Wisdom*, 70.

26. Ibid., 82–83.

27. Qāḍī al-Nuʿmān, *Daʿāʾim al-islām*, ed. Asaf A. A. Fyzee, 2 vols. (Cairo, 1951–61), 1:12. Partial English translation, Asaf A. A. Fyzee, *The Book of Faith* (Bombay, 1974), 14, n. 7.

28. For which texts were read to which levels, see Stern, "Cairo as the Centre." See also Paul Walker, "The Ismaili Daʿwa in the Reign of the Fatimid Caliph al-Hakim," *Journal of the American Research Center in Egypt* 30 (1993): 160–182, esp. 164–65.

29. Q 22:31; 16:100 are two of the many references.

30. Of course, rulers changing their coinage often required taxes and certain kinds of other payments to be made in their new issue coins, with a fixed exchange for the old coinage. This type of exchange was always to the advantage of the issuer of the new coins, and took place often. Such an exchange took place, in fact, under the direction of *wazīr* Yaʿcub ibn Killis, who made the previously issued dinar equal to only 75 percent of Fatimid Imam al-Muʿizz's new dinar, and then demanded payment of taxes in the new dinar. Aḥmad ibn ʿAlī al-Maqrīzī, *Ittiʿāẓ al-ḥunafā bi-akhbār al-aʾimmah al-Fatimiyīn al-khulafā*, 3 vols. (Qāhira: n.p., 1967–73), 1:146. I thank my colleague Jere Bacharach for constantly reminding me of this aspect of coinage change.

Still, the purity of these coins kept them in circulation a long time. Jewish merchants, Goitein informs us, collected payment in *Muʿizzī* in 983, 1004, 1026, and even as late as 1057. Goitein, *Mediterranean Society*, 1:236–37. These coins are understood today as "surpassing the standard of fineness of the best medieval gold coins," Andrew S. Ehrenkreutz and Gene W. Heck, "Additional Evidence of the Fatimid Use of Dinars for Propaganda Purposes," in *Studies in Islamic History and Civilization in Honour of Professor David Ayalon*, ed. M. Sharon (Jerusalem and Leiden: E. J. Brill, 1986), 146; W. Oddy, "The Gold Content of Fatimid Coins Reconsidered," *Metallurgy in Numismatics* 1 (1980): 99–188.

31. The semantic content, however, reads from the inner to the outer circles.

32. See Yves Marquet, "La pensée philosophique et religieuse du Qadi al-Nuʿman à travers *La Risala Mudhiba*," *Bulletin d'Études Orientales* 39–40 (1987–88): 141–81, where he provides a corpus of Qurʾanic verses cited by Qāḍī al-Nuʿmān.

33. Some phrases on the Fatimid issues were found on the coins of their contemporaries. The legend, *ṣalla Allahu ʿalayhi wa ʿala ālihi* (May God bless Him [the Prophet Muḥammad] and his family) appeared on Fatimid dinars. Some scholars consider this an Alid phrase, but I understand it, in this medieval context, to be simply a non-Abbasid statement. The detailed arguments behind either stance are not as germane here to the main point as is the reality that this phrase appeared on Fatimid coinage, on the coinage of the Sunni Ikhshidids beginning in 947/356, and on the coinage of the Imāmī Shīʿī Hamdanid, Sayf

al-Dawla, beginning in 944/333. What is important is that although this phrase occurred in the writing on the Ikhshidid and Hamdanid coins, they maintained the Abbasid format for the display of the writing. For a provocative discussion of this coinage, and one with which I do not fully agree, see Ramzi Jibran Bikhazi, "The Struggle for Syria and Mesopotamia (330–58/941–69) As Reflected on Hamdanid and Ikhshidid Coins," *American Numismatic Society Museum Notes* 28 (1983): 137–73.

34. See note 6 above.

35. See note 26 above.

36. Norman D. Nicol, "Islamic Coinage in Imitation of Fatimid Types," *Israel Numismatic Journal* 10 (1988–89): 58–70, plates 10 & 11.

37. *Madīnat al-salām* is the mint site.

38. Sulṭān al-Dawlah's (r. 1012–21/403–12) issue in 407 (1016) is especially interesting because it seemed to straddle the fence. The design on the obverse side displayed concentric circles, while that on the reverse retained the Umayyad-Abbasid format.

39. Jean-Claude Garcin, "Typonymie et topographie urbaines mediévales à Fustat," *Journal of the Economic and Social History of the Orient* 27 (July 1984): 113–35; "Pour un recours à l'histoire de l'espace vécu dans l'étude de l'Egypte Arabe," *Annales Economie, Société, Civilizations* 30 (1980): 437–65; Wladyslaw Kubiak, *Al-Fustat Its Foundation and Early Urban Development* (Warsaw: Wydawn, Universytetu Warszawskiego, 1982); Janet Abu-Lughod, *Cairo: 1001 Years of the City Victorious* (Princeton: Princeton University Press, 1971).

40. Primarily of Shāfiʿī and Mālikī.

41. See especially Goitein, *Mediterranean Society*, 4:1–104, where he details the marriage negotiations in which the bride stipulated that she would always reside in Fusṭāṭ. This section also mentions apartment housing shared by Muslims and Jews.

42. Ibid. This evidence leads Goitein to describe the area as housing a bourgeois population. He discusses zoning and its implications, esp. pp. 15–21.

43. He did not impose the Ismāʿīlī calendar on the population. He did suppress, however, the pronouncing of the formula "Allahu Akbar" (God is Most Great) after prayer. See Sanders, *Fatimid Cairo*, 45 and nn. 32–33.

44. Sawirus ibn al-Muqaffaʿ, *History of the Patriarchs of the Egyptian Church*, translated and annotated by Antoine Khater and O. H. E. Burmester, 4 vols. (Cairo: Societé de l'Archéologie, 1943), vol. 2, pt. 2. This volume covers the years 880–1066.

45. That an Ismāʿīlī uniformity was required is strongly suggested by the episodes reported in *Al-Khitat* where men carrying a Sunni text inside the city were beaten and sometimes executed. For one such incident, see al-Maqrīzī, *al-Khitat* 2:341.

46. Cairo was approximately 1 km. 200 m. x 1 km. or 1 ¼ miles x $^{6}/_{10}$ mile. See *MAE*, vol. 1, chap. 3, on the foundation of Cairo.

47. See note 3 above.

48. *MAE*, vol. 1, chap. 4 on the mosque of al-Azhar and related plates.

49. It seems likely that the mosque built during his reign would have displayed this sign. What is unusual about the articulation of the walls on the inner court-

yard is the presence of a circle motif, new in Egypt in this mosque. When these were put in the mosque is unclear. What was in these circles originally is also unclear. It could have been concentric circles of writing. What is clear, however, is that what fills the circles now was chosen by the Comité de Conservation.

50. Al-Maqrīzī, *Al-Khitat* 1:135; also found in al-Maqrīzī, *Itti'āẓ*, 1:140–42; and in Ibn Muyassar, *Akhbār Miṣr (Annales d'Egypte)*, ed. Henri Masse (Cairo: Impr. de l'Institut français d'archéologie orientale, 1919): 94.

51. Al-Maqrīzī transmits the reaction of pilgrims to Mecca (Egyptians, Syrians, and Khurasanis) who saw this ornament. They found it grander than earlier gifts they had either seen or heard of. Al-Maqrīzī, *Al-Khitat* 1:135; and *Itti'āẓ* 1:140–42.

52. Paul Balog, "Monnaies Islamiques rare Fatimites et Ayyubites," *Bulletin de l'Institut d'Egypte* 36 (1953–54): 327–41.

53. Ibn al-Muqaffa', *History of the Patriarchs*, vol. 2, 146–47 (English); 97–98 (Arabic).

54. This mosque was originally begun by the *wazīr* Ya'cūb ibn Killis during the reign of Imam-Caliph al-'Azīz who said the *khutba* in this structure. In 1012–13/403 various furnishings in the mosque were completed by Imam-Caliph al-Ḥākim. See *MAE*, vol. 1, chap. 5; Jonathan M. Bloom, "The Mosque of al-Hakim in Cairo," *Muqarnas* 1 (1983): 15–36. In this same year, Imam-Caliph al-Ḥākim completed other mosques outside the royal city: one at al-Maqs to the northwest of Cairo, and one in Rāshīda to the south built on the Birkat (lake) al-Habish. Al-Maqrīzī, *Al-Khitat* 2:133, 283–85. Since these mosques are no longer extant we do not know whether any of these buildings displayed writing. The only mention that I have found about writing on mosques—other than that which is discussed in the text—is by Abū Ṣāliḥ who noted that a mosque on the edge of Birkat al-Habish (south of Fusṭāṭ) had a minaret and that Imam al-Ḥākim's name was displayed on it. Abu Salih, al-Armani, *Churches and Monasteries*, 130.

55. Al-Maqrīzī, *Al-Khitat* 2:341.

The text is as follows: "In the year 395 slander and monstrosity occurred concerning Abu Bakr and 'Umar. . . . It was written in Safar of this year [395] on all of the mosques and on the old mosque of Fusṭāṭ (Miṣr), outside and inside, and on all of its sides (walls) and on the gates of shops, and rooms and on tombs, insulting the ancestors and cursing them. It was variegated and colored with colors and gold. And that was done on the doors of houses and bazaars. And people were forced to [do] that."

56. Such curses would include the Kharaji, too; however, they were so few and so isolated that they would not provoke significant ire. At this time, however, the Fatimid army had defeated an Ibadi group in the central Maghrib.

57. For these issues concerning public meaning in architecture, see Manfredo Tafuri, *Theories and History of Architecture* (New York: Harper & Row, 1976), esp. chap. 5, "Instruments of Criticism."

58. For a provocative discussion of group space within an urban area and the ways in which it was marked, see Natalie Zemon Davis, "The Sacred and the Body Social in Sixteenth-Century Lyon," *Past and Present* 90 (1981): 40–70.

59. This Ismā'īlī practice was part of the larger Shī'ī practice. Curses were put on the walls and gates of *masjids* in Baghdad in 963/35. G. Makdisi, *Ibn 'Aqil et la*

resurgence de l'Islam traditionaliste au XIè siècle (Damascus: n.p., 1963), 312. From 1051–53/443–45 gold inscriptions praising ʿAlī and Muḥammad (but not directly cursing Abū Bakr and ʿUmar) were put on a gate in Karkh. Ibn al-Jawzī, *Al-Muntaẓam fī tārīkh al-mulūk wa-l-umam*, 18 vols. (Beirut: Dār al-Kutub, 1992), 8: 149–50, 154, 157, 172–73. I want to thank Michael Morony for calling my attention to these instances.

60. There was perhaps more oral cursing, because there are prohibitions against cursing.

61. Al-Maqrīzī, *Ittiʿāẓ* 2:54, 96. He also saw it as an attempt to urge people into the Ismāʿīlī *daʿwa*. He mentions how effective this policy was for men and for women. See also Heinz Halm, "Der Treühander Gottes: Die Edikte des Kalifen al-Hakim," *Der Islam* 63 (1986): 11–72, esp. 34–38.

62. Al-Maqrīzī, *Ittiʿāẓ* 2:65; for comments on the revolt as a whole, see 60–67. For a political interpretation of these events, see Thierry Bianquis, *Damas et La Syrie Sous La Domination Fatimide (395–468/969–1076)*, 2 vols. (Damascus: The University of Paris, 1986) 1: 279–85.

63. Al-Maqrīzī, *Ittiʿāẓ* 2:96.

64. We are left only with Abū Ṣāliḥ's minimal notation about the Rāshīda mosque which Imam-Caliph al-Ḥākim built the same year that he completed the mosque outside the Bāb al-Futūḥ. If we are able ever to know that it did, in fact, display writing prominently on the outside, the thesis here is further supported. By such an action, Imam al-Ḥākim would then have surrounded Fusṭāṭ with writing. The Rāshīda mosque was built outside, and to the south of Fusṭāṭ, and was a mosque for prayer by Ismāʿīlīs. Al-Ḥākim tore this mosque down and then rebuilt it, suggesting that it was far smaller in scale than that outside the Bāb al-Futūḥ.

65. In contrast, those attending the al-Azhar mosque obviously had to first have access to the royal city. Thus, generally speaking, in this period the congregation of the al-Azhar mosque were mainly residents of the royal city.

66. Many examples of the use of the Bāb al-Futūḥ exist in the *Ittiʿāẓ* and the *Al-Khitat*. Al-Maqrīzī, *Ittiʿāẓ* 2:84 is one rather dramatic example. See also Sanders, *Fatimid Cairo*, for procession routes.

67. The only mosque in the entire urban area that rivaled the mosque of al-Ḥākim in size was that of Aḥmad ibn Ṭūlūn.

68. Sanders, *Fatimid Cairo*, 55–57.

69. For example, it might be quite possible for the *surāt al-Nūr* (the Light) to have been placed on the minaret to evoke for Ismāʿīlī beholders the *bāṭin* dimensions of those verses concerning the light of the Imam; as well as, as Bloom suggested ("Mosque of al-Hakim," 20), to imply the function of the minaret and, I should add, to convey several other understandings of these verses in various exegetical works. *Asbāb al-nazūl*, literally, "the causes for the coming down," is the collection of accounts that documents the conditions or reasons that caused God's messages to be given to the Prophet Muḥammad. As such, they served a Sunni population.

70. For a synthetic study of these changes, see Yaacov Lev, "The Fatimid Army, A.H. 358–427/968–1036 C.E.: Military and Social Aspects," *Asian and African Studies* 14 (1980): 156–92; Yaacov Lev, "Army, Regime and Society in Fatimid Egypt

358–487/968–1094," *International Journal of Middle East Studies* 9, no. 3 (1987): 337–66; see also Jere L. Bacharach, "African Military Slaves in the Medieval Middle East: the Case of Iraq (869–955) and Egypt (868–1171)," *International Journal of Middle East Studies* 13 (1981): 471–95.

71. *MAE* 1:85–98, and S. Flury, *Die ornamente der Hakim-und Asher-moschee* (Heidelberg: Carl Winters, 1912).

72. Ḥamīd al-Dīn Aḥmad ibn ʿAbd Allah al-Kirmānī, d.c. 1021/411, in *Rāḥat al-ʿaql* (Peace of Mind), ed. M. Kamil Hussein and M. Mustafa Hilmy (Cairo: Dar al-Fiqr, 1953), uses innumerable concentric circle diagrams as memory aids. All but one have lines of writing in the center circle.

73. The medallion is about ⅓ meter (1 ft.) in diameter. These are Creswell's measurements. *EMA*, vol. 1, chap. 5.

74. These heights are approximate because Creswell's measured drawings give measurements of the parts of the minaret to each other. As a true ground was not established, elevations cannot be established.

75. Walker, *The Wellsprings of Wisdom*. The word "Allah" is treated specifically in five out of the forty wellsprings: wellsprings 1, pp. 45–50; 23, pp. 79–85; 30, pp. 91–93; 32, pp. 94–95; 39, pp. 107–9.

76. This sign of Ismaʿilism is about 4 ½ meters (14.7 ft.) from the ground.

77. Bloom, "Mosque of al-Hakim," 35.

78. Stern, *Early Ismaʿilism*, chap. 1, "The Earliest Cosmological Doctrines," 3–29, relates that al-Murshid was a member of the entourage of Jawhar, and composed a treatise said to be related by Imam al-Muʿizz: "He (God) created a light and produced out of this light a creature" (p. 18, paragraph 132 in the Arabic text).

79. The easiest reference for the writing program on this mosque is Bloom, "Mosque of al-Hakim," 34–36, where a useful summary table translates and cites the phrases both in the Qurʾān and in their listing in the *MCIA, RCEA*, with references to plates in the *MAE*.

80. Sanders, *Fatimid Cairo*, 56.

81. The inscription is incomplete; the date is missing.

82. *MAE* 1:93. This canting is still readily visible from inside the bastion.

83. Creswell notes the projection of the moulding, *EMA* 1:96. I measured the depth of this inscription and that on the upper register of the northern minaret, and found that they were approximately the same, about four centimeters (1 ½ in.). This depth seems to be maintained over the minaret surface, although I could not readily check surfaces.

84. Sanders, *Fatimid Cairo*, 56.

85. *MAE* 1:68–71.

86. For the content of these bands see: *RCEA*, nos. 2090–92; Bloom, "Mosque of al-Hakim," nos. 2–4, p. 34.

87. Irene A. Bierman, "Near East Gallery," *Arts of Asia* 22, no. 3 (May–June 1992): 120–27, esp. 120–22, no. 84. Martin Lings and Yasin Hamid Safadi, *The Qurʾan: Catalogue of an Exhibition of Qurʾan Manuscripts at the British Library* (London: World of Islam Publishing Co. Ltd. for the British Library, 1976), 25, no. 11. Jonathan M. Bloom, "Al-Maʾmun's Blue Koran?" *Revue des Études Islamiques* 54 (1986): 59–65.

88. I have used the photograph from Flury's study of the mosque (1904) rather

than a contemporary photograph because the original writing is more clearly discernible there.

89. Sanders, *Fatimid Cairo*, 55–57, and nn. 104–9.

90. *MAE* 1:83–84. The entire frieze along the *qibla* may also have been canted. This canting was preserved in the recent restoration so that it is still possible to read the writing in the central aisle easily.

91. See Nuʿmān ibn Muḥammad, al-Qāḍī, *Taʾwīl al-daʿāʾim*, ed. Muḥammad Ḥasan al-Aʿẓamī (Miṣr: Dār al-maʿārif, 1967), the sections on Imamate.

92. Creswell, *MAE* 1:58–90, gives a detailed history of the bastions, or salients as he calls them. His archaeological/architectural studies enabled him to clarify that on the northern bastion yet a second outer wall was added in the time of Badr al-Jamālī when he built the new northern wall of Cairo (1087/480). Thus the outer surface we see today on the northern minaret is one which conformed to the bastion of al-Ḥākim but is different from it. The western bastion is the original one from the time of al-Ḥākim. Bloom, "Mosque of al-Hakim," 20–21, reconfirms Creswell's statements.

93. Thus the minarets of the mosque of al-Ḥākim were destroyed above the bastion line which is basically the roof line. The Fatimid period minarets of the mosques of al-Azhar, al-Aqmar, and Ṭalāʾiʿ also fell and were replaced in the early fourteenth century (and then later in the Ottoman period, and removed by the French). See Irene A. Bierman, "Urban Memory and the Preservation of Monuments," In *The Restoration and Conservation of Islamic Monuments in Egypt*, ed. Jere L. Bacharach (Cairo: American University Press, 1995): 1–12. An elaborate support system inside the bastions maintained access to the minarets, and an ability to see the carved writings.

94. *MAE* 1:88, where he remarks that the marble from the northern salient would have provided all but about ten meters of the length of the marble needed to put the inscription over the new Bāb al-Futūḥ which Badr al-Jamālī built.

95. The inscription runs approximately fifty centimeters (15 ¼ ft.). *MAE* 1:87 lists the verses, Q 33:56; 9: (part of) 108; 14:26–28; 62:9.

96. The verses in full are:

33:65

Surely God and His angels bless the Prophet. You who believe call for blessings upon him and salute him with an appropriate salutation.

9: (part of) 107

And those who built a mosque to cause harm and unbelief, and to cause disunion among the unbelievers, and as a refuge for him who made war against God and His Messenger before. They will swear: we desired nothing but good. And God bears witness that they are certainly liars.

24:26–28

Unclean women for unclean men, and unclean men for unclean women; good women for good men, and good men for good women; these are declared free from what they say. For them is forgiveness and an honorable sustenance. You who believe, enter not houses other than your own house, until you have asked permission and saluted those therein; this is better for you that you may be mindful; But if you find no one therein, enter them not until permission is given to you; and if it is said to you, Go back, then go back; This is purer for you. And God is the knower of what you do.

62:9

You who believe, when the call is sounded for the prayer on Friday, hasten to remembrance of God and leave off trafficking. That is better for you, if you know.

97. Sanders, *Fatimid Cairo*, 59–60.

98. For a readily available reference to this incident, see Bianquis, *Damas et la Syrie* 1:302–3; and s.v. "*Djarrahid*," Encyclopaedia of Islam, new ed. (Leiden: E. J. Brill, 1960–95).

99. Most *wazīr wasta* were executed. He also executed ʿAbd al-ʿAzīz ibn al-Nuʿmān, the grandson of Qāḍī al-Nuʿmān. He executed al-Faḍl ibn Ṣāliḥ, the general who led the defeat of Abū Rakwa, as well as Hasan ibn ʿUmar and Ḥusayn ibn Jawhar.

100. These measures are well known: Christians were made to wear heavy crosses in public; Jews had to wear black belts and turbans. Selling wine was prohibited as was the public celebration of Christian festivals. Churches were torn down (mosques were put up in their place, e.g., the Rāshīda mosque was built upon a Jacobite church), which culminated in the destruction of the Holy Sepulcher in Jerusalem (1009–10). Imam-Caliph al-Ḥākim later relaxed these measures and permitted churches to be rebuilt and the Holy Sepulcher to be reconstructed.

These measures have to be seen against a background of the other measures he took toward shaping the public morality: honey and raisins were prohibited for they could be used to make wine and beer. He prohibited eating lupine, watercress, and *mulūkhiyya* (a soup made from pounded greens) as well as fish without scales. Music was outlawed. No one (male) could appear in a public bath without a loin cloth; chess was prohibited. Women were forbidden to go to cemeteries and to public baths and to display jewelry in public. Most of these measure are detailed in al-Maqrīzī, *Al-Khitat* 2:286–88; Ibn al-Muqaffaʿ, *History of the Patriarchs*, vol. 2, 174–209 (English); 112–37 (Arabic).

These rules were not always enforced, but al-Ḥākim would ride out on a donkey both daily and at night, often with a small retinue to escape recognition, so that he could observe daily life. M. A. Shaban, *Islamic History: A New Interpretation A. D. 750–1055 (A. H. 132–448)*, 2 vols. (Cambridge: Cambridge University Press, 1976), 2:206–11, suggested that these measures show his acute sense of how to stabilize a growing agricultural-economic problem resulting from the neglect of the irrigation system and the shrinkage of arable land. What these measures show is an attention to public behavior and a highly tuned normative intent. In this context, the warnings to Muslims in the public text on the bastions seem quite appropriate.

101. *MAE* 1:87 recounts the story of asking Samuel Flury to identify, by the style of the inscription, the group responsible for displaying the inscription because it did not contain a name or date. Flury decided that the writing belonged to Badr al-Jamālī, although some stylistic differences existed between the presentational mode of this inscription and all others sponsored by him. What convinced Creswell of the date of the inscription—the time of al-Ḥākim's adding the bastions to the minarets—was the bonding and fit of the marble into the stonework masonry of the bastion itself.

102. It seems that the *kiswa* Nāṣir-i Khusraw saw in Mecca that had been sent

by Imam al-Mustanṣir may have displayed a public text. Nāṣir-i Khusraw describes the *kiswa* as having three arches on each side and bands. *Safar-nāma*, 133.

103. Ibid., 77–79.

104. Sanders, *Fatimid Cairo*, esp. chaps. 3–5.

105. See chap. 4.

106. Mary Douglas and Baron Isherwood, *The World of Goods* (New York: Basic Books, 1976), 64–65.

107. For an interesting insight into these perspectives, Daniel Dayan and Elihu Katz, "Electronic Ceremonies: Television Performs a Royal Wedding," in *On Signs*, ed. Marshall Blonsky (Baltimore: The Johns Hopkins University Press, 1985), 16–32.

108. Exactly what *būqalamūn* was in terms of a cloth is not known. But some of the properties are known from a later description by Nāṣir-i Khusraw (*Safar-nāma*, 64). He states that in "Old Cairo they make all types of pottery—they make cups, bowls and plates . . . and paint them to resemble the *būqalamūn* so that different colors show depending on how the article was held" (*Safar-nāma*, 93). Apparently, then, *būqalamūn* was a fabric that appears to be a different color when the light strikes it differently. Edward Meader suggested to me that *būqalamūn* might have been what is known today as "shot-silk" and what in Italy in the eleventh century and later was known as "Saracen silk." See his "Costumes Worn by Christians in Michelangelo's Sistine Chapel," Il Convegno Internazionale di Studi Michaelangelo, La Cappella Sistina, March 1990 (forthcoming).

109. Khusraw, *Safar-nāma*, 82.

110. Ibid., 82–87.

111. Ibid., 66.

112. Ibid., 79. *Buq, dohol*, and *kaseh* are the instruments mentioned.

113. See especially Khusraw, *Khvān al-Ikhvān*, 178, 182 ff.

Notes to Chapter 4

1. While the basic periodization in this text is by the dates of the patriarchs, events effecting the Coptic community, and indeed the entire population of Miṣr are recorded. Ibn al-Muqaffaʿ, *History of the Patriarchs*, vol. 3, pt. 1, is relevant to this second half of Fatimid rule.

2. These problems have been well documented in the medieval sources—Muslim, Christian and Jewish. A basic list includes: al-Maqrīzī, *Ittiʿāẓ* 2:325–34, 273–76, 280–97; Ibn al-Muqaffaʿ, *History of the Patriarchs*, vol. 2, pt. 3, 290–315. Twentieth-century analysis of these times includes: De Lacy O'Leary, *A Short History of the Fatimid Khaliphate* (London: K. Paul, Trench, Trubner & Polk Ltd., 1923), 210–216; Bernard Lewis, "An Interpretation of Fatimid History," *Colloque International sur l'histoire du Caire, 27 mars–5 avril 1969* (Cairo: General Egyptian Book Organisation, 1972), 287–95.

3. Abū Najm Badr al-Jamālī al-Mustanṣirī al-Ismāʿīlī was *wazīr* from 1073–1094/466–87. Armenian in origin, he was a mamluk who was manumitted and joined the Fatimid army. He headed an Armenian contingent of troops loyal to him. Before coming to Cairo, he had been governor of Damascus. A convert

to Islam, his *madhhab*, or rite, is agreed upon by many writers as Ismāʿīlī. Still others insist he remained Armenian at heart.

4. Al-Maqrīzī, *Al-Khitat* 1:335.

5. William Hamblin, "The Fatimid Army during the Early Crusades" (Ph.D. diss., University of Michigan, 1984), 19–27.

6. See al-Maqrīzī, *Al-Khitat* 1:305, 337, 364. Some details about this period are found in *MAE* 1:119. For an interpretation of some of the effects of these problems, see Paula Sanders, "From Court Ceremony to Urban Language: Ceremonial in Fatimid Cairo and Fustat," in *The Islamic World from Classical to Modern Times*, ed. C. E. Bosworth, Charles Issawi, Roger Savory, and A. L. Udovitch (Princeton: Princeton University Press, 1989), 316–18.

7. In this fortification and expansion of the walls of Cairo he included the mosque of al-Ḥākim within the city. This was the moment that the great defensive gateways were built: Bāb al-Naṣr, Bāb-al-Futūḥ, and the Bāb Zuwayla as we know them today. Details on the archaeology and architecture of these gates and their enlargement are provided by *MAE*, vol. 1, chaps. 10, 11.

8. Al-Afḍal, Badr al-Jamālī's son, who succeeded his father as *wazīr*, moved his residence to Fusṭāṭ. Al-Maqrīzī, *Al-Khitat* 1:451–52; Ibn al-Muqaffaʿ, *History of the Patriarchs* 3:35–36.

9. Sanders, *Fatimid Cairo*, 73–82, 94–98, 127–34.

10. The distance to the mosque of Aḥmad ibn Ṭūlūn from the Bāb al-Futūḥ along the Great Street is about three kilometers (1.9 miles). Walking that distance today can be accomplished in about forty-five minutes. Processions, of course, must have covered the distance at a more stately pace.

11. See especially the map by Louis Massignon, plate 2, in his article "La cité des morts au Caire," *Bulletin de l'Institut Français d'Archaeologie Orientale* 57 (1958): 25–79.

12. This mosque is published in *MAE* 1:241–46; its exterior inscriptions are recorded in *MCIA*, Egypte 2:171; *RCEA* 8:146–47; for an interpretation different from the one offered below, see Caroline Williams, "The Cult of ʿAlid Saints in the Fatimid Monuments of Cairo, Part I: The Mosque of al-Aqmar," *Muqarnas* 1 (1983): 37–53. Another mosque, known as the Fruitsellers Mosque (al-Fakahani) was built by Imam-Caliph al-Ẓāhir in 1149/544 in the southern part of Cairo. Today only the doors are Fatimid. For the reign of this Imam-Caliph, see O'Leary, *A Short History;* and "Fatimids," *Encyclopaedia of Islam*.

13. This mosque as been published, albeit somewhat schematically, by Creswell, *MAE* 1:275–388. Its modern restoration was undertaken in difficult social circumstances and times, both local and international. World War II, for instance, halted the reconstruction before the Comité de Conservation des monuments de l'art Arabe solved the problem of the minaret. The original Fatimid minaret was destroyed in the earthquake of 1303/702. For all of the issues, see *Comité de Conservation des monuments de l'art Arabe, compte rendus des exercises*, 1911: 22; 1912: 81; 1913: 52; 1915–19: 550–51, 728–29; 1930–32: 96–98, 103–19; 1936–40: 249, 273–76; 1941–45: 56. See also Bierman, "Urban Memory," 1–12. The inscription on the exterior of this mosque was published in *RCEA*, no. 3231; *MCIA*, no. 46. This inscription is incomplete in these texts and has been published complete in *Journal Asiatique* (1891), plate 1; and in *Comité de Conservation* 1915–19:

41–42. These inscriptions were read by Youssouf Effendi Ahmed, Inspecteur du Services. The upper band of the inscription was totally effaced at the time the comité undertook the restorations. The state of this cornice inscription was conveyed to me by Dr. ʿAbd al-Azīz Sadiq from the last living survivor from the comité who worked on this reconstruction. Thus, while it is known that two bands of writing originally existed, the semantic content (even the aesthetic dimensions) of the upper band remain unknown to us today.

14. In 1089, Badr al-Jamālī replaced the original mausoleum built by a ninth century Abbasid governor, with a larger structure. Yusuf Ragib, "Al-Sayyida Nafisa, sa légende, son culte, et son cemetère," *Studia Islamica* 44 (1976): 68–69.

15. The extent of his power is most tellingly revealed in a collection of letters from Imam al-Mustanṣir, his mother, and others to the Sulayhids of the Yemen: ʿAbd al-Munʿim Majid, ed., *Al-Sijillāt al-mustanṣirīyya (Correspondence de l'Imam al-mostancir)* (Cairo, 1954). See also Husain F. al-Hamdani, "Letters of al-Mustansir bi'allah," *Bulletin of the School of Oriental and African Studies* 7 (1933–35): 307–24.

16. Al-Qalqashandī, *Ṣubḥ al-aʿsha* 4:270; *MCIA*, vol. 1, pt. 4, Arabia, 95. The Fatimid color was white; see chap. 1.

17. Geoffrey Khan, "The Historical Development of the Structure of Medieval Arabic Petitions," *Bulletin of the School of Oriental and African Studies* 53 (1990), pt. 1, 8–30, esp. 29, where he comments about the role of Badr al-Jamālī in setting the titulature and format.

18. Gaston Wiet, "Une nouvelle inscription Fatimide au Caire," *Journal Asiatique* (1961): 13–30. Some evidence suggests that this practice was also followed by others in the ruling group. For example, ʿAlī Pasha recorded a mosque (no longer extant, known only by this account) off the Great Street with a large plaque over the entry port bearing the name of ʿAmir Zaʿim al-Dawla Juwamard, a retainer of *wazīr* al-Afḍal, dated 1102/496. ʿAlī Pāshā Mubārak, *Al-Khitat al-tawfiqīyya al-jadīda*, 10 vols. (Cairo: Būlāq, 1306H), 2:85–86. He quotes al-Maqrīzī, *Al-Khitat* 2:85–86, the latter suggesting that people felt that this structure was a *mashhad* for Jaʿfar al-Sādiq.

19. *EMA* 2:336 and plate 97b. Creswell notes that the restoration could "not have amounted to much." But for the purposes here we know that he put a plaque on the outside of the structure on the southern entrance of the northeast side of the *ziyāda*.

20. *CIA*, Egypte, vol. 1, no. 11, plate 2; no. 1, plate 17. The marble plaque is 260 cm x 45 cm and displays four lines of Arabic. It was located on the northeast corner, by a main door which today is walled up.

21. Wiet, *CIA*, Egypte 1:31–32 discusses this inscription. Al-Maqrīzī, *Al-Khitat* 2:268 comments about the condition of the districts of al-Qaṭāʾiʿ and al-ʿAskar. See also Yaacov Lev, *State and Society in Fatimid Egypt* (Leiden: E. J. Brill, 1991), 99.

22. See *MAE*, vol. 1, chap. 10; ʿAlī Pāshā Mubārak, *Al-Khitat al-tawfiqīyya* 2:83, for the inscription on the Bāb al-Barqiyya near al-Azhar in the name of Badr al-Jamālī.

23. A marble plaque is recorded in *MCIA*, Egypt 1:63–64; *RCEA* 7:248–49. This action is mentioned in al-Maqrīzī, *Ittiʿāẓ* 3:449.

24. This inscription and the similar ones over the doorway into the mosque and on the interior of the Nilometer are known only through the description,

translation and drawings of Marcel in *Description de l'Egypte*, 128–29, 151–84. *MAE* 1:217–18 published an abbreviated synopsis of Marcel's work. The mosque was destroyed by French inattention barely a decade after Marcel recorded its existence.

The plaque, according to Marcel, was 70 cm. x 569 cm. (27 ½ in. x c.18 ½ ft.). Marcel notes that the only way to see this inscription was by boat.

25. This list of what is extant is but a small portion of what Badr al-Jamālī constructed. He, for instance, built a new palace for himself in Cairo so he did not have to live in the palace where preceding *wazīrs* had lived. Al-Maqrīzī, *Al-Khitat* 1:438, 461, 464.

26. Marcel, *Description de l'Egypte*, 128–29, 151–84.

27. Ibid., 196–98.

28. Ibid., 194.

29. This phrase, which while used in the Qur'ān to begin chapters, was nonetheless very commonly used in social practice. It is interesting to note that the first two words of this phrase, *bismi ʿlahi*, in the Name of God, were, of course, used by all Christian groups who spoke and wrote Arabic to begin their salutations, "In the name of God, . . . " which continued differently from the Muslim one, and often differently among Christian rites.

30. Q 9:18 (beginning only): "Only he can maintain the mosques of God who believes in God and the Last Day, and maintains the *ṣalāt* and pays the *zakāt* and fears God"; and part of 61:13: "Help from God and Proximate Victory."

31. See chap. 3.

32. For the abandonment of the processions, see Sanders, *Fatimid Cairo*, 67–69.

33. He was known by his title—al-Ma'mūn. His name was Abū ʿAbd Allāh ibn al-Ajall.

34. He was the son of a Fatimid *dāʿī* in Iraq and entered the service of the previous *wazīr*, al-Afḍal. He was arrested in 1125/519, accused of plotting against Imam al-Āmir, and executed (along with his brothers) in 1128.

35. Imam al-Āmir was put on the throne when he was five years old by *wazīr* al-Afḍal.

36. Ibn al-Ṣayrafī, *Al-Ishāra ila man nāla al-wizārah*, ed. ʿAbd Allah Mukhliṣ (Cairo, 1924), 11, editor's comment.

37. Al-Maqrīzī, *Al-Khitat* 2:169.

38. Ibn Muyassar, *Akhbār Miṣr*, 62.

39. See note 12 above.

40. The reconstruction of this mosque was completed in the 1990s. At that time the south third of the facade was built anew by replicating the extant third.

41. Nāṣir-i Khusraw, *Safar-nāma*, 133–34. Nāṣir-i Khusraw's description says that "below and above these bands the distance was the same, so that the height was divided into three parts." This tripartite equal division was not replicated on the facade. *Safar-nāma*, 133.

42. It might even be suggested that the gray-white stone medium of the facade which gave the name "al-Aqmar"—the moonlit—to the structure was equivalent to the white, Fatimid royal color of the covering.

43. For their appearance in Ifriqiya, see Jonathan M. Bloom, "The Origins of Fatimid Art," *Muqarnas* 3 (1985): 23–25.

44. Al-Maqrīzī, *al-Khitat* 2:451; ʿAlī Mubārak, *al-Khitat al-tawfiqīyya* 3:73.

45. *RCEA* 8:146–47; and in Williams, "Cult of ʿAlid Saints," 43.

46. This inscription is about twenty-four feet from ground level.

47. They are about four meters (13 ft.) above ground. These figures are approximate because ground level then is hard to fix.

48. See chap. 1.

49. Williams, "Cult of ʿAlid Saints," 44–46 presents a different view.

50. Consult Ibn al-Muqaffaʿ, *History of the Patriarchs*, vol. 3, pt. 1, for the many instances of comments about the appropriateness of the titles conferred on the *wazīr*.

51. Al-Maqrīzī, *Al-Khitat* 2: 388–90, 422, 430–32, 436–37, 445–50, 490–91, 502–3 lists thirteen feasts throughout the year in which the space was used: commemoration of the death of Husayn; ʿĀshūra (10 Muḥarram); the births of Ḥusayn (5 Rabīʿ I); Fāṭima (20 Jumāda II); ʿAlī (13 Rajab); Ḥassan (15 Ramadan); investiture of Ghadīr Kumm; birthday of reigning caliph—al-Āmir—(12 Muḥarram); *ʿīd al-fitr* (1 Shawwāl); *ʿīd al-aḍḥa* (10 Dhu'l Ḥijja); Beginning of year (1 Muḥarram); *maulid al-nabī* (12 Rabīʿ I); departure of the caravan to Mecca; plus, some celebration even of Christian feasts like the Epiphany. See also Doris Behrens-Abouseif, "The Facade of the Aqmar Mosque in the Context of Fatimid Ceremonial," *Muqarnas* 9 (1992): 29–38.

52. *MAE* 1:245, quoting al-Maqrīzī and Ibn ʿAbd al-Ẓāhir.

53. Sanders, *Fatimid Cairo*, 35, 93, 97.

54. Sanders, *Fatimid Cairo*, 35, 93, 97; al-Maqrīzī, *Al-Khitat* 1:466.

55. The Nizārīs were the branch of Ismāʿīlīs who ruled at the Alamut in the Elburz mountains. They were responsible for a variety of unsettling actions in the eastern Mediterranean in this period. It is even suggested that they were responsible eventually for the poisoning of Imam al-Mustaʿlī.

Williams, "Cult of ʿAlid Saints," 44–47, suggests that references to the Alids (the family of ʿAlī) on the al-Aqmar mosque were ways of combatting the Nizārī problems. Here I cannot understand the basis of her argument because the Nizārīs were also Alids. Thus, rather than being "combatted" by the Alid references on this structure, they would have been included by them. See also Christopher S. Taylor, "Reevaluating the Shiʿi Role in the Development of Monumental Funerary Architecture: The Case of Cairo," *Muqarnas* 9 (1992): 1–10.

56. Nizārīs formulated three levels of understanding. The *bātin* and the *ẓāhir* shared most salient aspects with the Fatimid Ismāʿīlīs. In the dimension of the *ḥaqīqa* the formulation was mostly theirs alone. This is expounded most clearly in Nāṣir al-Dīn Muḥammad b. Muḥammad al-Ṭūsī, *Rawḍat al-taslīm*, ed. and trans. W. Ivanow (Leiden: E. J. Brill, 1950).

57. At this time a significant contest exists over who is able to claim the past and in what way. Imam al-Ḥākim becomes an important pivot in the polemics of this period.

58. S. M. Stern, "The Succession to the Fatimid Imam al-Amir, the Claims of the Later Fatimids to the Imamate, and the Rise of Tayyibi Ismailism," *Oriens* 4 (1951): 194.

59. Bierman, "Art of the Public Text," 286.

60. Al-Maqrīzī, *Al-Khitat* 2:273, 291, 311 ff. details the beginnings in the shifts

in power at the Fatimid court that served as prelude to this incident; 2:156 mentions the *jihād* declared by Riḍwān; *Itti'āẓ* 3:159–60 provides the main account of the specific upheaval discussed here.

61. Stern, "The Succession," 193–235; Paula Sanders, "Claiming the Past: Ghadir Khumm and the Rise of Hafizi Historiography in Late Fatimid Egypt," *Studia Islamica* 75 (1992): 81–104.

62. Ṣalāḥ al-Dīn (Saladin), a Shāfi'ī, the *wazīr* of the last Fatimid Imam-Caliph, took advantage of yet another crisis moment in Fatimid Ismā'īlī succession to end at last the Fatimid Imamate-Caliphate in 1171/567. Ṣalāḥ al-Dīn put himself on the throne as Sultan, and firmly put Egypt under Sunni (Shāfi'ī and Mālikī predominantly) law and practice. See Andrew S. Ehrenkreutz, *Saladin* (Albany: State University of New York Press, 1972).

63. Bahrām al-Armanī served as *wazīr* from 1134–37/529–32. Many charges were leveled against him by the Muslim wealthy elite of favoring Armenian Christians specifically. He seems to have encouraged emigration of Armenians into Egypt and to have given Armenians positions in the government. The specific charge was that he favored Armenians over other qualified people, specifically over members of traditional (Muslim) scribal families, like that of Riḍwān's. In fact, there is some indication that Coptic Christians were not all that happy with the staffing. Al-Maqrīzī, *Itti'āẓ* 3:155–56; Marius Canard, "Un vizir Chrétien de l'époque Fatimite: L'Arménien Bahram," *Annales de l'Institut d'Études Orientales de la Faculté des Lettres d'Alger* 12 (1954): 84–113.

Some difference of opinion exists as to the background of Bahrām al-Armanī. For a detailed account of his coming to power, see al-Maqrīzī, *Itti'āẓ* 3:155–56. Ibn al-Muqaffa' states that Bahrām['s family] came from an area near Acre with Badr al-Jamālī and that Bahrām, himself, was a governor of a province in the Delta (*History of the Patriarchs*, vol. 3, pt. 1, 46).

64. Ibn al-Muqaffa', *History of the Patriarchs*, 3:48.

65. Riḍwān, according to al-Maqrīzī, considered overthrowing the Imamate-Caliphate in favor of a Sunni government. *Itti'āẓ* 3:142, 166.

66. This event was so critical in shifting the treatment of Christians in the Cairo urban area that Ibn al-Muqaffa' records it, *History of the Patriarchs*, vol. 3, pt. 1, 49–50, where he makes the point that Riḍwān was the first *wazīr* that barred Christians from office (along with burning churches and doubling the *jizya* [tax] on Christians as well as Jews).

67. He fled with his troops to his brother in Qus: al-Maqrīzī, *Itti'āẓ* 3:161–65; Ibn Muyassar, *Akhbār Miṣr*, 82–83; Abū Ṣāliḥ, *Churches and Monasteries*, 235–39, records that Bahrām became a monk in the White Monastery near Akhmim.

68. Claude Cahen, Yusuf Ragib, and Mustafa Anouar Taher, "L'achat et le waqf d'un grand domaine Égyptien par le vizir Fatimide Tala'i' b. Ruzzik," *Annales Islamologiques* 14 (1978): 6, where it suggests that his family was either Armenian or Kurdish in origin.

69. He was killed in 1160/556 by some soldiers as he was going to the palace. His daughter was married to the Imam-Caliph. See Ibn al-Muqaffa', *History of the Patriarchs*, vol. 3, pt. 1, 77–78. Al-Maqrīzī, *Itti'āẓ* 3:217.

70. See note 12 above.

71. Mentioned in *MAE* 1:275, quoting the same source.

72. The only full reading of the inscription is found in *Comité de Conservation des monuments de l'art Arabe, comptes rendus des exercices*, 1915–19 where it was read by Yousouf Effendi Ahmad, Inspecteur du Service. *RCEA*, no. 3231; *MCIA*, no. 46 are both incomplete. Reproduced in *Journal Asiatique* (1891). When the comité undertook the restoration of this mosque the writing in the other bands was severely effaced. In the upper band were Qur'anic quotations from 9:129 (*sūrat al-barā'a'*, The Immunity); 12:64 (*sūrat Yūsuf*, Joseph); and 3:188–95 (*sūrat āl 'Imrān*, The Family of Amran).

73. Ibn al-Muqaffa', *History of the Patriarchs*, 78–79, 46–47.

74. Ṣalāḥ al-Dīn for instance maintained the concentric circle design for a time to ensure as much as possible a smooth economic transition.

75. The only exception appears to be Najim al-Dīn Muḥammad ibn Masal who held the position of *wazīr* for two months in 1149/544 before he was killed.

76. Substantial citations from Ibn al-Ṭuwayr have been preserved in the *Tārikh al-duwal wa'l-mulūk* of Ibn al-Furat (d.c. 1500); however, these are found in the first three volumes, as yet unpublished and available only in a unique Vienna ms. which I have not seen.

77. Al-Maqrīzī, *Al-Khitat* 2:281. This is part of a description given by Ibn al-Ṭuwayr which begins on p. 280. No silk inscribed textiles from this period are yet known. The great majority of the textiles have silk woven bands but the ground of the textile is linen. Plenty of evidence exists for the collection, trade, wearing, and use as payment-in-kind of linen ground fabrics with silk inscribed borders. These records are found in profusion in the Geniza documents, and represent a nonofficial, yet wealthy segment of the population.

Consult S. D. Goitein, *Letters of Medieval Jewish Traders* (Princeton: Princeton University Press, 1973), and *Mediterranean Society*, vol. 1; Yedida Stillman, "Female Attire of Medieval Egypt: According to the Trousseau Lists and Cognate Material from the Cairo Geniza," (Ph.D. diss., University of Pennsylvania, 1972).

78. Al-Maqrīzī, *Al-Khitat* 1:444–48 gives the entire description; this specific ceremony is described and analyzed in Sanders, *Fatimid Cairo*, 88–93; it was mentioned by Marius Canard, "Le cérémonial Fatimite et le cérémonial Byzantin: Essai de comparison," *Byzantion* 21 (1951): 355–420.

79. *Sūra* 61, *sūrat al-Ṣaff* (The Ranks). Similar phrases, although not these exact words, are found in *sūra* 48: 1 and 3, [*sūrat al-Fatḥ* (The Victory)], where *fatḥan mubīnan* (clear victory) and *naṣran 'azīzan* (great help) are mentioned. These latter phrases appeared in the writing before the mihrab on the interior of the mosque of al-Ḥākim (see chap. 3). The exact phrase on these banners is also on the plaque with Badr al-Jamālī's name on the mosque on Roda Island, and the Nilometer.

80. *Ṭirāz* is the word used in al-Maqrīzī. What the word signified is hard to sort out. Etymologically speaking, the word means embroidery, but textiles from this period extant today displaying writing in which the semantic content states that they were fabricated in the *tirāz* workshops are not embroidered. They are woven. In seeking a referent for this term in the Middle Ages, and not in contemporary textile catalogues, we might speculate that *tirāz* referred to a category of border or band that had basic qualities recognized by all who saw them. These qualities may or may not have been vested in a specific technique (weaving or embroidery); they may have been in design or in color.

81. Al-Qalqashandī, *Ṣubḥ al-aʿsha* 3:473–74. This section, which starts on p. 472, begins with a coronation ceremony.

82. *Dībāj* usually is translated as brocade. Judging from the kinds of textiles described as *dībāj* the word seems to be used quite non-scientifically as it is today. Today, in popular use, brocade is used to describe textiles of many differing techniques but which display gold or silver threads, or both. Such may have been its use in the medieval period.

83. Al-Maqrīzī, *Al-Khitat* 2:423.

84. This brings up the tangential question of how the weaving establishments known as *tirāz al-khāṣṣa* (special or private) and *tirāz al-ʿāmma* (public or common) were related to production of cloth for court ceremonial. Undoubtedly, simply because of the quantity demanded, they must have been used to produce textiles for the processions and for the *kiswa* for the Kaʿba. But to date no record has come to light that clarifies these institutions. We know that during (at least one) New Year's ceremony the accounts of the *tirāz* were read out loud (al-Maqrīzī, *Al-Khitat* 1:442–44) which suggests that the income from these establishments went into the equivalent purses or treasuries, namely, the *bayt māl al-muslimīna* (or *al-ʿāmma*) and the *bayt māl al-khāṣṣ* (or for the maintenance of the palace). But what these establishments produced and who bought what is not clear.

85. There is possibly one other instance. The description in al-Qalqashandī of the troops cited in note 81 above (vol. 3, p. 273) begins by stating that "the two most important of the banners are those known as the Standard of Thanks (or Praise) to God (*liwaʾ āy al-ḥamd*)." Perhaps there were inscribed banners, too, although the description says "known" (*al-maʿrūfān*). It does not say the banners displayed words of "thanks."

86. This word can refer specifically to the cloth (or "clothing") which covers the Kaʿba in Mecca. In the Fatimid period, it was a term which referred also to the annual, occasionally more often than annual, distribution of clothing—or money for clothing—to the members of the ruling group, including the troops. What precisely these outfits looked like in this period is unclear from the texts. We are told small details, such as how certain groups wrapped turban ends around their chins, but no pattern emerges.

87. For these Ibn al-Maʾmūn leaves us a report, al-Maqrīzī, *Al-Khitat* 1:410. For the early period, see Ibn Tayy's account, al-Maqrīzī, *Ittiʿāẓ* 3:415; see also *Al-Khitat* 1:409. Here the account mentions robes of gold fabric encrusted with jewels and pearls.

88. Al-Maqrīzī, *Ittiʿāẓ* 3:51. As before, these descriptions are relatively general.

89. In Wehr's Dictionary (1961) "inscribed" is the meaning given for the word *manqūsh*. But in the medieval dictionaries, both Lane and the *Lisān al-ʿarab*, the word means "embellished" or "colored" when applied to cloth. Goitein talks about this term appearing in the Geniza records where Moses Maimonides replied to a Jew who asked about praying in front of a wall where the stucco decoration was *manqūsh*. Maimonides replied that "figures were certainly a distraction. . . . close one's eyes when praying." Goitein, *Mediterranean Society* 4:121.

90. For an accessible reference to the verses Qāḍī al-Nuʿmān mentions and their referent consult Marquet, "La pensée philosophique," 141–81.

91. This is an argument made by Cameron with regard to Byzantine ritual,

"The Construction of Court Ritual," 106–9. It is also an element in the argument of Bernard Cohen about official ceremony in Victorian India, "Representing Authority in Victorian India," in *The Invention of Tradition*, ed. Eric Hobsbawm and Terence Ranger (Cambridge: Cambridge University Press, 1992), 165–209. See esp., Sanders, *Fatimid Cairo*, 91, for a diagram of the New Year's procession that is a good example of the issue at hand.

92. Substantial changes took place in the tax system in the later Fatimid period. For a good basic understanding of the early period see Kosei Morimoto, *The Fiscal Administration of Egypt in the Early Islamic Period* (Kyoto: Dohosha, 1981), esp. 222–57, where the late Fatimid period is discussed. See also Eliyahu Ashtor, *A Social and Economic History of the Near East in the Middle Ages* (London: Collins, 1976)—this text should be used for "fact" rather than interpretation.

93. The question of color can be investigated in two ways. In *Mediterranean Society* 1:106–8, notes 41–60, Goitein tells us about the colors of fabrics ordered by the Geniza people as well as about dye stuffs and dyers. Alternately, we can look at the color analysis of fabrics from the area and period. Most of this latter work has been done by R. Pfister, "Matériaux pour servir au classement des textiles Egyptiens postérieurs a la Conquête Arabe," *Revue des Arts Asiatique* 10 (1936): 1–16, 78–85. Official Fatimid practices related to color are quite different from the coeval Byzantine practices where use of color is legislated.

94. See the section in this chapter on wazīr Bahrām al-Armanī.

95. White, *Monasteries*, pt. 3.

96. *MAE* 1:220–22.

97. *MAE*, vol. 1, plates 116–21 for a quick review of the arched mihrabs.

98. Yusuf Ragib's meticulous study—"Deux monuments Fatimides au pied du Muqattam," *Revue des Études Islamiques* 46 (1978): 91–117, esp. 97—states that this structure cannot be more specifically dated than to the last Fatimid century, a view with which I agree—contrary to the dates of Creswell, *MAE* 1:236; and Caroline Williams, "The Cult of ʿAlid Saints in the Fatimid Monuments of Cairo, Part 2: The Mausolea," *Muqarnas* 3 (1985): 39–60, 49.

99. See Bierman, "Art of the Public Text," 284–86 for an analysis of the writing in this building and the audience it addressed.

100. Occasionally the name of the donor with one or two titles is found inside: e.g., the mihrab al-Afḍal gave to the Aḥmad ibn Ṭūlūn mosque. *MAE* 1:220–22.

101. See especially the persuasive dissertation of Christopher S. Taylor, "The Cult of the Saints in Late Medieval Egypt" (Ph.D. diss., Princeton, 1989), chap. 1, for an assessment of religious piety at this period, and "Reevaluating Shīʿi Role in Development of Monumental Funerary Architecture," pp. 1–10. See also Ibn Muyassar, *Akhbār Miṣr* and al-Maqrīzī, *Al-Khitat*, for multiple references for the rebuilding and repair of the mausolea throughout all of the urban area. Clearly these structures were constantly being upgraded, to use a late twentieth century term.

102. The use of officially sponsored writing in this manner went in tandem with other practices of expanding a solid Muslim base within the ruling group and in the urban area that supported it. *Wazīrs* allowed some mosques to restore the Sunni call to prayer; and the position of the Chief Judge (*qāḍī al-quḍāt*) was

shared by representatives of more than one *madhhab*. Adel Allouche, "The Establishment of Four Chief Judgeships in Fatimid Egypt," *Journal of the American Oriental Society* 105 (1985): 317–20.

103. ʿAlī ibn Abī Bakr al-Harāwī, *Kitāb al-Ishārāt ila maʿrifat al-ziyārāt*, trans. Janine Sourdel-Thomine (Damascus, 1953), *Guide des lieux de pélerinage*. Al-Harāwī visited Cairo in 1176–77 just after the fall of the Fatimids and the rise to power of their last *wazīr* Ṣalāḥ al-Dīn. He lists well over a hundred shrines or commemorative structures for various kinds of people important in Muslim culture—for example, jurists such as al-Shāfiʿī, Qurʾān reciters, as well as holy people who were not members of the family of the Prophet. See also Yusuf Ragib, "Essai d'inventaire chronologique des guides à l'usage des pélerins du Caire," *Revue des Études Islamiques* 41 (1973): 259–80.

Notes to Afterword

1. Al-Maqrīzī states that Riḍwān, the Sunni *wazīr* of Imam-Caliph al-Ḥāfiẓ, considered overthrowing him. *Ittiʿāẓ* 3:142.

2. *CIA*, Egypte, vol. 1, appendix, 726–27; *MAE*, vol. 2, plate 7c.

3. *CIA*, Egypte 1:80–85. *MAE*, vol. 2, fig. 15 shows the location of the inscriptions.

4. Bierman, "Urban Memory," 1–12.

5. The al-Ḥākim mosque retains the exterior from the period of Badr al-Jamālī. Its current interior is a modified version of that period. The exterior of the al-Azhar mosque is greatly layered and modified. See ibid., 3.

6. Ibid., 4; German Institute of Archaeology Cairo, *Mausoleum des Sultans as-Saleh Nagm ad-Dīn Ayyūb* (Cairo, 1993), and *Minaret of Madrasa of as-Saleh Nagm ad-Dīn Ayyūb*, report on the restoration projects of the German Institute of Archaeology in the District of Gamaliya (n.p., n.d.).

7. The *madrasa* of al-Zahir Baybars is no longer extant.

8. The Ayyubids built on the west side too, but the structures are not extant today.

9. He became Sultan twice: 1294–95 and 1299–1309/693–94 and 698–708.

10. See Nairy Hampikian, "Restoration of the Mausoleum of al-Salih Najim al-Din Ayyub," in Bacharach, *Islamic Monuments*, 46–58; *MAE* 2: 94–103.

11. *RCEA*, vol. 2, nos. 4219, 4220; *CIA*, Egypte 1:576.

12. Sultan Qalāʾūn's complex also included a hospital—but it was behind, not flanking the street. His family and retainers were avid builders. See Caroline Williams, "The Mosque of Sitt Hadaq," *Muqarnas* 11 (1994): 55–56.

13. *RCEA*, vol. 13, Qalāʾūn nos. 4850; 4852, 4853; *CIA*, Egypt, vol. 1, nos. 83, 84, plate 25; al-Nāṣir Muḥammad, *RCEA*, vol. 13, no. 5006; *CIA*, Egypte, vol. 1, nos. 1, 133, 762.

14. *MAE*, vol. 2, plate 96.

15. For an easy reference to the function and social role of the structures discussed here, see Carl F. Petry, *The Civilian Elite of Cairo in the Later Middle Ages* (Princeton: Princeton University Press, 1981), appendix 1.

16. See chap. 4.

17. *MAE*, vol. 2, plates 104b, 104c. This structure is discussed also in Richard Parker, Robin Sabin, and Caroline Williams, *Islamic Monuments in Cairo, A Practical Guide*, 3rd edition (Cairo, 1985) where there is handy reference to the inscription.

18. Bierman, "Urban Memory," 8.

19. We need to consider the facades of both the mosque and synagogue before their recent expansions and restorations.

Bibliography

Abu-Lughod, Janet. *Cairo: 1001 Years of the City Victorious*. Princeton: Princeton University Press, 1971.

Abu Salih al-Armani. *The Churches and Monasteries of Egypt and Some Neighbouring Countries*. Translated by B. T. A. Evetts. Oxford: The Clarendon Press, 1895.

Alhazen. *The Optics of Ibn al Haytham*. Translated by A. I. Sabra. 2 vols. London: Warburg Institute, University of London, 1989.

ʿAlī Pāshā Mubārak. *Al-Khitat al-tawfiqīyya al-jadīda*. 10 vols. Cairo: Būlāq, 1306H.

Allouche, Adel. "The Establishment of Four Chief Judgeships in Fatimid Egypt." *Journal of the American Oriental Society* 105 (1985): 317–20.

Arts Council of Great Britain. *The Arts of Islam*. London: Westerham Press Ltd. Council of Great Britain, 1976.

Ashtor, Eliyahu. *A Social and Economic History of the Near East in the Middle Ages*. London: Collins, 1976.

Avi-Yonah, Michael. "The Ancient Synagogue at Caesarea: Preliminary Report." *Bulletin Rabinowitz* 3 (1960): 44–48.

———. "Ancient Synagogues." *Ariel* 32 (1973): 29–43.

———. "Une école de mosaïque à Gaza au sixième siècle." In *La mosaïque greco-romaine II*, IIe Colloque International pour l'étude de la mosaïque antique, Vienna, 1971. Paris: A. & J. Picard, 1975.

———. "La mosaïque juive dans les relations avec la mosaïque classique." In *La mosaïque greco-romaine*, Colloque International sur la mosaïque greco-romaine, Paris, 1963. Paris: Editions du Centre National de la Recherche Scientifique, 1965.

Avi-Yonah, M., and M. Makhouly. "A Sixth-Century Synagogue at 'Isfiya." *Quarterly Department of Antiquities Palestine* 3 (1933): 118–31.

Avigad, Nahman. *Discovering Jerusalem*. Nashville, Camden, New York: Thomas Nelson Publishers, 1980.

Avni, G., and S. Rosen. "Negev Emergency Survey—1983/1985." *Excavations and Surveys in Israel* 4 (1985): 86–87.

Bacharach, Jere L. "Administrative Complexes, Palaces, and Citadels: Changes in the Loci of Medieval Muslim Rule." In *The Ottoman City and Its Parts*, edited by Irene A. Bierman, Rifaʿat A. Abou-El-Haj, and Donald Preziosi. New Rochelle: A. D. Caratzas, 1991.

———. "African Military Slaves in the Medieval Middle East: The Case of Iraq (869–955) and Egypt (868–1171)." *International Journal of Middle East Studies* 13 (1981): 471–95.

———, ed. *The Restoration and Conservation of Islamic Monuments in Egypt*. Cairo: American University Press, 1995.

Bakhit, M. Adnan, and Robert Schick, eds. *The History of the Bilad al-Sham During the Umayyad Period*. Fourth International Conference of the History of Bilad al-Sham, 1987. Amman: University of Jordan and Yarmouk University, 1989.

Balog, Paul. "Monnaies Islamiques rare Fatimites et Ayyubites." *Bulletin de l'Institut d'Egypte* 36 (1953–54): 327–41.

Baramki, D. "Al-nuqush al-ʿarabiyya fī al-bādiya al-sūriyya." *Al-Abḥāth* 17 (1964): 317–46.

Barth, Fredrik, ed. *Ethnic Groups and Boundaries, The Social Organization of Difference*. London: George Allen Unwin, 1969.

Bates, Michael. "History, Geography and Numismatics in the First Century of Islamic Coinage." *Revue Suisse de Numismatique* 65 (1986): 231–63.

———. "Islamic Numismatics." *Middle East Studies Association Bulletin* 12, no. 2 (1978): 1–6; 12, no. 3 (1978): 2–18; 13, no. 1 (1979): 3–21; 13, no. 2 (1979): 1–9.

———. "Shiʿi Inscriptions on Buyid and Fatimid Coins." Paper delivered at the Annual Meeting of the Middle East Studies Association, Chicago, November 1983.

Bateson, Gregory. *Steps to an Ecology of the Mind*. New York: Ballantine Books, 1972.

Baxandall, Michael. *Painting and Experience in Fifteenth-Century Italy*. Oxford: Oxford University Press, 1972.

Behrens-Abouseif, Doris. "The Facade of the Aqmar Mosque in the Context of Fatimid Ceremonial." *Muqarnas* 9 (1992): 29–38.

Ben-Dov, Meir. *In the Shadow of the Temple*. Translated by Ina Friedman. New York: Harper & Row, 1982.

Bergman, Ingrid. *Late Nubian Textiles*. Vol. 8 of *The Scandinavian Joint Expedition to Sudanese Nubia*. Stockholm: Esselte Studium, 1975.

Bianquis, Thierry. *Damas et la Syrie sous la domination Fatimide (395–468/969–1072)*. 2 vols. Damascus: The University of Paris, 1986.

Bierman, Irene A. "Art and Politics: The Impact of Fatimid Uses of *Tiraz* Fabrics." Ph.D. diss., University of Chicago, 1980.

———. "The Art of the Public Text: Medieval Rule." In *World Art Themes of Unity in Diversity, Acts of the 26th International Congress of the History of Art*, edited by Irving Lavin. 3 vols. Philadelphia: Penn State University Press, 1989.

———. "Cairo: A Parallax of Judgment." In *Identities in Medieval Cairo*, edited by Irene A. Bierman. Working Papers, Gustav E. von Grunebaum Center for Near Eastern Studies. Los Angeles: Gustav E. von Grunebaum Center for Near Eastern Studies, 1995.

———. "Near East Gallery." *Arts of Asia* 22, no. 3 (May–June 1992): 120–27.

———. "Urban Memory and the Preservation of Monuments." In *The Restoration and Conservation of Islamic Monuments in Egypt*, edited by Jere L. Bacharach. Cairo: American University Press, 1995.

Bierman, Irene A., Rifaʿat A. Abou-El-Haj, and Donald Preziosi, eds. *The Ottoman City and Its Parts*. New Rochelle: A. D. Caratzas, 1991.

Bikhazi, Ramzi Jibran. "The Struggle for Syria and Mesopotamia (330–58/941–69) As Reflected on Hamdanid and Ikhshidid Coins." *American Numismatic Society Museum Notes* 28 (1983): 137–73.

Blonsky, Marshall, ed. *On Signs*. Baltimore: The Johns Hopkins University Press, 1985.

Bloom, Jonathan M. "Al-Ma'mun's Blue Koran?" *Revue des Études Islamiques* 54 (1986): 59–65.

———. "The Mosque of al-Hakim in Cairo." *Muqarnas* 1 (1983): 15–36.

———. "The Origins of Fatimid Art." *Muqarnas* 3 (1985): 23–25.

Bosworth, C. E., Charles Issawi, Roger Savory, and A. L. Udovitch, eds. *The Islamic World from Classical to Modern Times*. Princeton: Princeton University Press, 1989.

Brish, Klaus. "Das Omayyadische Schloss in Usais." *Mitteilungen des Deutschen Archaologischen Instituts Abteilung Kairo* 19 (1963): 147–49.

Britton, Nancy Pence. *A Study of Some Early Islamic Textiles in the Museum of Fine Arts*. Boston: Museum of Fine Arts, 1938.

Broadbent, Geoffrey, Richard Bunt, and Charles Jenks, eds. *Signs, Symbols and Architecture*. Chichester and New York: John Wiley & Sons, 1980.

Brown, Peter R. L. "Art and Society in Late Antiquity." In *The Age of Spirituality*, edited by Kurt Weitzmann. New York: Metropolitan Museum of Art and Princeton Press, 1980.

Bulliet, R. *Conversion to Islam in the Medieval Period, An Essay in Quantitative History*. Cambridge & London: Harvard University Press, 1979.

Cahen, Claude, Yusuf Ragib, and Mustafa Anouar Taher. "L'achat et le waqf d'un grand domaine Égyptien par le vizir Fatimide Talaʾiʿ b. Ruzzik." *Annales Islamologiques* 14 (1978): 1–21.

Cameron, Averil. "The Construction of Court Ritual: The Byzantine Book of Ceremonies." In *Rituals of Royalty: Power and Ceremonial in Traditional Societies*, edited by David Cannadine and Simon Price. Cambridge and London: Cambridge University Press, 1987.

Canard, Marius. "Le cérémonial Fatimite et le cérémonial Byzantin: Essai de comparison." *Byzantion* 21 (1951): 355–420.

———. "Un vizir Chrétien de l'époque Fatimite: L'Arménien Bahram." *Annales de l'Institut d'Études Orientales de la Faculté des Lettres d'Alger* 12 (1954): 84–113.

Cannadine, David, and Simon Price, eds. *Rituals of Royalty: Power and Ceremonial in Traditional Societies*. Cambridge and London: Cambridge University Press, 1987.

Carruthers, Mary. *The Book of Memory, A Study of Memory in Medieval Culture*. Cambridge: Cambridge University Press, 1990.

Carter, Michael. "Language, Truth and Power in Classical Islam." Paper delivered at American Research Center in Egypt, February 1993.

Chelkowski, Peter J, ed. *Studies in the Art and Literature of the Near East in Honor of Richard Ettinghausen*. Salt Lake City: Middle East Center, University of Utah, 1974.

Chiat, Marilyn Joyce Segal. *Handbook of Synagogue Architecture*. Brown University Judaic Studies, no. 29. Chico: Scholars Press, 1982.

Christie, A. H. "The Development of Ornament from Arabic Script." *Burlington Magazine* 40 (1922): 287–92.

Clanchy, M. T. *From Memory to Written Record, 1066–1307*. London: Arnold, 1979.

Cohen, Bernard. "Representing Authority in Victorian India." In *The Invention of Tradition*, edited by Eric Hobsbawm and Terence Ranger. Cambridge: Cambridge University Press, 1992.

Combe, E(tienne). "Tissus Fatimides du Musée Benaki." In *Mélanges Maspero*. 3 vols. Cairo: L'Institut français d'archaéologie orientale, 1934.

Comité de Conservation des monuments de l'art Arabe, compte rendus des exercises, 1911–1913, 1915–19, 1930–32, 1936–40, 1941–45.

Conkey, Margaret. "Boundedness in Art and Society." In *Symbolic and Structural Archaeology*, edited by Ian Hodder. Cambridge: Cambridge University Press, 1982.

Corbin, H. *Trilogie Ismaélienne*. Tehran-Paris: Department of Iranology, Institute Franco-Iranian, 1961.

Coughenour, Robert A. "The Fifteen Churches of Umm el-Jimal." In *The Umm el-Jimal Excavations*, edited by Berton De Vries. Oxford: British Archaeological Reports, forthcoming.

Creswell, K. A. C. *Early Muslim Architecture*. New York: Hacker Art Books, 1979.

——. *The Muslim Architecture of Egypt*. 2 vols. Oxford: Clarendon Press, 1952–59.

Crowfoot, J. W. *Early Churches in Palestine*. London: Oxford University Press, 1941.

Curtin, Philip D. *Cross-Cultural Trade in World History*. Cambridge and New York: Cambridge University Press, 1984.

Dachraoui, Farhat. *Califat Fatimide au Maghreb*. Tunis: n.p., 1981.

Daftary, Farhad. *The Isma'ilis: Their History and Doctrine*. Cambridge: Cambridge University Press, 1990.

Dan, Joseph. "Midrash and the Dawn of Kabbalah." In *Midrash and Literature*, edited by Geoffrey H. Hartman and Sanford Budick. New Haven: Yale University Press, 1986.

Dauphin, Claudine. "Development of the Inhabited Scroll, Architectural Sculpture and Mosaic Art from Late Imperial Times to the Seventh Century A.D." *Levant* 19 (1987): 183–212.

——. "New Method of Studying Early Byzantine Mosaic Pavements (coding and a computed cluster analysis) with Special Reference to the Levant." *Levant* 8 (1976): 113–49.

Davis, Natalie Zemon. "The Sacred and the Body Social in Sixteenth-Century Lyon." *Past and Present* 90 (1981): 40–70.

Day, Florence E. "Dated Tiraz in the Collection of the University of Michigan." *Ars Islamica* 4 (1937): 420–26.

Dayan, Daniel, and Elihu Katz. "Electronic Ceremonies: Television Performs a Royal Wedding." In *On Signs*, edited by Marshall Blonsky. Baltimore: The Johns Hopkins University Press, 1985.

De Vries, Berton. "Urbanization in the Basalt Region of North Jordan in Late Antiquity: The Case of Umm el-Jimal." In *Studies in the History and Archaeology of Jordan II*, edited by Adnan Hadidi. Amman: Department of Antiquities Jordan, 1985.

——, ed. *The Umm el-Jimal Excavations*. Oxford: British Archaeological Reports, forthcoming.

Dennett, D. *Conversion and Poll Tax in Early Islam*. Cambridge: Harvard University Press, 1950.

Der Nersessian, Sirarpie. *Armenian Art*. London: Thames and Hudson, 1977.

Derrida, Jacques. *Writing and Difference*. Translated and with an introduction by Alan Bass. London: Routledge, Kegan Paul, 1978.

Desreumaus, A. "The Birth of a New Aramaic Script in the Bilad al-Sham at the End of the Byzantine Period." In *The History of the Bilad al-Sham during the Umayyad Period*, edited by M. Adnan Bakhit and Robert Schick. Fourth International Conference of the History of Bilad al-Sham, 1987. Amman: University of Jordan and Yarmouk University, 1989.

Diehl, Charles. *Constantinople*. Paris: H. Laurens, 1924.

——. "Les mosaïques de Sainte-Sophie de Salonique." In *Académie des inscriptions et belles-lettres monuments et mémoires*. Paris: Fondation Piot, 1909.

Diehl, Charles, M. Tourneau, and H. Saladin. *Les monuments Chrétiens de Salonique*. Paris: Ernest Leroux, 1918.

Dodd, Erica Cruikshank. "The Image of the Word." *Berytus* 18 (1969): 35–73.

Douglas, Mary, and Baron Isherwood. *The World of Goods*. New York: Basic Books, 1976.

Eco, Umberto. "Function and Sign: The Semiotics of Architecture." In *Signs, Symbols and Architecture*, edited by Geoffrey Broadbent, Richard Bunt, and Charles Jenks. Chichester and New York: John Wiley & Sons, 1980.

Ehrenkreutz, Andrew S. *Saladin*. Albany: State University of New York Press, 1972.

Ehrenkreutz, Andrew S., and Gene W. Heck. "Additional Evidence of the Fatimid Use of Dinars for Propaganda Purposes." In *Studies in Islamic History and Civilization in Honour of Professor David Ayalon*, edited by M. Sharon. Jerusalem and Leiden: E. J. Brill, 1986.

Ettinghausen, Richard. "Arabic Epigraphy: Communication or Symbolic Affirmation." In *Near Eastern Numismatics, Iconography, Epigraphy and History: Studies in Honor of George C. Miles*, edited by Dickran K. Kouymijian. Beirut: American University of Beirut, 1974.

Fine, Steven. "Synagogue and Sanctity: The Late Antique Palestinian Synagogue as a 'Holy Place.'" Ph.D. diss., Hebrew University, 1993.

Flury, Samuel. "Le décor épigraphique des monuments Fatimides du Caire." *Syrie* 17 (1936): 365–76.

——. *Die ornamente der Hakim-und Asher-moschee*. Heidelberg: Carl Winters, 1912.

Garcin, Jean-Claude. "Pour un recours a l'histoire de l'espace vécu dans l'étude de l'Egypte Arabe." *Annales: Economies, Société, Civilizations* 30 (1980): 437–65.

——. "Typonymie et topographie urbaines mediévales à Fustat." *Journal of the Economic and Social History of the Orient* 27 (July 1984): 113–35.

German Institute of Archaeology Cairo. *Mausoleum des Sultans as-Saleh Nagm ad-Dīn Ayyūb*. Cairo, 1993.

——. *Minaret of Madrasa of as-Saleh Nagm ad-Dīn Ayyūb*. N.p., n.d.

Gervers, Veronica, ed. *Studies of Textile History in Memory of Harold B. Burnham*. Toronto: Royal Ontario Museum, 1977.

Gibb, H. A. R. "The Arabic Sources for the Life of Saladin." *Speculum* 25 (1950): 58–72.

Goitein, S. D. *Letters of Medieval Jewish Traders*. Princeton: Princeton University Press, 1973.

——. *A Mediterranean Society*. 6 vols. Berkeley, Los Angeles, London: University of California Press, 1983.

Golombek, Lisa, and Veronica Gervers. "*Tiraz* Fabrics in the Royal Ontario Museum." In *Studies of Textile History in Memory of Harold B. Burnham*, edited by Veronica Gervers. Toronto: Royal Ontario Museum, 1977.

Gombrich, E. H. *Art and Illusion: A Study in the Psychology of Pictorial Representation, The A. W. Mellon Lectures in the Fine Arts*. Bollingen Series 35. Princeton: Princeton University Press, 1956.

——. *Meditations on a Hobby Horse and Other Essays on the Theory of Art*. London: Phaidon Publishers, 1963.

——. *Norm and Form: Studies in the Art of the Renaissance I*. London: Phaidon Publishers, 1966.

Goody, Jack. *The Interface Between the Written and the Oral*. Cambridge: Cambridge University Press, 1987.

——. *The Logic of Writing and the Organization of Society*. Cambridge: Cambridge University Press, 1986.

——. "Writing, Religion and Revolt in Bahia." *Visible Language* 20, no. 3 (1986): 318–43.

Goody, Jack, and Ian Watt. "The Consequences of Literacy." *Comparative Studies in Society and History* 5, no. 3. (1963): 304–45.

Grabar, A. "Recherches sur les sources juives de l'art Paléochretien." *Cahiers Archéologiques* 12 (1962).

——. "Un thème de l'iconographie Chrétienne: L'oiseau dans la cage." *Cahiers Archéologiques* 16 (1966): 9–16.

Grabar, Oleg. "Grafitti or Proclamations: Why Write on Buildings?" Paper delivered at the Annual Meeting of the College Art Association, Philadelphia, 1983.

——. "Notes sur les cérémonies Umayyades." In *Studies in Memory of Gaston Wiet*, edited by Myriam Rosen-Ayalon. Jerusalem: Institute of Asian and African Studies, Hebrew University of Jerusalem, 1977.

——. "Pictures on Commentaries: The Illustrations of the *Maqamat* of al-Hariri." In *Studies in the Art and Literature of the Near East in Honor of*

Richard Ettinghausen, edited by Peter J. Chelkowski. Salt Lake City: Middle East Center, University of Utah, 1974.

———. "Symbols and Signs in Islamic Architecture." *Architecture as Symbol and Self-Identity*. Proceedings of Seminar Four in the Series Architectural Transformations in the Islamic World, Fez, Morocco, October 9–12, 1979. Philadelphia: The Aga Khan Award for Architecture, c. 1980.

———. "The Umayyad Dome of the Rock in Jerusalem." *Ars Orientalis* 3 (1959): 51–84.

Grabar, Oleg, R. Holod, J. Knustad, and W. Trousdale. *City in the Desert, Qasr al-Hayr East*. 2 vols. Cambridge: Harvard University Press, 1978.

Gray, Basil, ed. *The Arts of the Book in Central Asia*. Paris: UNESCO-Shambala Publications, 1979.

Grierson, P. "The Monetary Reforms of ʿAbd al-Malik." *Journal of the Economic and Social History of the Orient* 3 (1960): 241–64.

Grohmann, Adolph. "The Origin and Development of Floriated Kufic." *Ars Orientalis* 2 (1957): 183–213.

———. "Tiraz." *Encyclopaedia of Islam*. 1st ed. Leiden: E. J. Brill, 1913–36.

Gutman, J. *The Image and the Word: Confrontations in Judaism, Christianity and Islam*. American Academy of Religion and Society of Biblical Literature, Religion and the Arts, Series 4. Missoula, Mont.: Scholars Press for the American Academy of Religion, 1977.

Hachlili, Rachel. "The Zodiac in Ancient Jewish Art: Representations and Signification." *Bulletin of the American School of Oriental Research* 228 (December 1977): 61–77.

Hadidi, Adnan, ed. *Studies in the History and Archaeology of Jordan II*. Amman: Department of Antiquities Jordan, 1985.

Halm, Heinz. *Kosmologie und Heilslehre der frühen Ismaʾiliya*. Weisbaden: Franz Steiner, 1978.

———."Der Treühander Gottes: Die Edikte des Kalifen al-Hakim." *Der Islam* 63 (1986): 11–72.

Hamblin, William. "The Fatimid Army during the Early Crusades." Ph.D. diss., University of Michigan, 1984.

al-Hamdani, Husain F. "Letters of al-Mustansir biʾallah." *Bulletin of the School of Oriental and African Studies* 7 (1933–35): 307–24.

———. "Some Unknown Ismaʿili Authors and Their Works." *Journal of the Royal Asiatic Society* (1933): 359–78.

Hampikian, Nairy. "Restoration of the Mausoleum of al-Salih Najim al-Din Ayyub." In *The Restoration and Conservation of Islamic Monuments in Egypt*, edited by Jere L. Bacharach. Cairo: American University Press, 1995.

al-Harāwī, ʿAlī ibn Abī Bakr. *Kitāb al-Ishārāt ila maʿrifat al-ziyārāt*. Translated by Janine Sourdel-Thomine. Damascus, 1953.

Hartman, Geoffrey H. and Sanford Budick, eds. *Midrash and Literature*. New Haven: Yale University Press, 1986.

Hawkes, Terence. *Structuralism and Semiotics*. Berkeley and Los Angeles: University of California Press, 1977.

Hilāl ibn al-Muḥassin al-Ṣābiʾ. *Rusūm dār al-khilāfah*. Baghdad: Matbaʾat al-ʿAni, 1964.

Hjort, O. "L'oiseau dans la cage: Exemples mediévaux à Rome." *Cahiers Archéologiques* 18 (1968): 21–31.

Hobsbawm, Eric, and Terence Ranger, eds. *The Invention of Tradition.* Cambridge: Cambridge University Press, 1992.

Hodder, Ian, ed. *Symbolic and Structural Archaeology.* Cambridge: Cambridge University Press, 1982.

Huettenmeister, Frowald, and Gottfried Reeg. *Die Antiken Synagogen in Israel.* 2 vols. Wiesbaden: Reichert, 1977.

Ibn ʿAbd al-Hadi, Yūsuf. *Thimār al-masājid fī dhikr al-masājid.* Edited by Asʿad Talas. Beirut: n.p., 1943.

Ibn ʿAbd Rabbihi. *Al-ʿIqd al-Farīd.* 7 vols. Cairo: Būlāq, 1332H.

Ibn al-Jawzī. *Al-Muntaẓam fī tārīkh al-mulūk wa-l-umam.* 18 vols. Beirut: Dār al-Kutub, 1992.

Ibn al-Muqaffaʿ, Sawirus. *History of the Patriarchs of the Egyptian Church.* Translated and annotated by Antoine Khater and O. H. E. Burmester. 4 vols. Cairo: Societé de l'Archéologie, 1943.

Ibn Muyassar. *Akhbār Miṣr (Annales d'Egypte).* Edited by Henri Masse. Cairo: Impr. de l'Institute français d'archéologie orientale, 1919.

Ibn al-Ṣayrafī. *Al-Ishāra ila man nāla al-wizārah.* Edited by ʿAbd Allah Mukhliṣ. Cairo, 1924.

Institut français d'archéologie orientale du Caire. *Répertoire chronologique d'épigraphie Arabe.* Le Caire: Impr. de l'Institut français d'archéologie, 1931–91.

Isaac, Benjamin, and Israel Roll. *Roman Roads in Judea I: The Legio-Scythopolis Road.* BAR International Series 141. BAR: Oxford, 1982.

Jakobson, Roman. "Closing Statement: Linguistics and Poetics." In *Style in Language*, edited by Thomas A. Sebeok. Cambridge: MIT Press, 1960.

Jameson, Frederic. *The Prison-House of Language.* Princeton: Princeton University Press, 1972.

Kendrick, A. F. *Catalogue of Muhammadan Textiles of the Medieval Period.* London: Victoria and Albert Museum, 1924.

———. *Catalogue of the Textiles from the Burying-Grounds in Egypt.* 3 vols. London: Victoria and Albert Museum, 1924.

Kessler, Cristel. "ʿAbd al-Malik's Inscription in the Dome of the Rock: A Reconsideration." *Journal of the Royal Asiatic Society* (1970): 1–14.

Khan, Geoffrey. "The Historical Development of the Structure of Medieval Arabic Petitions." *Bulletin of the School of Oriental and African Studies* 53 (1990): 8–30.

King, Geoffrey, C. J. Lenzen, and Gary O. Rollefson. "Survey of Byzantine and Islamic Sites in Jordan Second Season Report." *Annual of the Department of Antiquities Jordan* 27 (1983): 385–436.

al-Kirmānī, Ḥamīd al-Dīn Aḥmad ibn ʿAbd Allah. *Rāḥat al-ʿaql* (Peace of Mind). Edited by M. Kamil Hussein and M. Mustafa Hilmy. Cairo: Dar al-Fiqr, 1953.

Kouymijian, Dickran, ed. *Near Eastern Numismatics, Iconography, Epigraphy and History: Studies in Honor of George C. Miles.* Beirut: American University of Beirut, 1974.

Kraeling, Carl H., ed. *Gerasa City of the Decapolis*. New Haven: American Schools of Oriental Research, 1938.

Kress, Hedge, and Gunther Kress. *Social Semiotics*. Ithaca: Cornell University Press, 1988.

Kubiak, Wladyslaw. *Al-Fustat: Its Foundation and Early Urban Development*. Warsaw: Wydawn, Universytetu Warszawskiego, 1982.

Kuhnel, Ernst. *Catalogue of Dated Tiraz Fabrics*. With textile analysis by Louise Bellinger. Washington, D.C.: The Textile Museum, 1952.

———. *Islamische Stoffe*. Berlin: Ernst Wasmuth, 1927.

Kuwait National Museum. *Masahif Sanaʿ*. Kuwait, 1985.

Lamm, Carl Johan. "Dated or Datable Tiraz in Sweden." *Le Monde Oriental* 32 (1938).

Lane-Poole, Stanley. *Catalogue of Arabic Glass Weights in the British Museum*. Paris: Rollin, 1891.

Lapidus, I. "The Conversion of Egypt to Islam." *Israel Oriental Studies* 2 (1972): 256–57.

Launois, A. "Catalogue des monaies Fatimites entrées au Cabinet des Médailles depuis 1896." *Bulletin d'Études Orientales* 24 (1971): 19–53.

Lavin, Irving, ed. *World Art Themes of Unity in Diversity, Acts of the 26th International Congress of the History of Art*. 3 vols. Philadelphia: Penn State University Press, 1989.

Lechtman, Heather. "Style in Technology—Some Early Thoughts." In *Material Culture, Style, Organization, and Dynamics of Technology*, edited by Heather Lechtman and Robert S. Merrill. Cambridge, Mass.: West Publishing, 1976.

Lechtman, Heather, and Robert S. Merrill, eds. *Material Culture, Style, Organization, and Dynamics of Technology*. Cambridge, Mass.: West Publishing, 1976.

Lev, Yaacov. "Army, Regime and Society in Fatimid Egypt 358–487/968–1094." *International Journal of Middle East Studies* 9, no. 3 (1987): 337–66.

———. "The Fatimid Army, A.H. 358–427/968–1036 C.E.: Military and Social Aspects." *Asian and African Studies* 14 (1980): 156–92.

———. *State and Society in Fatimid Egypt*. Leiden: E. J. Brill, 1991.

Lewis, Bernard. "An Interpretation of Fatimid History." *Colloque International sur l'histoire du Caire, 27 mars–5 avril 1969*. Cairo: General Egyptian Book Organisation, 1972.

Lings, Martin, and Yasin Hamid Safadi. *The Qur'an: Catalogue of an Exhibition of Qur'an Manuscripts at the British Library*. London: World of Islam Publishing Co. Ltd. for the British Library, 1976.

MacCormack, Sabine. *Art and Ceremony in Late Antiquity*. Berkeley: University of California Press, 1981.

Machamer, Peter K., and Robert G. Turnbull, eds. *Studies in Perception: Interrelations in the History of Philosophy and Science*. Columbus: Ohio State University, 1978.

Madelung, Wilfred. "Aspects of Ismaʿili Theology: The Prophet Chain and the God Beyond Being." In *Ismaʿili Contributions to Islamic Culture*, edited by Seyyed Hossein Nasr. Tehran: Imperial Iranian Academy of Philosophy, 1398/1977.

Magdalino, P., and R. Nelson. "The Emperor in Byzantine Art of the Twelfth Century." *Byzantinische Forschungen* 8 (1982): 123–83.

Majid, 'Abd al-Mun'im, ed. *Al-Sijillāt Al-mustanṣirīyya (Correspondence de l'Imam al-mostancir)*. Cairo: n.p., 1954.

Makdisi, G. *Ibn 'Aqil et la resurgence de l'Islam traditionaliste au Xiè siècle*. Damascus: n.p., 1963.

Mango, C. *Byzantine Architecture*. New York: Abrams, 1976.

———. "The Byzantine Inscriptions of Constantinople: A Bibliographic Survey." *American Journal of Archeology* 55 (1951): 52–66.

Mango, C., and I. Sevcenko. "A New Manuscript of the De Cerimoniis." *Dumbarton Oaks Papers* 14 (1960): 247–49.

al-Maqrīzī, Aḥmad ibn 'Alī. *Itti'āẓ al-ḥunafā bi-akhbār al-a'immah al-Fatimiyīn Al-khulafā*. 3 vols. Qāhira: n.p., 1967–73.

———. *Al-Khitat*. 2 vols. Cairo: Būlāq, 1853.

Marçais, G., and G. Wiet. "Le voile de Sainte Anne d'Apt." *Académie des Inscriptions des Belles-Lettres, Fondation Eugène Piot, Monuments et Mémoires* 34 (1934): 65–72.

Marcel, J. J. *Description de l'Egypte, état moderne, II, IIe part*. Paris: n.p., 1822.

Marquet, Yves. "La pensée philosophique et religieuse du Qadi al-Nu'man à travers *La Risala Mudhiba*." *Bulletin d'Études Orientales* 39–40 (1987–88): 141–81.

Marzouk, Muhammad Abdel Aziz. "The Evolution of Inscriptions on Fatimid Textiles." *Ars Islamica* 10 (1942): 164–66.

———. "The Turban of Samuel ibn Musa, The Earliest Dated Islamic Textile." *Bulletin of the Faculty of Arts, Cairo University* 16 (December 1954): 143–51.

Massignon, Louis. "La cité des morts au Caire." *Bulletin de l'Institut Français d'Archaeologie Orientale* 57 (1958): 25–79.

Matériaux pour un Corpus Inscriptionum Arabicarum. Paris and Cairo: E. Leroux; Impr. de l'Institut français d'archéologie orientale, 1894–1985.

Meader, Edward. "Costumes Worn by Christians in Michelangelo's Sistine Chapel." Il Convegno Internazionale di Studi Michaelangelo, La Cappella Sistina, March 1990. Forthcoming.

Metropolitan Museum of Art. *Bulletin of the Metropolitan Museum of Art* 25 (1930): 129.

Miles, George C. *Fatimid Coins in the Collection of the University Museum, Philadelphia, and the American Numismatic Society*. New York: American Numismatic Society, 1951.

———. "Mihrab and 'Anazah: A Study in Early Islamic Iconography." In *Archaeologica Orientalia in Memoriam Ernst Herzfeld*, edited by George C. Miles. Locust Valley, N.Y.: J. J. Augustin, Inc., 1952.

Miles, George C., ed. *Archaeologica Orientalia in Memoriam Ernst Herzfed*. Locust Valley, N.Y.: J. J. Augustin, Inc., 1952.

Morimoto, Kosei. *The Fiscal Administration of Egypt in the Early Islamic Period*. Kyoto: Dohosha, 1981.

Morison, Stanley. *Politics and Script*. Oxford: Oxford University Press, 1972.

Morony, Michael. "The Age of Conversions: A Reassessment." In *Conversion and Continuity, Indigenous Christian Communities in Islamic Lands: Eighth to*

Eighteenth Centuries. Papers in Medieval Studies 9, edited by Michael Gervers and Ramzi Jibran Bikhazi. Toronto: Pontifical Institute of Medieval Studies, 1990.

———. *Iraq after the Muslim Conquest*. Princeton: Princeton University Press, 1984.

Mouraviev, Serge N. "Les caractères danieliens (identification et reconstruction)." *Revue des Études Arméniennes* 14 (1980): 55–85.

———. "Les caractères mesropiens (leur gènes reconstituée)." *Revue des Études Arméniennes* 14 (1980): 87–111.

Nanji, Azim. "Between Metaphor and Context: The Nature of Fatimid Isma'ili Discourse on Justice and Injustice." *Arabica* 37 (1990): 234–39.

Nāṣir-i Khusraw. *Kitāb-i Khvān al-Ikhvān*. Tehran: n.p., 1929.

———. *Safar-nāma*. Edited and annotated by Muhammad Dabir Siyaqi. Tehran: Zuvvar, 1956.

Nasr, Seyyed Hossein, ed. *Isma'ili Contributions to Islamic Culture*. Tehran: Imperial Iranian Academy of Philosophy, 1398/1977.

Naveh, Joseph. *Early History of the Alphabet, An Introduction to West Semitic Epigraphy and Paleography*. Jerusalem and Leiden: Magnes Press, Hebrew University and E. J. Brill, 1982.

Negev, Avrahm. *The Inscriptions of the Wadi Haqqaq, Sinai*. Jerusalem: Institute of Archaeology, 1977.

Nelson, R. L. "Symbols in Context." *Studies in Church History* 13 (1976): 97–119.

Nelson, Robert N. "An Icon at Mt. Sinai and Christian Painting in Muslim Egypt during the 13th and 14th Centuries." *Art Bulletin* 65, no. 2 (1983): 201–18.

Nicol, Norman D. "Islamic Coinage in Imitation of Fatimid Types." *Israel Numismatic Journal* 10 (1988–89): 58–70.

Nu'mān ibn Muḥammad, al-Qāḍī Abū Ḥanīfah. *The Book of Faith*. Partial translation by Asaf A. A. Fyzee. Bombay, 1974.

———. *Da'ā'im al-islām*. Edited by Asaf A. A. Fyzee. 2 vols. Cairo, 1951–61.

———. *Al-Majālis wa'l-musāyarāt*. Edited by al-Ḥabīb al-Fāqī, I. Shabbuḥ, and M. Al-Ya'lawī. Tunis: n.p., 1978.

———. *Ta'wīl al-da'ā'im*. Edited by Muḥammad Ḥasan al-A'ẓamī. Miṣr: Dār al-ma'arif, 1967.

Oddy, W. "The Gold Content of Fatimid Coins Reconsidered." *Metallurgy in Numismatics* 1 (1980): 99–188.

O'Leary, De Lacy. *A Short History of the Fatimid Khaliphate*. London: K. Paul, Trench, Trubner & Polk Ltd., 1923.

Ong, Walter J., S.J. *The Presence of the Word*. Minneapolis: University of Minnesota Press, 1967.

Parker, Richard, Robin Sabin, and Caroline Williams. *Islamic Monuments in Cairo, A Practical Guide*. 3rd edition. Cairo: 1985.

Parker, S. Thomas. *Romans and Saracens: A History of the Arabian Frontier*. American School of Oriental Research Dissertation Series, no. 6. Winona Lake, Wisc.: American Schools of Oriental Research, 1986.

Perizanyan, A. G. "Concerning the Origin of Armenian Writing" (in Russian). *Peredneaziatskij sbornik II*. Moscow: Izd-vo vostochnoi literatury, 1966.

Petry, Carl F. *The Civilian Elite of Cairo in the Later Middle Ages*. Princeton: Princeton University Press, 1981.

Pfister, R. "Matériaux pour servir au classement des textiles Egyptiens postérieurs à la Conquête Arabe." *Revue des Arts Asiatique* 10 (1936): 1–16, 78–85.

Poonawala, Ismail. *Bibliography of Ismaʿili Literature*. Malibu, Calif.: Undena Publications, 1977.

Preziosi, Donald. *Rethinking Art History: Meditations on a Coy Science*. New Haven and London: Yale University Press, 1989.

al-Qalqashandī. *Ṣubḥ al-aʿsha fī sināʿat al-inshāʾ*. 14 vols. Cairo: al-Muʾassasah al-Miṣriyya, al-ʿĀmma, 1964.

Ragib, Yusuf. "Deux monuments Fatimides au pied du Muqattam." *Revue des Études Islamiques* 46 (1978): 91–117.

———. "Essai d'inventaire chronologique des guides à l'usage des pélerins du Caire." *Revue des Études Islamiques* 41 (1973): 259–80.

———. "Al-Sayyida Nafisa, sa légende, son culte, et son cemetère." *Studia Islamica* 44 (1976): 68–69.

Reiske, J. J. *Corpus Scriptorum Historicum Byzantinorum*. 2 vols. Bonn: 1829–30.

Rogers, J. M. Review of *Calligraphy and Islamic Culture* by Annemarie Schimmel. In *Art International* 27, no. 4 (1984): 68.

Rosen-Ayalon, Myriam. "The First Mosaic Discovered in Ramla." *Israel Expedition Journal* 26 (1976): 104–11.

———, ed. *Studies in Memory of Gaston Wiet*. Jerusalem: Institute of Asian and African Studies, Hebrew University of Jerusalem, 1977.

Rosenthal, Franz. "Significant Uses of Arabic Writing." *Ars Orientalis* 4 (1961): 15–23.

Sabra, A. I. *Optics, Astronomy and Logic Studies in Arabic Science and Philosophy*. London: Variorum, 1994.

———. "Sensation and Inference in Alhazen's Theory of Visual Perception." In *Studies in Perception: Interrelations in the History of Philosophy and Science*, edited by Peter K. Machamer and Robert G. Turnbull. Columbus: Ohio State University, 1978.

Salem, Elie A. *Rusūm dār al-khilāfah, The Rules and Regulations of the ʿAbbasid Court*. Beirut: American University Press, 1977.

al-Samhudī, ʿAlī ibn ʿAbd Allah. *Khulāṣat al-wafāʾ bi-akhbār al-muṣtafa*. al-Qāhira: 1392H.

Sampson, Geoffrey. *Writing Systems*. Stanford: Stanford University Press, 1985.

Sanders, Paula. "Claiming the Past: Ghadir Khumm and the Rise of Hafizi Historiography in Late Fatimid Egypt." *Studia Islamica* 75 (1992): 81–104.

———. "From Court Ceremony to Urban Language: Ceremonial in Fatimid Cairo and Fustat." In *The Islamic World from Classical to Modern Times*, edited by C. E. Bosworth, Charles Issawi, Roger Savory, and A. L. Udovitch. Princeton: Princeton University Press, 1989.

———. *Ritual, Politics, and the City in Fatimid Cairo*. New York: SUNY Press, 1994.

Schapiro, Meyer. "Style." *Anthropology Today* (1969): 279–303.

Schick, Robert. "The Fate of the Christians in Palestine during the Byzantine-

Umayyad Transition, A.D. 600–750." Ph.D. diss., University of Chicago, 1987.

Schwabe, Moses. "The Synagogue of Caesarea and Its Inscriptions." In *Alexander Marx: Jubilee Volume on the Occasion of His Seventieth Birthday*. New York: Jewish Theological Seminary, 1950.

Scribner, Sylvia, and Michael Cole. *The Psychology of Literacy*. Cambridge: MIT Press, 1981.

Sebeok, Thomas A., ed. *Style in Language*. Cambridge: MIT Press, 1960.

Sed-Rajna, Gabrielle. *Ancient Jewish Art*. Seacaucus, N.J.: Chartwell Books, n.d.

Serjeant, R. B. "Material for a History of Islamic Textiles up to the Mongol Conquest," *Ars Islamica* 9–16 (1942–51).

Shaban, M. A. *Islamic History: A New Interpretation A.D. 750–1055 (A.H. 132–448)*. 2 vols. Cambridge: Cambridge University Press, 1976.

Sharon, M., ed. *Studies in Islamic History and Civilization in Honour of Professor David Ayalon*. Jerusalem and Leiden: E. J. Brill, 1986.

al-Sijistānī. *Kashf al-maḥjūb*. Edited with an introduction by Henry Corbin. Tehran: Institut Franco-Iranien, 1949.

Smith, G. Rex. "Some Umayyad Inscriptions of Bilad al-Sham—Paleographic Notes." In *The History of the Bilad al-Sham during the Umayyad Period*, edited by M. Adnan Bakhit and Robert Schick. Fourth International Conference of the History of Bilad al-Sham, 1987. Amman: University of Jordan and Yarmouk University, 1989.

Sokoly, Jochen A. "Between Life and Death: The Funerary Context of Ṭirāz Textiles." In *Islamisch Textilkunst des Mittelalters: Aktuelle Problem*. Riggisberg: Abegg-Stiftung, 1996.

Soucek, Priscilla P. "The Arts of Calligraphy." In *The Arts of the Book in Central Asia*, edited by Basil Gray. Paris: UNESCO-Shambala Publications, 1979.

Sourdel-Thomine, Janine. "L'ecriture Arabe et son evolution ornamentale." In *Ecriture et la psychologie des peuples, XXIIe semaine de synthèse*. Paris: A. Colin, 1963.

——. "Inscriptions et grafitti Arabes d'époque Umayyade à propos de quelques publications récentes." *Revue des Études Islamiques* 32 (1964): 115–20.

Stern, S. M. "Cairo as the Centre of the Isma'ili Movement." Colloque International sur l'histoire du Caire. Cairo: Ministry of Culture of the Arab Republic of Egypt, n.d.

——. "Isma'ili Propaganda and Fatimid Rule in Sind." *Islamic Culture* 23 (1949): 298–307.

——. *Studies in Early Isma'ilism*. Jerusalem: Magnes Press, Hebrew University, 1983.

——. "The Succession to the Fatimid Imam al-Amir, the Claims of the Later Fatimids to the Imamate, and the Rise of Tayyibi Ismailism." *Oriens* 4 (1951): 193–255.

Stillman, Yedida. "Female Attire of Medieval Egypt: According to the Trousseau Lists and Cognate Material from the Cairo Geniza." Ph.D. diss., University of Pennsylvania, 1972.

Stock, Brian. *The Implications of Literacy*. Princeton: Princeton University Press, 1983.

———. "Texts, Readers and Enacted Narratives." *Visible Language* 20, no. 3 (1986): 194–301.
Stone, Michael E., ed. *The Armenian Inscriptions from the Sinai*. Cambridge: Harvard University Press, 1982.
Street, Brian V. *Literacy in Theory and Practice*. Cambridge: Cambridge University Press, 1984.
Sukenik, E. L. *Ancient Synagogues in Palestine and Greece*. London: Oxford University Press, 1934.
———. *The Ancient Synagogues of Beth Alpha*. London: Oxford University Press, 1932.
———. "More about the Ancient Synagogue of Caesarea." *Bulletin Rabinowitz* 2 (June 1951): 28–30.
Svecenko, I. "The Early Period of the Sinai Monastery in the Light of Its Inscriptions." *Dumbarton Oaks Papers* 2 (1966).
al-Ṭabarī. *Ta'rīkh*. Vol. 5. Cairo: Maṭbaʿat al-Istiqāma, 1939.
Tafuri, Manfredo. *Theories and History of Architecture*. New York: Harper & Row, 1976.
Tāmir, ʿArif. *Al-Muʿizz li-Dīn Allah al-Fātimī*. Beirut: Dār al-Afaq al-Jadīda, 1982.
Taylor, Christopher S. "The Cult of the Saints in Late Medieval Egypt." Ph.D. diss., Princeton, 1989.
———. "Reevaluating the Shiʿi Role in the Development of Monumental Funerary Architecture: The Case of Cairo." *Muqarnas* 9 (1992): 1–10.
Terasaki, Emiko. "The Lack of Animal and Human Figural Imagery in the Public Art of the Umayyad Period." Master's thesis, UCLA, 1987.
Toynbee, A. *Constantine Porphryogennetos and His World*. Oxford: Oxford University Press, 1973.
Tsori, Nehum. "The Ancient Synagogue at Beth Sheʿan." *Eretz Israel: Archaeological, Historical and Geographical Studies* 8 (1967): 149–67.
al-Ṭusī, Nāṣir al-Dīn Muḥammad b. Muḥammad. *Rawḍat al-taslīm*. Edited and translated by W. Ivanow. Leiden: E. J. Brill, 1950.
al-ʿUsh, Abū al-Faraj. "Kitābāt al-ʿarabiyya ghayr mansūra fī Jabal Says." *Al-Abḥāth* 17 (1964): 227–316.
van Berchem, Margaret. *EMA*. Vol. 1, chap. 10, mosaics.
van Berchem, Max. *CIA*. Part 2, *Syrie du Sud*. Vol. 2, *Jerusalem: Haram*, 224–28, 248–51.
Van Milligen, Alexander. *Byzantine Churches in Constantinople, Their History and Architecture*. London: Macmillan, 1912.
Volov-Golombek, Lisa. "Plaited Kufic on Samanid Epigraphic Pottery." *Ars Orientalis* 6 (1966): 107–33.
von Bothmer, Hans-Caspar Graf. "Meisterwerke islamischer Buchkunst: Koranische Kalligraphie und Illumination im Handschriftenfund aus der Grosse Moschee in Sanaa." *Jemen, 3000 Jahre Kunst und Kultur des glücklichen Arabien*.
Vryonis, Speros, Jr. "Panegyris of the Byzantine Saint: A Study in the Nature of a Medieval Institution, Its Origin and Fate." *Sobornost* 12 (1981): 196–228.
Walker, John. *A Catalogue of Muhammadan Coins in the British Museum*. Vol. 1,

Arab-Sassanian Coins, and vol. 2, *Arab-Byzantine and Post Reform Coins*. London: British Museum, 1941–65.

Walker, Paul. "The Ismaili Daʿwa in the Reign of the Fatimid Caliph al-Hakim." *Journal of the American Research Center in Egypt* 30 (1993): 160–82.

——. *The Wellsprings of Wisdom*. Salt Lake City: University of Utah Press, 1994.

al-Washsha. *Kitāb al-Muwashshā*. Edited by R. E. Brunnow. Leiden: E. J. Brill, 1886.

Weitzmann, Kurt, ed. *The Age of Spirituality*. New York: Metropolitan Museum of Art and Princeton University Press, 1980.

Welch, Anthony. "Epigraphs as Icons: the Role of the Written Word in Islamic Art." In *The Image and the Word: Confrontations in Judaism, Christianity and Islam*, edited by J. Gutman. American Academy of Religion and Society of Biblical Literature, Religion and the Arts, Series 4. Missoula, Mont.: Scholars Press for the American Academy of Religion, 1977.

Welles, C. B. "Inscriptions." In *Gerasa City of the Decapolis*, edited by Carl H. Kraeling. New Haven: American Schools of Oriental Research, 1938.

Whitcomb, Donald. "Evidence of the Umayyad Period from the Aqaba Excavations." In *The History of the Bilad al-Sham during the Umayyad Period*, edited by M. Adnan Bakhit and Robert Schick. Fourth International Conference of the History of Bilad al-Sham, 1987. Amman: University of Jordan and Yarmouk University, 1989.

White, Hayden. *Tropics of Discourse: Essays in Cultural Criticism*. Baltimore: The Johns Hopkins University Press, 1978.

White, Hugh G. E. *The Monasteries of the Wadi 'N Natrun*. Metropolitan Museum Expedition. 8 vols. New York: The Metropolitan Museum of Art, 1933.

Wiet, Gaston. "Une nouvelle inscription Fatimide au Caire." *Journal Asiatique* (1961): 13–30.

Williams, Caroline. "The Cult of ʿAlid Saints in the Fatimid Monuments of Cairo, Part 1: The Mosque of al-Aqmar." *Muqarnas* 1 (1983): 37–53.

——. "The Cult of ʿAlid Saints in the Fatimid Monuments of Cairo, Part 2: The Mausolea." *Muqarnas* 3 (1985): 39–60.

——. "The Mosque of Sitt Hadaq." *Muqarnas* 11 (1994): 55–56.

Williamson, Calle. "Monuments of Bronze: Roman Legal Documents on Bronze Tablets." *Classical Antiquity* 6, no. 1 (April 1987): 160–83.

Wilson, C. W., and H. S. Palmer. *Ordnance Survey of the Peninsula of Sinai*. Southampton: Ordnance Survey Office, 1869.

Zarkashī, Muḥammad ibn Bahadur. *Iʿlām al-sājid bi-aḥkā al-masājid*. Cairo: n.p., 1384H.

Index

CPSIA information can be obtained at www.ICGtesting.com
Printed in the USA
BVOW02s1236060814

361805BV00001B/88/P